Violence and Society in the Early Medieval west

Violence and Society in the Early Medieval West

Edited by

Guy Halsall

THE BOYDELL PRESS

First published 1998
The Boydell Press, Woodbridge

Transferred to digital printing

ISBN 978-0-85115-849-5

The Boydell Press is an imprint of Boydell & Brewer Ltd
PO Box 9, Woodbridge, Suffolk IP12 3DF, UK
and of Boydell & Brewer Inc.
668 Mt Hope Avenue, Rochester, NY 14620, USA
website: www.boydellandbrewer.com

A CiP catalogue record for this book is available
from the British Library

This publication is printed on acid-free paper

CONTENTS

CONTRIBUTORS

Dr *N. B. Aitchison* 7 Rydal Road, Longlevens, Gloucester, GL2 0NT

Dr *Ross Balzaretti* Department of History, University of Nottingham, University Park, Nottingham, NG7 2RD

Matthew Bennett esq. Department of Communication Studies, RMA Sandhurst, Camberley, Surrey, GU16 4PQ

Dr *T. S. Brown* Department of History, University of Edinburgh, William Robertson Building, 50 George Square, Edinburgh, EH8 9JY

Dr *Julie Coleman* Department of English, University of Leicester, University Road, Leicester, LE1 7RH

Dr *Paul Fouracre* Department of Historical and Cultural Studies, Goldsmith's College, University of London, New Cross, London, SE14 6NW

Professor *Luis A. García Moreno* Universidad de Alcala de Henares, Facultad de Filosofia Y Letras, Seminario de Historia Antigua, Colegio de Malága, E-28801 Alcala de Henares, Spain

Dr. *Guy Halsall* Department of History, Birkbeck College, University of London, Malet Street, London, WC1E 7HX

Guy A. E. Morris esq. Flat 5, Bessborough Mansions, 122 Regency Street, Pimlico, London, SW1P 4AP

Professor *Janet L. Nelson* Department of History, King's College, University of London, Strand, London, WC2R 2LS

Dr *S. J. Speight* Department of Continuing Education, University of Nottingham, University Park, Nottingham NG7 2RD

Dr *Nancy L. Wicker* Art Department, Mankato State University, MSU 42/PO Box 8400, Mankato, Minnesota 56002-8400, USA

ABBREVIATIONS

AB	*Annals of St-Bertin*
AC	*Annals of Clonmacnoise*
AF	*Annals of Fulda*
AFM	*Annals of the Four Masters*
AI	*Annals of Inisfallen*
ARF	*Royal Frankish Annals*
Arn	Arnorr Þjorðarson
ASC	*Anglo-Saxon Chronicle*
AT	*Annals of Tigernach*
AU	*Annals of Ulster*
Bersi	Bersi Skaldtorfuson
BjH	Bjarni Hallbjarson gullbrarskald
Böl	Bölverkr Arnorsson
Capit.	*Capitularia Regum Francorum*
CC	*Codex Carolinus*
CDL	*Codex Diplomaticus Langobardiae*
CS	*Chronicum Scotorum*
DB	Domesday Book (refs to Phillimore edition)
Edað	Eyjolfr daðaskald
Ed. Roth.	*Edictum Rothari*
EH	Bede, *Ecclesiastical History of the English People*
EHD	*English Historical Documents*
Epp.	*Epistolae*
Gldr	Þorbjorn hornhlofi, *Glymdrapa*
GND	William of Jumièges, *Gesta Normannorum Ducum*
Hal	Eyvindr Finnsson, *Haleygjabal*
Halli	Halli stirði
HD	Simeon of Durham, *Historia Dunelmensis*
Hfr	Hallfroðr Ottarsson
HL	Paul the Deacon, *Historia Langobardorum*
HR	Simeon of Durham, *Historia Regum*
LC	*Liber Constitutionum* (Burgundian Law)
LH	Gregory of Tours, *Histories*
LHF	*Liber Historiae Francorum*
Liut. Leg.	*Liutprandi Leges*
LL	*Book of Leinster*
LP	*Liber Pontificalis*
LRB	*Lex Romana Burgundionum*
LV	*Leges Visigothorum*
MGH	*Monumenta Germaniae Historica*
MR	Moltke 1985

NR	*Norges Innskrifter med de Yngre Runer*, 1951, Annet Binde, V, and *Norges Innskrifter med de Yngre Runer*, 1954, Tredje Binde
PL	J. P. Migne (ed.), *Patrologiae Cursus Completus. Series Latina*
PLS	*Pactus Legis Salicae*
Ott	Ottarr Svarti
OV	Orderic Vitalis, *Ecclesiastical History*, references are given to the volume and page number of Chibnall's edition
Schiaparelli	*Codice Diplomatico Longobardo*
Sigv	Sigvatr Þorðarson
SM	*Sveriges runinskrifter*, 1935, Fjärde bandet
SRG	*Scriptores Rerum Germanicarum in usum Scholarum*
SRM	*Scriptores Rerum Merovingicarum*
SS	*Sveriges runininskrifter*, 1924–36, Trejde bandet
Steinn	Steinn Herdisarson
SU	*Sveriges runinskrifter*, 1940–43, Sjätte bandet; *Sveriges runinskrifter*, 1949–1951, Åttonde bandet; and *Sveriges runinskrifter*, 1953–1958, Nionde bandet
SV	*Sveriges runinskrifter*, 1964, Trettonde bandet
TH	Giraldus Cambrensis, *Topographia Hiberniae*
Tindr	Tindr Hallkelsson
Þfagr	Þorleikr fagri
ÞjóðA	Þjóðolfr Arnorsson
Þkolb	Þorðr Kolbeinsson
Þorf	Þorfinnr munnr
Valg	Valgarðr a Velli
Vell	Einarr Helgason, *Vellekla*
VP	Gregory of Tours, *Vita Patrum*

Note on citation of primary sources

Where a citation has a primary source's title followed by a colon, the succeeding reference is to the page number of the edition or translation used. Elsewhere, where no colon is used, the reference is to book (upper case Roman numerals), chapter (arabic numerals) or verse (lower case Roman numerals) of the original source. Unless otherwise stated, all translations of primary sources are taken from the published translation listed in the bibliography.

Violence and society in the early medieval west: an introductory survey

Guy   Halsall

SICHAR AND CHRAMNESIND

At Christmas 585, in Manthelan in the Touraine, Sichar, a prominent local, entertained a number of other Tourangeaux, including a certain Austregisel. Hearing of this, the village priest, Sichar's friend, sent a retainer (*puer*) to invite the party-goers over for a drink. One of the men invited, for some reason, drew his sword and killed the *puer*. At this, Sichar armed himself and went to exact revenge upon Austregisel. Not to be outdone, Austregisel took up his weapons and met Sichar and his followers. Sichar's party emerged worst from the ensuing fight. Several wounded *pueri* were left in the church house and Sichar fled the village, injured. Austregisel now reassembled his own forces, stormed the priest's house, killed Sichar's *pueri* and stole some valuables left there. A court hearing was called which, unsurprisingly, found in Sichar's favour.

At this juncture, Sichar attacked the house of one Auno, in whose hands his stolen goods were, slew him, his son, and his brother Eberulf, as well as some of their slaves (*servi*), and recovered his property. Now Bishop Gregory of Tours, the narrator of the whole incident, stepped in and tried to end this, as he called it, 'civil war' (*bellum civile*), offering, from church funds, to compensate Chramnesind, Auno's son, for the death of his father, brother and uncle; Chramnesind refused. Not long afterwards, Sichar, on his way to Poitiers, beat one of his slaves, where-upon the latter gravely wounded him with his own sword. The slave was mutilated and killed, but the rumour went around that Sichar was dead. Hearing this, Chramnesind attacked his house, killed his slaves and burnt both Sichar's house (*domus*) and those of the other people who held land in the *villa*, or small rural district. Once again a tribunal was held. The outcome was that Chramnesind should forfeit half the compensation; the church of Tours paid the remainder. There the matter rested, temporarily.

A year or two later, by now close friends, sharing meals and even on occasion a bed, Sichar and Chramnesind were dining one night. Evidently a certain amount of alcohol was imbibed. Sichar pointed out that Chramnesind ought to be grateful to him for slaughtering his relatives for he was now rich on the compensation received. At this, Chramnesind felt ashamed for not avenging his relatives properly, blew out the lights and dealt Sichar a lethal blow to the head with his axe. Hanging Sichar's body on the fence-post of his house, he rode off to the court of Childebert II of Austrasia to justify himself. Sichar had been under the protection of Childebert II's mother, Brunechildis, who was not pleased, and Chramnesind fled to the region of Bourges. Chramnesind obtained a second hearing before the king, maintained that he had killed Sichar in vengeance but lost his property in punishment. Nevertheless he soon received it back, via one of the queen's *domestici*. [1]

So, from one drunken brawl, a violent series of events unfolded lasting the best part of two years and leading to at least thirteen deaths.[2] The story (Gregory of Tours, *LH* VII.47, IX.19) is one of the best known of all tales of early medieval violence, and has often been studied or cited (cp. Auerbach 1953, ch. 4; Wallace-Hadrill 1962; James 1983; Sawyer 1987: 29-31). It is an extremely appropriate focus for the introduction to this volume, referring, as it does, to many issues raised by the essays contained here.

VIOLENCE AND HISTORIOGRAPHY

The speed with which the factions at Manthelan resorted to armed, lethal violence is an apposite illustration of what many see as the intrinsic violence of the early medieval period: 'Anglo-Saxon society was so violent that a central fact of its politics, its way of life, even, was fighting and making war' (John 1966: 132).

Eric John was hardly alone in expressing this idea of the 'violent'

---

1. This arrangement, whereby the queen gave Chramnesind's property to her *domesticus*, who then returned it to Chramnesind, looks like an elaborate, deliberate ploy to maintain the effectiveness and prestige of Brunechildis' tutelage. Although Sichar's killing was legitimate, had she not made a show of punishing Chramnesind for it, her 'protection' would not have seemed worth having; Fustel de Coulanges 1890: 235-47 for the heavy obligations of patronage.

2. The priest's *puer*, Sichar's four *pueri*, Auno, Eberulf, Auno's son, Auno's slaves (at least two), Sichar's slaves (at least two), and Sichar himself.

early Middle Ages, and at least some early medieval people shared the view that deadly, alcohol-induced violence, such as at Manthelan, was common: 'From one, an irascible ale-swiller, a man full of wine, a sword's edge will thrust out the life on the mead bench; previous to that his words will have been too hasty' (*The Fortunes of Men*).

Gregory of Tours' oeuvre contains many other outbreaks of this kind of fighting (*LH* V.32, VI.32, VII.3, X.27; *VP* 8.vii), and similar, well-known, set-piece descriptions of violence are easily found: they are strewn through the papers in this volume. We find a similar concern with frequent violence in non-narrative written sources. Anglo-Saxon poetic treatments of 'the way of things', like *The Fortunes of Men* or its companions, *The Gifts of Men*, and *Maxims I* and *II*, treat warfare and violence, as Eric John said, as central to Anglo-Saxon life. Venantius Fortunatus composed an epitaph for a deacon killed with an axe whilst sleeping (*Carmina* IV.15), and, whilst obviously deploring the crime, Venantius makes no hint that it was extraordinary. Sermon collections can present similar pictures; Valerian of Cimiez saw resort to armed violence as a typical means of settling disputes over estate boundaries (*Homily* 20.iii).

The use of weaponry to symbolise various social identities is attested by written and unwritten sources. The bestowal of weapons upon a young man when he came of age is well known; the association of a knight with his sword more so. The excavation of countless mainland European cemeteries of the late fourth to eighth centuries, and later in the 'Viking world', further confirms the way in which weaponry could symbolise age, class or rank, or ethnicity (Halsall 1995a: 255, 267; Härke 1992). It is unhelpful to see the choice of weaponry as a symbol as haphazard, or to equate it simply with the wearing of ceremonial swords in modern British state rituals, a statement of rank perhaps, but saying little or nothing about actual violence. The sword borne by a knight of the garter is significant for its historical content, not for what it says about the functions of the bearer, let alone the realities of power and its acquisition. The early medieval sword, spear or shield, helmet or armour, and, perhaps especially, war-horse, were current symbols of violent action, representing expensive and efficient items of military equipment. There was nothing 'ceremonial' about them. Even the Sutton Hoo helmet, which, as often remarked, shows few signs of use, was symbolically important not as an archaic hangover, but as a potent demonstration of contemporary military power and authority. The best analogy for the display of power through these symbols is not the knight of the garter but the militiaman or rebel toting an AK47: the sub-machine-gun amply demonstrates the source of power and the means whereby it was achieved, maintained and defended. What symbolized a young adult male in sixth-century northern Gaul, or perhaps distinguished Frank from Gallo-Roman or Anglo-Saxon from Romano-Briton, or, later, which distinguished an aristocrat from a simple free commoner was the likelihood of his participation in at least certain types of armed violence. These symbols therefore add meaningfully to the literary picture of warfare and other violence.

The early medieval world, like thirteenth-century Todi, was 'a world of thin skins, short fuses and physical violence' (Lesnick 1991: 72). It *was* a violent era; such can be said easily and without controversy. How violent, whether more or less violent than preceding and succeeding eras, is naturally less easy to state and, perhaps, less profitable to consider. Nevertheless, these questions feature strongly in the period's historiography. A few *causes célèbres* deserve brief mention to highlight how violence has loomed large in ways of seeing the early Middle Ages.

The first concerns the violence of the 'transition' from the ancient world to the medieval. Leaving aside the still unresolved issue of the role of barbarian 'invasion' in ending the Roman empire (for a recent statement, see Heather 1995a), historians have long compared the Roman period with its successors in terms of their respective levels of violence. Samuel Dill memorably contrasted the late Roman and Merovingian periods:

> 'The "Roman Peace" which gave the world almost unexampled calm and prosperity, has vanished. As in our own days [for Dill, the 'roaring twenties'], passion, greed and bold disregard of moral tradition have followed great wars and triumphs of military strength. . . . The long tranquillity of the Roman sway ended in the violence and darkness of the Middle Age' (Dill 1926: 306–07).

More recently his thesis has been revived by Ralph Mathisen (1993). Of course, as one reviewer caustically remarked, the comparisons are, given the different sources available, largely nonsensical: '. . . comparing Gregory and Sidonius on violence is as meaningful as comparing the films of Quentin Tarantino with those of Merchant Ivory productions' (Loseby 1995: 336).

The supposedly 'elemental' violence of the early Middle Ages has, however, a far larger historiographical role to play than simply pointing up the purported shortcomings of the Merovingians vis-à-vis their leisured fifth-century precursors. It has taken centre stage in the study of the origins of the phenomenon known as feudalism. Ganshof's schematic statement of 'what feudalism was' is a convenient starting point. Ganshof (1964, ch. 1) believed that people entered relationships of dependence on their more powerful fellows for protection in an age of untrammelled violence. He was neither alone nor original in holding this view. In the previous century, Fustel de Coulanges (1890: 336–426) associated the rise of immunities, which, he thought, led ultimately to the collapse of royal power, with attempts to protect people from the depredations of unscrupulous officials. Brunner (1887) famously linked violence and 'feudal' institutions by connecting the establishment of aristocratic feudo-vassalic relations with the need to maintain specialist warriors equipped with weapons, armour and war-horse. Increased military specialization helped separate the aristocracy from the remainder of the free population (for more recent incarnations of the idea, see White 1962: 1–38; Beeler 1971: 12–13).

Many of these ideas have been heavily criticized (on Charles Martell see Wood 1995, and the papers collected in Jarnut, Nonn & Richter (ed.) 1994). Bachrach (1970; 1983) tackled the technical military aspects of Brunner's hypothesis. The historiography of feudalism has been thoroughly addressed by Susan Reynolds (1994). Nevertheless, the military specialization of the Frankish aristocracy is still, probably correctly, regarded as very important in the socio-economic differentiation of this class (Leyser 1984; Nelson 1989; Goetz 1995: 456; but see Reuter 1985: 88–90; 1990: 395–401). And, to medieval people in the theorization of the *ordines* of their society, aristocrats were *bellatores*: those who fight (or, more accurately, those who make war, which is an important difference).

Bloch (1962: 39–42) invoked violence, this time the ninth-century Viking, Magyar and Arab attacks, as a cause of his 'first age of feudalism'. The Viking phenomenon is another aspect of early medieval history and archaeology which has turned upon questions of violence. Were the Vikings as violent and destructive as contemporary sources portrayed? This debate has raged since the 1960s, when Peter Sawyer (1962, ch. 6) questioned the validity of contemporary depictions of Viking raiders (also Sawyer 1982a, ch. 6; countered by Wormald 1982), and does not seem to have lost its historical currency (Foot 1991). Reuter (1985; 1990) has cogently linked the socio-political changes of the late Carolingian period, and the differences between West and East Frankish politics, to differing abilities to wage foreign warfare.

The connections between violence and 'feudalism' have another, important, dimension, the debate over the 'feudal revolution' of c. 1000,[3] and the 'peace of God' movement.[4] Some historians (e.g. Bois 1992; Bisson 1993) hold that social change around the end of the first millennium was marked by an upsurge of violence, associated with increasing 'seigneurial' power, and symbolized notably by the construction of castles (cp. Debord 1992). Related to this is the argument that a

---

3. This debate has become something of a growth industry, sparked by the work of Poly and Bournazel (1991), and, most controversially, Bois (1982): see Barthélemy 1992; Bisson 1993; Guerreau 1990; Rosenwein 1993. A useful collection of essays is brought together in *Médiévales* 21 (1991). *Past and Present* 152 (1996), which arrived just as this introduction was being finished, and 153 (forthcoming) contain further important contributions.

4. See, above all, Hoffman 1964; Head & Landes (eds) 1992; Nelson 1994.

dynamic of the 'feudal mode of production', or at least the spread of
seigneurial power, was aristocratic violence, terrorizing the peasantry
and forcing them into further dependence upon castle-building lords
(Hilton 1971; White 1986: 260–61). This is probably the most current
early medieval historical debate involving the questions of violence and
society.

THE PROBLEMS OF THE SOURCES

All these debates raise the issue of the use of sources. The comparison
of Gregory of Tours' Gaul with that, 100 years earlier, of Sidonius Apollinaris is a case in point. We cannot take varied sources together as an
undifferentiated whole in the examination of violence. As Loseby (1995:
336) makes clear, different genres required subjects such as violence to
be treated in different ways, or indeed not treated at all. Gregory of
Tours had a clear moral purpose in recording episodes like the Sichar
and Chramnesind story (cp. Goffart 1988, ch. 3; Fouracre, below: 61–
62). This is not to say that such violence was rare or unusual; the regular-
ity of such tales in Gregory's works, coupled with the slow pace of his
narrative, implies that 'headline-grabbing' violence was frequent. It
simply serves to stress that differing types of work had different
agendas. Paul Fouracre (ch. 2) underlines this point in his careful
analysis of the relative violence of the late Merovingian and early Carolingian periods (see also Fouracre 1990 and 1995; Reuter 1985: 91), drawing particular attention to the use of hagiographical sources.

The problems of the sources occur not only when trying to compare
regions or periods covered by different evidential forms. When we have
the same types of written data, apparently giving similar pictures of violence at various times and places, this can, equally, simply result from
the demands of genre. Hence we must look closely for subtle reworkings
and redefinitions of old themes. Especially over long periods, the same
words, as Nelson (1994: 168) has said in review of Magnou-Nortier
(1992), need not necessarily have had the same meanings.

These difficulties thus render meaningless, except where one has
analogous types of evidence with similar concerns but giving different
indications, any comparisons of levels of violence, let alone moral judgements of the period. Ironically, rather than (as he thought) subjecting
his evidence to critical attention, Dill's castigation of Merovingian
violence simply reproduced a contemporary point of view (i.e Gregory
of Tours'). Ross Balzaretti (below: 175) makes the same point about
historians' attitudes to female violence in Lombard (or Langobard) Italy.
Source criticism is thus a thread running through this collection. Tom
Brown (ch. 3) makes sense of Agnellus of Ravenna's famous account of
one of the most intriguing of all cases of early medieval violence; Nick
Aitchison (ch. 5) unravels the moral, political and possibly ritual under-

tones behind the language of otherwise terse Irish Annals; Guy Morris (ch. 7) deals importantly with the problems of using Scandinavian poetry embedded in later sources; Julie Coleman's survey of the treatment of rape in different forms of Old English literary source (ch. 10) shows how the same type of violence could evince quite varied responses, depending upon the kind of work being written; Sarah Speight (ch. 8) examines the different attitudes of early twelfth-century chroniclers to the 'Harrying of the North'; and Nancy Wicker (ch. 11) applies similar source-critical methods to archaeological cemetery data.

LEGITIMATE AND ILLEGITIMATE, PRIVATE AND PUBLIC

Violence in different periods and places within the early medieval era might be compared and contrasted, and the issue of source criticism highlighted, by consideration of its legitimacy. What types, and levels, of violence were considered legitimate or acceptable, and by whom? Two 'dimensions' may be considered: 'vertical', encompassing the attempts of those who tried to govern early medieval societies to limit 'legitimate' violence to that approved by them or carried out on their orders; and 'horizontal', covering the ways in which communities defined the legitimacy or illegitimacy of violent acts. The two should not be rigorously opposed. Early medieval government was not, indeed could not be, a simple matter of coercion and imposition (see Speight, ch. 8, for the difficulties involved in the violent imposition of a new order). The currently fashionable 'consensus model' of early medieval politics rightly stresses the ways in which local communities actively subscribed to incorporation into a political unit. One reason for this was to obtain arbitration of disputes, restriction of certain types of violence and protection from others (on this, Fouracre, below: 71). Furthermore, we often study 'community' ideas of legitimate violence via legislation issued by the state (e.g. García Moreno, ch. 1; Balzaretti, ch. 9). Nevertheless, the 'vertical' and 'horizontal' dimensions are convenient.

Early medieval rulers habitually tried to distinguish between violence which they approved or ordered, and that which they did not. Such distinctions were rarely articulated in terms of legitimacy and illegitimacy. Often, they concentrated upon the maintenance of the royal peace; violence was especially to be condemned when it took place within spaces, or on occasions, protected by the king: royal halls or palaces (e.g. Ine 6; Alfred 7; *Ed. Roth.* 36), cities in which the king was resident (*Ed. Roth.* 37–38); royal assemblies or the army (e.g. *PLS* 63; *Ed. Roth.* 6, 8; Alfred 38), with protection sometimes broadened to journeys to or from such assemblies (*Ed. Roth.* 17–18); and, naturally, the church (*Ed. Roth.* 35; Ine 6.i). Sometimes these extended more general attempts to ban violence in certain spaces, households in Anglo-Saxon law (Hlothhere-Eadric 11, 13–14; Ine 6.2–3; Alfred 39), walled cities in Lombard Italy

(*Ed. Roth.* 39–40), or the principle of ecclesiastical sanctuary established in late Roman times. Rulers protected their officers and heavily penalized violence against them (e.g. *PLS* 54; *Ed. Roth.* 374), and at various times took other social groups under their protection. The legitimacy of rule was often expressed in terms of the control of illegitimate violence and the protection from it of vulnerable sections of society (Morris, ch. 7; Reuter 1996; Kershaw forthcoming).

Illegitimate violence, violating the king's peace and protection, was condemned by the use of words like *seditio* or *praesumptio* and punished with death or extremely heavy fines. It was presumption, in Lombard Italy, to form an armed band and attack a village (*Ed. Roth.* 19). The same law also declared it presumption to take vengeance without recourse to law and the arbitration or judgement of royal officers (see below: 23). It was sedition to expel a judge or attack another *civitas* without royal backing (*Liut. Leg.* 723 AD, 6; Ratchis' Laws 10), or for the unfree to arm themselves (*Ed. Roth.* 280). Louis the Pious, like his successors, even outlawed sworn, armed groupings of the unfree in the face of Viking assault (*Capit.* I, 148.vii; Nelson, below: 96).

The legitimacy of violence thus also hinged upon the legitimacy of armed bands. Attempts to control armed gangs are a *Leitmotif* of post-Roman law.[5] The *Pactus Legis Salicae* (42–43) legislated against *contubernia*, apparently gangs of equals, as did *Lex Ribuaria* (67), which used the Germanic term *Hariraida*. Lombard, Burgundian and Visigothic law contained similar clauses (*Ed. Roth.* 19, 263; *Liut. Leg.* AD 733, 5; *LRB* 18.i; *LV* VIII.2–3) and in seventh-century Wessex Ine's laws contain probably the most famous attempt to restrict and condemn armed bands: 'We call up to seven men thieves, between seven and thirty-five is a band, beyond that is an army' (Ine 13.1). Often taken, wrongly, as evidence that early medieval armies could number as few as thirty-five men (Sawyer 1962: 120), this is a royal attempt to outlaw unofficial groupings of armed men by assigning appropriate levels of crime – and punishment – to gatherings of various sizes (for a similar tripartite categorization of levels of violence, see Nelson 1996). It has been observed (most recently Keynes 1995: 26) that similarities between Ine's code and Wihtred of Kent's (cp. Ine 20 and Wihtred 28) suggest that they were issued together as part of a peace- or alliance-making process. This law can thus be seen as part of an attempt to maintain peace within and between kingdoms; Ine extended the king's peace over particularly wide areas (e.g. Ine 6.iv). This raises the important point that statements about the legitimacy of armed force are heavily dependent upon their context, as is underlined when we consider Charlemagne's tough

---

5. As it is also a *Leitmotif* of the essays in this collection; see García-Moreno, below: 50–51; Brown, below: 80–81; Nelson, below: 96; Morris, below: 149–50; Balzaretti, below: 186–87.

legislation about illegal armed gatherings (*trustes* or *conjurationes*);[6] his reign saw particularly determined attempts to make the state effective at the local level and to ban all violence not closely supervised by royal officials (below: 25–26; see Nelson, below: 92–94, for Carolingian ideologies of internal peace). Similarly, the Lombards dealt more harshly with unauthorized armed gatherings than did the Anglo-Saxons and Franks and this may well relate to the strength of the Lombard kingdom (for instance, recently, Harrison 1993). García Moreno (below: 48–50) shows how the rigour of attempts to define legitimate violence varied from one Visigothic king to the next. The severity of the punishment of armed bands and the seriousness of attempts to restrict them, like the extent of the areas, and the inclusiveness of the social groupings, laid under royal protection, thus varied according to perceptions of royal power.

Drawing lines between authorized and unauthorized violence or armed groups was never easy in the early Middle Ages (García Moreno, below: 52). Shaw (1984) has shown the difficulty which the Roman state had in closing up the grey areas between legitimate and illegitimate violence. Unlike Roman emperors, barbarian kings had little or no coercive force independent of their aristocracy. In many, if not most, early medieval polities, the very same people condemned at one turn for violently overawing a locality, or for gathering an 'illegal' armed band, might, at the next, be called upon to provide those armed men for the army, or be appointed to govern that region.[7] This point is underlined by the various senses, ranging from value-neutrality to outright condemnation, of the word *contubernium*.[8] Precise political circumstances largely determined the clarity of the definition of legitimate or illegitimate violence. Particularly crucial was the need for royal patronage in the legitimation of local authority, the extent to which independent means of maintaining such pre-eminence existed, and consequently the ability of rulers to strip regional magnates of their powers and re-

---

6. *Capit.* I, 20.xiv, xvi, *Capit.* I, 28.xxxi. On *conjurationes* see Brunner 1979: 17–20. The word may have lost its pejorative undertones to some extent towards the end of our period. See Althoff 1982; Frase 1989: 284–87.

7. Neatly illustrated by the fact that the violence condemned by Liut. *Leg.* 723 AD, 6, is only sedition if it does not have royal backing; the possibility that such armed action might be royally sponsored is clearly acknowledged. Note also the career of Childeric the Saxon, found wandering with an armed band (*LH* VII.3), appointed duke (*LH* VIII.28), and later involved in the revolt of the Nuns at Poitiers, and out of royal favour (*LH* X.22).

8. Thus the word is apparently used pejoratively in *PLS* 42–43; *Vita Desiderii*, 1 seems to use it to describe worldly gatherings, such as the royal court, and contrasts the *contubernia* of the sinful with the crowds (*catervuis*) of the humble; but some hagiography simply uses the word to describe a saint's band of followers. The word originally meant a group of legionaries who shared a tent.

distribute lands and offices amongst competitors for local supremacy.

Our definitions of legitimate and illegitimate violence thus turn on the extent to which violence could be termed 'private' or 'public' (although these terms are rare in the sources). Such distinctions, though, for reasons just discussed, are and were never straightforward. Early medieval legislation recognized the scope which existed in small-scale rural societies for 'public' office-holders to abuse their position for 'private' ends[9] and, at a higher level, 'private' factional rivalry for the control of the court (Fouracre, ch. 2; Brown, below: 78–82) could be represented as being for the protection of the 'public' good. A 'private' score might be settled, and a rival removed, by accusations of treason, or *infidelitas*, and the violence employed thus represented as 'public'. The same ambiguity can be seen in Aitchison's (ch. 5) examination of power struggles within royal Irish *derbfine*. Are violent rivalries between kings and magnates (cp. Reuter 1991b: 312–13; Morris, ch. 7) 'private' or 'public'? The Visigothic church's eternally flexible attitude to the legitimacy of violence against the king (García Moreno, ch. 1) makes the same point.

Legitimation or condemnation of violence was often a simple matter of vocabulary. Words for unauthorized armed force were used to condemn larger-scale rebellion and political illegitimacy. In some ways this continued the Roman application of terms for bandit, like *latro* (Shaw 1984) and *bacauda* (Van Dam 1985, ch. 3), to usurpers, rebels, and wielders of illegitimate local authority in general, although the precise vocabulary changed. Paul's rebellion in Septimania in 672 is described as *seditio* (*Historia Wambae* 7, 8, 9, 12, 13, 14, etc.), *conjuratio* (*ibid.* 5, 8, 9, 11), *perfidia* (*ibid.* 5, 6, 7, 8, 9 etc.) and *infidelitas* (*ibid.* 6), all part of the vocabulary used to describe illegitimate violence. Austrasian rebels formed a *conjuratio* (*Revised Annals s.a.* 785), possibly motivating Charlemagne to ban sworn gatherings except where the oath was one of loyalty to him, although he had forbidden illegal armed bands earlier in his reign. A Viking force on the Thames was decried as a *hlop* (*ASC s.a.* 879; cp. Ine 13.i). Actions against rebels could be declared to be without sin or blame; the Pope absolved Charlemagne and the Franks of all guilt for military action against the recalcitrant Tassilo of Bavaria (*ARF s.a.* 787), and similar pronouncements were made by the Visigothic church.

Here, too, there was great diversity within our period. Whereas early Merovingian kings could justify decisive military operations against over-mighty subjects (e.g. *LH* IX.9–10, 12), and apparently arbitrary acts of violence (e.g. *LH* VIII.36), by declaring their opponents guilty of *lèse majesté* (*crimen maiestatis lesi*: *LH* V.25, VI.37, IX.13, IX.14) in Roman style, this was not as possible in the late seventh century, as Childeric II

---

9. Cp. Ratchis, 10; *Capit.* I, 82.viii; *PLS* 51; *Lex Ribu.* 87.

found to his cost (*LHF* 45). By the ninth century, powerful Carolingians like Charles the Bald had to prepare the ground carefully for the execution even of habitual *infideles* like Bernard of Septimania (Nelson 1992: 139–40), and the long-term price which Charles' father, Louis the Pious, paid for his brutal suppression of Bernard of Italy is well known. As the political role of aristocratic consensus increased, so the treatment of rebels became correspondingly muted. By the end of our period, rulers who emerged from the political traditions of tenth- and eleventh-century France, including the Norman kings of England, could not afford to alienate their nobility by unduly harsh treatment of defeated opponents (Strickland 1994). From this specific political climate grew the supposedly more civilized and 'chivalric' conduct of aristocratic warfare, recently studied by John Gillingham (1992; 1994). The comparisons which Gillingham notes between this warfare and that of the late Anglo-Saxons, Irish and Welsh seem, however, to stem, on the one hand, from the differences between French consensus-based polities and the powerful late Anglo-Saxon state (on which, see e.g. Campbell 1975), and, on the other, from the differences between warfare *within* such a polity and that waged *between* Irish and Welsh kingdoms, rather than from fundamental variations in economy and urbanism. Again, diversity in politics and political organization was reflected in changing attitudes to illegitimate violence or armed force.

Sentiments about violence and the means of its legitimation were heavily culturally specific, and consequently when early medieval cultures collided the results could be dramatic. This might be shown most clearly in the relationships between Christian Europe and the ninth-century Vikings (Halsall 1992 for a basic statement). It has been cogently claimed (Sawyer 1962; 1982a) that Viking raids were not qualitatively different from most other early medieval warfare (although see Leyser 1994a: 48–49 for interesting discussion of tactical differences between Vikings and Franks); it can, however, also be closely argued (Wormald 1982) that the effects of Viking assaults upon Christian Europe were indeed significant, and could not have been produced if Viking attacks were indeed just 'extensions' of 'normal' Dark Age activity (Sawyer 1962: 196).

This apparent dichotomy or impasse can be resolved if we see violence and violent relationships as communication – a discourse between the parties involved. A violent act sets in train a series of actions aimed at resolving the dispute which brought it about or at retaliating for it. To read the intentions or significance of violence, to know what kinds of reply are deemed 'correct', or to try to anticipate the responses of opponents or third parties, requires mutual acceptance of norms, especially those governing the legitimacy of these actions. Such norms are often founded on religious belief and spiritual sanction, and this is especially true in considering the ritual side of violence.

Where the actions of one side are not based upon these norms, as was obviously the case with pagan Vikings, the other will not be able to understand them, put them into perspective, or know how to respond. Regardless of how the perpetrators see them, their actions will always seem to break the rules, and, in short, to be extreme, unfettered violence. This lack of comprehension surely generated the ninth-century terror of the Vikings and the effects which this in turn produced, and helps us to reconcile this terror and its consequences with the fact that, from an abstracted viewpoint, Viking warfare encompassed the same types of action, fought for the same purposes, as western European Christian warfare. It partly (but only partly) explains the desire of ninth-century Christian leaders to have any defeated Viking leaders baptized. Conversion to Christianity would establish shared rules of conduct, essential, for example, in giving meaning and effective religious support to the swearing of oaths (Halsall 1992: 9; Nelson, below: 91–92).

Ninth-century pagan Vikings were, however, an extreme case, using maritime technology to strike directly overseas from unknown home-lands (Sawyer 1982b). Similar points might be made about other cultural clashes such as those between seaborne Saracen pirates and the Christians of the Mediterranean littoral, or those which arose immediately from the sudden appearance of new 'barbarian' foes, like Huns or Magyars. Generally, though, where cultures bordered each other on dry land, the establishment of frontiers, the effects of time and the accumulation of knowledge could combine to moderate the effects of culture contact. Reuter (1985: 92; 1991a) shows the political dialogue which could take place across the East Frankish Reich's Slavic frontiers in spite of religious difference, and once Vikings settled in Normandy or northern England the nature of their contacts with Franks or Anglo-Saxons changed significantly, helped, naturally, by conversion to Christianity.

These points highlight the church's role in establishing the legitimacy of violence. Church councils often considered violent acts, and penitentials drew up long lists of the religious penalties for violent crimes, which considered numerous mitigating circumstances (Nelson, below: 101; Speight, below: 171; Coleman, below: 199). Like secular attitudes, these varied from place to place and from century to century, but the church can be seen to act with a greater sense of continuity of tradition, through respect for canon law and previous conciliar decisions. Obviously, its particular concern was to make any violence against the church and its property wholly illegitimate, a concern also very frequently seen in hagiography. In Gregory of Tours' miracle collections such violence is almost invariably visited by lethal and prompt divine vengeance (e.g. below, n. 23).

At a higher level, the church promulgated distinct ideas about the legitimacy of warfare and the nature and desirability of peace.[10] Gregory of Tours railed against *bellum civile*, which pejorative term he extended from royal inter-Frankish warfare down to the fighting between Sichar and Chramnesind; yet, whilst taking some delight in pointing out the futility of foreign wars, he apparently had less scruples about this kind of warfare (*pace* Goffart 1988: 219–20). Indeed, Clovis served as a model ruler for him, as a latter-day Old Testament warrior-king. Civil war posed a particular problem for Carolingian churchmen (Nelson, ch. 4; 1996). The legitimacy or otherwise of rebellion also featured strongly in ecclesiastical thought about violence. This, naturally, hinged upon the legitimacy or otherwise of the rule against which arms were raised (Aitchison, below: 117–18). In certain circumstances, the Fathers could be seen to legitimize the killing of a 'tyrant'; Reynolds (1987) usefully surveys this thought, though his precise application of the theory to Merovingian assassination remains tenuous. Visigothic churchmen had particular difficulty reconciling themselves to rebellion, lending their whole-hearted support to the religious underpinning of Visigothic kingship and the anathematizing of rebellion against the anointed king, yet, at the same time, being led by their own need for strong royal protection to acquiesce in successful usurpations, justifying them, again, as reactions against tyranny (García Moreno, below: 57; Collins 1983: 120–22).

Yet again, though, in spite of the church's attention to its own body of tradition, change through time can be perceived. Partly this can be seen in the introduction, or more usually reintroduction, of particular elements of patristic thinking on the subject. Often it was a reaction to changing political circumstances, as is seen clearly in the Visigothic situation described above. It can also be seen in the West Frankish church's gradual appropriation of the previously royal role in legitimizing, restricting, and arbitrating over the consequences of violence, as kingly authority declined in the tenth and eleventh centuries. This found particular expression in the peace and truce of God movements, and in the acts of the associated peace councils, although many of their concerns can, in very general terms, be traced as far as the Merovingian period (Magnou-Nortier 1992).

So far we have discussed our 'vertical' dimension. Ideas of legitimate force promulgated by lay and ecclesiastical rulers can be brought into contact with those of local communities by discussion of early medieval banditry, a sadly neglected topic (though see Reuter 1996). We saw earlier how difficult it was for kings to control armed bands. One upshot

---

10. Kershaw, forthcoming, will add valuably to the voluminous literature on this subject, which cannot be surveyed here. See also: Markus 1983; Prinz 1971; Renna 1980. Fried (ed.) 1996 came to hand only as the final touches were being put to this volume.

appears to have been the downgrading of the term *latro*, which in Roman times was used to describe a particular, abnormal, level of violent activity above and beyond the norms of criminal activity (Shaw 1984). It was punished particularly savagely and, as mentioned, the word's semantic range was extended to cover rebellion and forms of warfare (e.g. Ammianus Marcellinus, XVII.13.xxvii and *passim*). Early medieval armed bands were not commonly or consistently dealt with severely; members of a *hlop* (band) in Ine's West Saxon code (12, 14) receive lesser punishment than thieves, and members of *contubernia* in Salic Law are fined fairly lightly (*PLS* 42–43), provided that no criminal action was committed. *Latrocinium* is not commonly used to describe the gathering or use of these armed forces; *seditio* appears most commonly. *Latro*'s semantic scope in early medieval sources spans habitual criminals and (apparently armed) robbers; sometimes *latrones* are simply equated with *fures* (thieves).[11] Only the lower reaches of the word's range of meanings in the Roman period are perpetuated into the early Middle Ages. It seems that *latrones* could be people who refused to abide by the decisions of the local court.[12] A large corpus of law banned dealings with *latrones*,[13] and Frankish legislation made the pursuit of *latrones* a communal responsibility (*PLS* 93; Callendar Murray 1988). Thus, rather than being wielders of armed force who, in our 'vertical' dimension, potentially stood between the state and effective government of the localities, *latrones* now apparently lie outside this vertical scale, as criminals expelled by the community, although often retaining links with it. This argument is supported to some extent by the fact that the vernacular words *wargus* or *wearg* appear to be synonymous with *latro*. Sidonius (*Epp.* VI.4.i) mentions *vargi* abducting women and selling them as slaves; *PLS* 66 uses the verb *wargare* to mean abduction. *Wargus* is used in Frankish law (*PLS* 55.iv; *Lex Ribv.* 88) to describe someone out-lawed for grave-robbing, and again an interesting comparison with Sidonius' writings emerges; the latter described the grave-robbers whom he had chased from his family tomb (*Epp.* III.12.ii) as *latrones*. One Carolingian capitulary actually uses the word *wargida* to describe some-one's condemnation by their community (*Capit.* I, 27.iv). That *wearg*

---

11. cp. *Capit.* I, 20, xxiii (Frankish version), and xii (Lombard version); *Capit.* I, 139.xv; and the similarity between early Anglo-Saxon laws about *þeofas* (thieves) and continental legislation about *latrones*: Wihtred 25–26; Ine 12, 15.ii, 16, 28, 36, 72–73.

12. Such, at least, would be one conclusion from Childebert II's Decrees II.5; III.1; *Capit.* I, 64.xi. This conclusion is to some extent supported by the strong similar-ity between certain laws on *latrones* and those relating to runaway slaves, *fugitivi*: see *LV* IX.1.xxi.

13. On sheltering *latrones*, see: *LV* IX.1.xix; *LRB* 18.i; *Capit.* I, 59.v; *Ed. Roth.* 22. On settling with *latrones* 'out of court', see: *Lex Baiuariorum* 9.xvii; *PLS* II.80; III.89.

could be used to describe monsters and evil spirits is also significant, but the point is driven home by the fact that the *latrones* of the Vulgate (e.g. Matt. 27.xxxv-xliv) become the *wergus* of the Old English *Dream of the Rood* (l.31).

Community attitudes towards the legitimacy of violence are naturally difficult to establish. Violence was only condemned when it was perceived to be criminal, which normally depended upon an accusation being brought against the perpetrator. Violence within households was rarely the subject of legislation, presumably because, apart from abused wives whose families brought charges against their husbands, such violence would be unlikely to come to court. Lombard law recognized the legitimacy of violence by the head of the household against his children or wards (*Liut. Leg.* AD 731, 4), as long as this was in the cause of discipline or instruction (Balzaretti, below: 179). Wicker (ch. 11) examines the related issue of Scandinavian attitudes towards female infanticide, particularly from the archaeological data, and in doing so interestingly explores an area of conflict between the 'vertical' and 'horizontal' dimensions of the legitimation of violence. Few laws attempted to limit violence by a master against his slaves. Visigothic law briefly attempted to impose restrictions on killing one's own slaves (*LV* VI.5.xii), but these were short-lived and ineffectual (Bonnassie 1991: 20–21; García Moreno, below: 56). This acknowledgement of the legitimacy of such violence by the head of a household is perhaps linked to the laws' concern to maintain the inviolability of a man's house or *curtis* (see above; but see Callendar Murray 1994 for critique of some traditional ideas of *Hausherrschaft*). Classes of people, like pregnant women (*PLS* 24.v; Alfred 9), or young boys (*PLS* 24.i), were, at particular times and places and for various reasons, also protected by heavier *wergilds*. The fact, though, that in Visigothic Spain, unlike Merovingian Gaul, the old merited a lower *wergild* than adults in their prime, reinforces the point that the laws' concern was usually to penalize damage to a family rather than that to protect the individual (Halsall 1995a: 63–64; 1996) and reveals, again, the wide scope for cultural diversity, also manifested in differing attitudes to violence by and towards women (Balzaretti, ch. 9; Coleman, ch. 10), the punishment of adultery (García Moreno, ch. 1), infanticide (Wicker, ch. 11) and so on.

A general principle, attested throughout our period, appears to have been that if violence took place in public, or if it was publicly acknowledged, this might alleviate its consequences. In some cases to make an act of violence public was to declare its legitimacy. Thus, according to *Lex Ribuaria* (80), a man caught in the act of breaking and entering might be killed without threat of punishment, but the body must be publicly displayed (cp. Ine 35). This, obviously, was why Chramnesind hung Sichar's body on his fence-post.

However, the laws specify that the opposite, the concealment of a murder, was a heinous crime; throwing a body down a well, or covering it with sticks or bark, trebled the fine for homicide envisaged by the authors of the *Pactus Legis Salicae* (*PLS* 41.iv, vi, vii). There are three possible reasons for these concerns. The first is that to conceal a body was probably seen as an admission that the killer had no reason to commit the crime; the second is that it was perhaps seen as dishonourable and doubly blameworthy to refuse to acknowledge the consequences of one's actions; thirdly, and related to this, the concealment of a crime might lead to punishment, or vengeance, being exacted on an innocent party, and that in turn might lead to spiralling violence within a community (cp. *PLS* 41.xiv). Not unconnected with these ideas were laws condemning violence at night to heavier penalties (*Ed. Roth.* 32–33); and those which dealt with other forms of indirect, or otherwise concealed, violence: secret hirings of assassins (*PLS* 28; *Ed. Roth.* 11), assaults through witchcraft (*PLS* 19, 64) and poison (*PLS* 19; *Ed. Roth.* 139–42), or even lending weapons to another (Æthelberht 18–19; *Ed. Roth.* 307; Alfred 19).

The dichotomy between public (or open) and concealed, legitimate and illegitimate, could, particularly in Anglo-Saxon and Scandinavian evidence, be carried over into other areas of crime, such as theft, robbery and even the destruction of woods (cp. Ine 43, 43.i). The thief in *Beowulf* is to be condemned because of the secrecy of his actions (Andersson 1984). This attitude may be what condemns the *þeof* of Ine's code (12) to death, whereas the *hloþere* (member of a band) could clear himself with an oath of 120 hides, or a fine of 120 shillings (Ine 14). In Scandinavia the act of *rán*, or plunder (discussed by Morris, ch. 7), was held to be more legitimate if carried out openly (Miller 1986). Laws on theft and robbery typically also maintained the particular protection afforded to the house, *villa* or *curtis* (e.g. *PLS* 11), as did those on kidnapping (García Moreno, below: 51–52) and armed bands (*PLS* 14.vi-vii; Æthelberht 17).

VIOLENT STRATEGIES AND RELATIONSHIPS, AND THE SETTLEMENT OF DISPUTES

Violent relationships can often be seen as a discourse, structured around shared norms. That this discourse frequently aims at the solution of disputes goes without saying, and violence can be used directly to settle a dispute.[14] One party may obtain a satisfactory outcome simply by attacking its opponents. One rival for local power may achieve victory by the effective, if unsubtle, expedient of killing or physically incapacitating

---

14. On dispute settlement see Davies & Fouracre (eds) 1986; Caplan (ed.) 1995; Roberts 1983.

the other; someone aggrieved after suffering a violent injury or wrong may achieve satisfaction by inflicting a similar injury in return; disputed ownership of land or property may be resolved by the violent ejection or dispossession of one party. The relationship between assailant and victim is direct, and relates, furthermore, directly to the resolution of the dispute; put even more simply, a disputant's aim is achieved by violent action against his or her opponent.

This was possible in the early Middle Ages, but not always. One needed to take account of the possible reactions of third parties, again raising the issue of the legitimacy of violence. Some parties were simply incapable of undertaking direct and open violent action against their rivals, opponents or oppressors, or of being sure that such action would be accepted as legitimate. Where this is the case, violence becomes in a sense indirect. A publicly violent stance might be adopted, without carrying out any actual violence; a limited, ritualized or token act of violence may be perpetrated, or violence against a third party carried out. Some or all of these options may be used together. The violence does not terminate the dispute, but draws the community's attention to it. Highlighting the wrong done, the existence of a grievance, and the right (theoretically) to take violent action brings pressure upon third parties to arbitrate and end the dispute. Examples may be found in the use of violence against saints' relics by aggrieved religious, especially monastic, communities (Geary 1994a; 1994b), as well as in those communities' suspension of the usual spiritual services for secular society (not just their aggressors or opponents). These sanctions were often accompanied by public, heavily ritualized, declarations of the religious community's grievance and the source of the wrong. Secular examples of limited or restricted violent action aimed at highlighting a dispute and bringing about arbitration and settlement have been studied in the context of twelfth-century Tuscany by Chris Wickham (unpublished).

To distinguish between these types of violent action is analytically important, but it is not always easy to coin adequate terms to differentiate them. Marx (1972), in a useful anthropological examination of personal violence, used the terms 'rational' and 'irrational'. Here, 'rational' implies that the violence has a clear aim in mind, which is achieved by the violence used; 'irrational' that the end in mind is not, and cannot be, achieved by the violence used (it 'holds no chance of a way out of the impasse'; *ibid.*: 299). Thus, underprivileged Israeli Bedouin cannot gain the increased benefits they desire by physical attack on state officers (*ibid.*: 293–300); in fact this would be counterproductive. But they draw attention to the dispute by sit-ins, public threats of violence, smashing up the official's office and furniture, or in extreme cases by violence against spouses and children or threatened suicide; rarely does an official suffer more than a grabbed arm or a slapped face. Interestingly, those who actually assaulted officials could 'afford to lose' (*ibid.*: 297). Nevertheless, whether we like it or not, because of these words' usual connotations, the vocabulary of 'rationality' today implies too much of a moral judgement.

Coser used the terms *realistic* and *non-realistic* to differentiate between types of conflict:

> 'Conflicts which arise from the frustration of specific demands within the relationship and from estimates of gains of the participants, and which are directed at the presumed frustrating object, can be called *realistic conflicts*, insofar as they are means towards a specific result. *Nonrealistic conflicts*, on the other hand, although still involving interaction between two or more persons, are not occasioned by the rival ends of the antagonists, but the need for a tension release of at least one of them. In this case the choice of antagonists depends on determinants not directly related to a contentious issue and is not oriented towards the attainment of specific goals' (Coser 1965: 49).

Wickham (unpublished) coins the term 'strategic' for violence which draws attention to, but does not in itself resolve, disputes. This seems a preferable alternative, and I have adopted it in the remainder of this introduction. By the same token, violence aimed directly at the achievement of ends becomes 'tactical' violence, which accords with the *Shorter Oxford English Dictionary*'s definition of tactical.

Related to the issue of tactical and strategic violence, as becomes clear in the quote from Coser, is that of the relationships involved in violent acts. In most tactical violence the primary relationship involved is that between aggressor and victim. This can be broadened to include supporting kin-networks where vengeance may be wrought on a murderer's kin instead of the murderer himself, or, in warfare, an enemy's subjects or followers, without affecting the general point. In some cases, however, the primary relationship involved in the violence is not that between assailant and assaulted. In modern examples we might cite certain 'drive-by' killings in less privileged urban areas of the USA, or strategic, or, as Marx (1972) would term it, 'irrational' attacks by straitened Bedouin on their wives or children. The primary relationship in some 'drive-by' killings is that between the shooter and the members of the gang within which prestige is sought, or of which membership is desired; the victim often has no prior relationship with the killer. Although the victims of domestic Bedouin violence have previous relationships with their attackers, and are sometimes seen by them as causing the attack, the principal causal relationship is really between the attacker and the administrators of Israeli state benefits. Most of this violence is strategic, but it need not be.

Perhaps the best examples of early medieval violence where the primary relationship involved is not that between attacker and attacked are to be found in early medieval endemic warfare, where the primary relationships are those between the ruler or lord and his followers or magnates. Wars were undertaken to provide the booty so essential to early medieval politics (Reuter 1985; Reuter 1990 for the consequences of failing to take plunder), to provide opportunities to demonstrate valour or military prowess, and thus obtain rewards, and to display the military ability of the leader to his followers (and potential rivals). This was a kind of 'tension release'. The victims were in some ways incidental, though the choice of target was usually justified by some real or alleged insult or wrong. One instance might be Theuderic I's 525 attack on the Auvergne. Here, Gregory of Tours' account (*LH* III.11, admittedly confused: Wood 1994: 51–54) makes it clear that the primary causal relationship involved was that between Theuderic and 'his Franks' who had threatened to desert him for his brothers if he did not lead them on campaign. The Auvergnats simply happened to have mistakenly invited Theuderic's half-brother Childebert to be their king when Theuderic was rumoured killed in Thuringia. It is thus important to retain a distinction between the different causal relationships involved in violent action. They permit one way at least of usefully differentiating between different types of violence and dispute settlement within early medieval political units.

FEUD, VENGEANCE AND 'CIVIL' WAR

Feud is often regarded as central to early medieval life, looming large in innumerable discussions of violence and law in this period.[15] Yet, given that the body of academic historians can all too often be regarded as a 'feuding society', it is odd that notions of feud so often remain vague.[16] As a definition, that quoted by Bennett at the beginning of his chapter seems uncontroversial. Most would agree that a feud is a relationship of lasting hostility between groups, marked by periodic, cyclical, reciprocal

---

15. References to works on early medieval feud can be found in Bennett's chapter, below. To these may be added Byock 1982; Callendar Murray 1983; Davis 1969, Goebel 1976, ch. 1; Miller 1983a; 1983b; O'Brien 1996; Reuter 1991b; Smail 1996. The idea that the 'feud', or, as will be argued here, 'customary vengeance', is a Germanic legal principle (Wallace-Hadrill 1962: 121; Callendar Murray 1983: 135) is undermined by its existence in medieval Celtic societies (Davies 1969), let alone in modern Bedouin ones! Anthropology: Boehm 1984; Gluckman 1962; Peters 1975. Black-Michaud 1975: 1–24 comprehensively surveys the anthropological literature up to the early 'seventies.

16. Gillingham (1994: 36) seems untypically confused: 'These feuds were property disputes waged with violence, but violence controlled so as not to escalate into the blood-feud.' Quite what the difference between feud and 'the' blood-feud was remains unspecified.

violence. As Sawyer (1987) has argued, it is actually very difficult (but, I would argue, *contra* Sawyer, not impossible) to find this kind of violent relationship in the early medieval west. Yet the feud remains locked centrally within our concepts of what this period 'was like'. So, many definitions of feud have been proposed (Bennett, below: 127–29), usually bending the general definition, but still failing to fit the early medieval data closely or indeed at all. It is time to wrench ourselves free of this construct. Feud, as understood in modern definitions, was not generally practised in the early Middle Ages; what early medieval people called *faehðe*, or similar, was something rather different.

Understanding 'true' feud means acknowledging its 'structural' and 'temporal' aspects. Feud is a long-term phenomenon. Each killing or attack simply retaliates for the opposition's previous assault. Several writers highlight the fact that feud can be seen as a form of exchange (Black-Michaud 1975: 80–85; Bourdieu 1977; Miller 1990: 182ff.).[17] Killings create a 'debt' paid off by retaliatory violence, only to place the other side in the position of debtors. Although a group is justified in exacting revenge for a previous attack, their retaliation does not end the conflict; it merely justifies the other side's next blow. Thus 'true' feud is terminated with difficulty, and never through violence (unless one group exterminates the other).

One aspect of Black-Michaud's thesis (1975: 63–80) needs refinement. This concerns what Wallace-Hadrill (1962: 143) called the 'dormant' feud. Although each cycle of violence might be justified by a previous 'wrong' shamefully, or incompletely, compensated, instead of all feuds always existing meaningfully in the minds of the participants, some 'feuds' are actually periodically reinvented to justify discrete acts of violence. This still counts as feud for Black-Michaud, as for Wallace-Hadrill. But if, rather than having a continuous state of violence and enmity, we have a series of independent incidents taking place to solve immediate problems, and the active and contingent selection from the past of particular episodes to justify or explain them, it does not seem analytically useful to link them into a spuriously continuous 'chain' of events and call that feud. This selection of past violent acts to justify present ones is important as an indication of a particular mentality which saw vengeance as legitimate and 'correct', but it does not, of itself, indicate a 'feuding society'. As Roy (1994) argues in her excellent study of a Bangladeshi riot, a violent act or quarrel forever alters any relation-

---

17. White (1986: 250) questions the 'exchange' simile. Acharias of Marmande, during a raid on his enemies, killed some probably unrelated bystanders, for which he later compensated. Thus, for White, 'the notion that Acharias' killings constituted an exchange begins to look like a legalistic or anthropological fiction.' But from the evidence cited, *pace* White's view, it seems clear that the violence in which Acharias was involved was not a feud. See below.

ship, and is always there to be remembered and to inform future action. It should be noted that Black-Michaud (1975: 78–79) discusses how in 'true' feuding societies, enmity is kept alive in the participants' consciousness by the use of songs or stories (often performed by women).

Black-Michaud (1975, ch. 4) also argues that feud is a means of structuring society in the effective absence of other kinds of socio-political organization. Periodic outbursts of violence highlight and thus reaffirm or redefine the lines along which society is ordered.[18] Feuds can, as he and others (recently, White 1986) have argued, only really take place between groups of roughly equal socio-political power, where there is no 'higher' political authority which is capable of ending the dispute, either through the participants' mutual acceptance of its right to arbitrate, or through its ability to stamp out the dispute forcibly.

The use of time in this kind of bloody exchange is interesting (Bourdieu 1977: 6–7); immediate retribution can indicate power effectively, yet can also simply pass the initiative straight back to the other side. A delayed response can be more potent, in that it keeps the initiative, maintains the relationship of 'debt' between the groups, and puts the other side on the defensive as they live in perpetual awareness that retaliation may take place at any time. To keep vengeance waiting may be a sign of power, yet to delay too long might be construed as signifying weakness. The social practice of the feud involves, therefore, a difficult balancing act involving knowledge of the possibilities of action and of the mores constraining it, the latter including the responses of third parties. Excellent applications of this sort of social theory to medieval evidence can be found in the work of William Ian Miller (1986; 1990).

Compurgation and compensation payments, phenomena well known to early medievalists (recently, O'Brien 1996), feature in the strategies of feuding societies (Black-Michaud 1975: ch. 3), but in rather different ways. The collective swearing of oaths can act as a demonstration of kin solidarity, indicating that a kin-group is ready to fight in defence of one of its members. Successful oath-swearing thus, at least temporarily, produces a stand-off and (sooner or later) a probable escalation to violence. This *may* differ subtly from the use of compurgation in early medieval societies, where recent studies suggest that oath-swearing was aimed at establishing community consensus on an individual's guilt or otherwise. Similarly, rather than terminating the dispute, the payment of compensation simply indicates that one side currently (and however temporarily) cannot pay the debt of blood. Accepting compensation is often

---

18. Another key element of Black-Michaud's treatment of feud concerns its ecological dimension, occurring in situations of 'total scarcity'. Although this can be argued for some feuding societies, such as 'Saga Iceland', or the early modern border and highland regions of Scotland, it does not apply to some early medieval instances of feud.

regarded as dishonourable, and is no long-term substitute for equalling the score violently (Black-Michaud 1975: 12, 109–18).

Stressing feud's structural and temporal aspects permits a definition which is neither so vague that a broad array of forms of violence may be included under a single heading, nor so narrow that only one very culturally specific type of violence may be called feud. We can still recognise some early medieval conflicts as feuds, but most supposed 'feuds' of the early medieval west are in fact something else. An individual or group injures another individual or group; the latter then either retaliate, vengeance being seen as justifiable and apparently ending the dispute, or, through the threat of violence, they produce a resolution through compensation, equally appearing to settle the issue. This partly, but far from entirely, results from the fact that our sources rarely allow us to trace a conflict over a long period (Fouracre, below: 61 n. 2). Nevertheless, the evidence as its stands almost invariably shows us tales of violence in one or, at most, two acts. There is scant reference to long-standing enmities producing the recorded outbreaks and little or no indication that, after the narrated outbursts, lasting hostility led to further violence. Nor is it easy to find the mechanisms used to keep feuds burning.

There are critical differences between feuding and what I would call 'legal' or (perhaps better) 'customary vengeance'. Here, compensation is an alternative to vengeance; the threat of vengeance serves to bring about a legal settlement through compensation. What is more, such a settlement, by either alternative, is legitimate and honourable. In feud, when the aggrieved party attacks its opponents, this simply passes the acknowledged grievance to the other side, reversing the roles and relationships. Early medieval sources give us no reason to suppose that, when a person or group injured another party, paid no compensation and thus suffered an avenging attack, they had any right to feel offended or aggrieved, or that retaliation for vengeance was in any way legitimate. We see the law of Talion. To early medieval people, two wrongs did make a right.

Other useful distinctions between feud and 'customary vengeance' may be highlighted by returning to the question of violence in dispute-settlement. In feud, each act of violence is, in a way, 'strategic', calling attention to the dispute, rather than solving it in itself (though it may produce an attempt to arbitrate and end the feud), and marshalling support for one side or the other. If violence is resorted to as 'customary vengeance' then, provided it is carried out in the correct way, it terminates the dispute. The 'strategic' element within 'customary vengeance' is the *threat* of violence. Public declarations of the intent to seek vengeance call attention to the dispute and bring about arbitration and settlement. These declarations may be seen in the ways in which aggrieved parties made it obvious that they held an opponent in *odium*, proclaimed their *ira* or *inimicitia*, or, in certain cases, declared defiance. This is illustrated for eleventh-century Touraine by the cases cited by White (1986).

'Customary' vengeance presents as many opportunities for social practice as does feud. This is clear from White's (1986) study. Some aggrieved parties put off or refused compensation, and rejected attempts to mediate, apparently for quite lengthy periods. This was evidently an effective strategy, highlighting the wrong suffered and its seriousness, and allowing the aggrieved party to make the most out of their rivals' contrition and attempts to end the dispute, giving them a temporary local political ascendancy. However, we may also suppose that holding out for too long would risk turning opinion against the aggrieved party.

The existence of customary vengeance, as distinct from feud, has implications for the nature of 'state' control in the localities. Rather than being a means of keeping order *faute de mieux*, in the effective absence of centralized 'law and order' maintenance,[19] we may see it as quite the opposite. The threat of vengeance is used strategically to bring about arbitration and end the dispute. This arbitration and settlement, however, are frequently carried out by a state appointee, the local count (or equivalent) or his deputies. Mutual acceptance of the state officers' right to arbitrate and settle disputes is important in maintaining an active state presence in the localities, and in binding the latter into a single political unit. Instead of a rather weary acceptance of political impotence, and a consequent legitimation of a 'self-help' 'system' whereby local peace was maintained by the threat of mutually destructive violence, kingly backing for 'customary vengeance' was an active strategy for increasing control (see Gregory of Tours, *VP* 8.vii as an example, and *Ed. Roth.* 19, mentioned above: 8). Royal promulgation of legislation acknowledging or legitimizing the procedures of 'customary vengeance' is thus unsurprising, or at least requires less convoluted explanation than has sometimes been offered in the past. Indeed, given the rarity with which vengeance seems to have actually been exacted, the frequency with which declarations of *faida* or *inimicitia* were aimed at bringing about arbitration through governmental officers, and the extent to which such officers monopolized the legitimation of vengeance, it may be unwise to continue to classify early medieval 'feud' as a 'self-help' mechanism at all (*contra* Kaiser 1983: 56).

Although the general principles of customary vengeance are attested in most parts of early medieval Europe, we must bear in mind regional

---

19. The idea of a collapse of central authority after the end of the Roman empire, and thus the need to find local peace-keeping mechanisms, has a long and venerable historiography stretching back to Brunner and Fustel in the late nineteenth century and represented by such recent works as Lynch 1986 and Mathisen 1993.

and chronological diversity. The practice, as opposed to the principles, and the precise mechanisms used to arbitrate and resolve disputes varied according to time and place,[20] and the ways in which early medieval kings intervened in such disputes changed in line with the (at least imagined) extent and possibilities of effective political control at a local level (see the comparison of Edmund I of England's and Charlemagne's legislation on vengeance, below, and compare both of these with the Salian kings' non-intervention in such violence; Reuter 1991b; also Kaiser 1983).

We can distinguish feud from customary vengeance in practice. When the text is subjected to close scrutiny, the famous 'feud' of Sichar and Chramnesind is (*pace*, for the most recent example, Reuter & Wickham 1995: 5 n. 8) revealed to be nothing of the sort. Tension was clearly already in the air in Manthelan. The killing of the servant of the priest, to whom Sichar was bound by *amicitia*, and the violent rejection of the priest's invitation to hospitality constituted grave offences. Although there is no hint that Austregisel was responsible for the retainer's death it seems reasonable to conjecture that the murderer was somehow linked to him. Yet Austregisel himself was more than willing to resort to violence, hinting that both sides were waiting for an opportunity to settle their rivalry thus. Perhaps, as Wallace-Hadrill (1962: 140) wrote, it was simply a case of the party having 'reached an advanced stage'. Nevertheless, after the killing of Sichar's *pueri*, the two parties were brought before a *iudicium*, and Austregisel legally penalized. This settled the issue. Austregisel did not dispute the sentence, and disappears from history. Wallace-Hadrill (*ibid.*) inserted a wholly unsubstantiated conjecture into the story, and greatly blurred the issue, by stating that Austregisel was a relative of Sichar's opponents in the second act of the saga. Gregory mentions no kinship between Austregisel and Auno. In fact, this would be unlikely, as what is apparently happening is that the court has put disputed property in the hands of a neutral third party, pending a final decision (probably related to the fact that, as subsequent events made clear, Sichar was under the protection [*in verbo*] of Queen Brunechildis[21]) or formal transaction.

This is 'customary vengeance'. The same can be said of very nearly all other medieval 'feuds'. Those described by Koziol (1992), White (1986) and even, in a later period, Wormald (1983), look, not like anything which would satisfy modern understandings of feud, but like individual wrongs avenged by violence or resolved by the threat of vengeance (on

---

20. The choice between using royal (or ducal or comital) officers or subordinates, bishops (James 1983), or local monasteries or saints' cults (White 1986; Koziol 1992), for instance, is heavily dependant upon the specifics of society and politics at the time and place in question.
21. Above, n. 1.

concepts of vengeance in Lombard Italy, which generally support the argument proposed here, see Sutherland 1975). Even the spiralling bloodshed in Tournai described by Gregory (*LH* X.27, and termed feud, wrongly in my view, by Halsall 1995a: 66, and Goffart 1989: 275) is probably more helpfully to be seen, in the context of Chlothar II's minority, as an unusually violent, but short-lived, local power-struggle (Gregory simply calls it *disceptatio*, a dispute). Similarly, the later Merovingian aristocratic violence studied by Paul Fouracre (below: 63–66) should be seen as armed struggle for political power rather than 'feud' (and see Brown, below: 78–82 for such violent rivalries in Rome). Although our evidence gives us, chronologically, only a snap-shot of violence, there is little suggestion of lasting hostility as a long-term principle of social relations, as in feuding societies. [22]

The argument can be pursued by examination of laws expressly concerned with revenge. Probably the best known of all such legislation is the Anglo-Saxon code 'II Edmund', entitled by Whitelock (*EHD* I, no. 38) 'Edmund's code concerning the blood-feud'. Here legislation restricts the use of vengeance, which can only be carried out against the killer himself, not against any of his kin, if the latter refuse to support him; the slayer, if he calls upon his friends for support, has a year to pay compensation; if vengeance is carried out against the killer's kin contrary to the regulations, the avenger is outlawed; procedures for sanctuary and for the safe payment of compensation are set out. Throughout the code, nothing is said about the possibility that someone who legally avenges a murdered kinsman must then 'bear the *faehðe*' himself. Illegal vengeance becomes the king's affair, not that of the murderer's kinsmen (II Edmund 1.iii).

Similar conclusions emerge from a study of the lengthy treatment of vengeance in Charlemagne's 'Programmatic capitulary' (*Capitulare Missorum Generale*) of 802 (*Capit.* I, 33.xxxii). King (trans. 1987: 240–41) translates *inimicitia* as 'feud', which is a little misleading. This edict, unlike Edmund's, 140 years later, attempts to ban *all* vengeance, which is very important, revealing significantly different perceptions of royal power. Charlemagne attempted to remove all means of dispute settlement except those operating through his officers. A murderer must agree to pay compensation, and, when this is given, the victim's relatives should accept compensation and not, in enmity (*inimititia* [*sic*]), add to the evil already done. Anyone taking vengeance will be punished. Again, the range of possibilities envisaged does not include revenge by the kin of a murderer killed in vengeance.

---

22. Reuter 1991b: 303: 'Feud, in the form of a vendetta between families or groups extending over several generations, is, as far as I can see, not proven in the eleventh century'; 'We may not interpret any violent action as feud in the narrow sense' (*ibid.* 300).

It was important, however, to make it clear that a killing had been carried out as legitimate vengeance. Chramnesind hung Sichar's body on his fence to make the killing public and proclaim its legitimacy. We find the 'publication' of legitimate killings appearing frequently throughout Gregory's work: Childebert II had Magnovald's body thrown into the street (*LH* VIII.36); the bodies of Eberulf's men were dragged from the building in which they were killed and exposed (*LH* VII.29);[23] the same fate befell the corpses of Guntramn Boso and his followers (*LH* IX.10).

Nevertheless, the term feud is applicable in some instances. One, perhaps ironically in view of the usually supposed 'Germanic' nature of 'feuding', is documented in Provence (Geary 1994c). Here a dispute between a group of knights and the monastery of St-Victor, Marseille, was kept alive by acts of violence (although not fatal) and also by repeated public (and unsuccessful) attempts to end the conflict. As Geary (1994c: 157) argues, surely correctly, one of the reasons why the dispute was never settled is that it served periodically to define the lines along which this local society in 'stateless' France was structured. Each act of violence was 'strategic', including the monks' use of spiritual 'weapons'. This seems to fit our definition of feud.

Gillingham (1994: 34) has argued for the existence of feud during the 'anarchy' of William the Bastard's minority which, if his case were proven, would underscore the argument presented here. However, the only case of feud adduced (as opposed to customary vengeance-killing) can only be seen as such if one accepts, *a priori*, the interrelationship of quite possibly discrete acts of political violence, and Bennett (below: 132–33) presents a more persuasive argument against this, demonstrating the specific political circumstances pertaining to the mutilation of William Giroie.

The other, obvious, examples of 'true' feud, although slightly outside our period, concern those of 'saga Iceland' (Byock 1982; Miller 1990; although see Sawyer 1987). Here the definition is satisfied; here, too, we see feud in a stateless context, and thus feud as a means of structuring local society by periodically demanding that people situate themselves on one side or other of a particular dispute. As the saga of Bergthora and Hallgerd (*Njál's Saga*; Miller 1990: 182–84) shows, compensation was only received as a temporary measure, until 'the debt of blood' could be paid.

Another instance of feud may be the possibly cyclical, reciprocal violence between the rival Gothic groups of Alaric and Sarus in the late fourth and early fifth centuries (García Moreno 1994: 5–7). This

---

23. Here, interestingly, Gregory portrayed the slaughter of Eberulf and his men as divine vengeance: *Dei ultio*.

example relies upon insecure genealogical reconstructions of the participating bodies, but, if accepted, would fit our model. The Goths, a
wandering agglomeration of armed bands (e.g. Liebeschuetz 1990; 1992)
can be seen as located within an, at that point, fairly ineffectual state
(the Roman empire), and this possible 'feud' could well have served
periodically to define the outlines of Gothic society. Perhaps, though,
this too can be seen more simply and helpfully as warfare for political
control.

Mention of warfare raises the final possible instance of early medieval
feuding. Much border raiding and hostility between neighbouring
polities seems to have operated along the lines of feud. In literature we
can see this in the strife between Geats and Swedes in *Beowulf* (ll.
2472–90; Cross 1971). The intermittent warfare between Frank and continental Saxon between the sixth and eighth centuries seems to have
been carried out in tit-for-tat reprisal attacks, and here we have evidence,
albeit problematical, of songs sung (by women) to keep alive old
enmities (*Vita Faronis* 78; Wood 1994: 163; cp. *LHF* 41; Fouracre 1984:
5, and below: 64 for doubts). The eleventh-century warfare between
Danes and Norwegians (Morris, ch. 7) can also be seen in this light.
Again, though, 'feuds' may have been periodically reinvented rather
than being perpetually in the minds of the protagonists (cp., in the context of Frankish-Thuringian warfare, Theuderic I's speech recorded in
Gregory *LH* III.7; the tenth-century Welsh *Armes Prydein* may be another
example). Irish warfare (e.g. Hughes 1972: 154; Byrne 1973: 146–47 for
'revenge warfare') seems to follow the 'feud' model, and so, probably,
did all 'endemic' early medieval warfare, where justification for annual
border raids or smaller-scale military plundering expeditions (as implied,
for example in the Laws of Hywel Dda) was required. Even Augustine
could consider just a war waged to avenge an injury (*Quaestiones in
Heptateuchum* VI.10; Cross 1971: 271; Markus 1983). In warfare it is
possible to see spiralling reciprocal violence, with each attack justified by
the one before. Again, this kind of violent relationship is important in
drawing the lines on the political map, helping to define identities in the
absence of higher, 'legal' authority (Morris, ch. 7). For this kind of warfare, occurring during a momentary lapse in 'higher' authority, we might
cite the hostilities which broke out between the Loire valley *civitates* in
the confusion following Chilperic I's murder (584; Gregory, *LH* VII.2).
This war was eventually stopped by the intercession of royal officers,
and, presumably, the re-establishment of royal control, but only as it
entered its third phase (the crucial 'revenge for revenge' stage characteristic of feud, but typically absent from our records of lower-level civic
violence).

Two problems arise from the schema set out here. The first concerns
'customary' vengeance-killing which becomes feud, through secondary
retaliation on the part of the original aggressors. This is possible, but

difficult to detect in our evidence, partly perhaps because of the existence of many forces (community, 'state' and church) militating against
such escalation, and, related to this, because this escalation only occurs
with frequency in particular socio-political situations, as noted. The
second problem is terminological; individual acts of violence within a
feud are usually discussed as revenge or vengeance; above, for clarity, I
have restricted myself to the word revenge.

Early medieval people had no clear term for the social relationship
which we would define as feud. The Germanic words *faehðe, faithu* or
faida mean legal vengeance, usually as a right or threat. At some point
the modern feud (or German *Fehde*) has widened to mean on-going
relationships based upon this right.[24] The early medieval word meant
something different from its modern descendant, and this is what lies at
the root of the whole problem. *Faehðe* was a right on the part of one
side;[25] feud is a reciprocal relationship. The Germanic words may
indeed, as Wallace-Hadrill (1962: 122–23) said, 'lurk behind' Latin terms
like *inimicitia*.[26] They have the sense of hostility and enmity, but we
should remember that hostility, or enmity, is by no means necessarily
feud; and it is not justifiable to stretch their semantic range to make
them automatically mean feud. Declarations of enmity were strategic,
used to publicise the threat of vengeance and to bring about a resolution, and so the time-scale implicit in early medieval *inimicitia* was
(subject to the strategies of social practice mentioned earlier) a limited
one. When violence broke out it was usually talked of simply as a dispute. If contemporaries wanted a word for lasting hostile relationships,
they seem simply to have used the words *bellum* or *werra* – war (see
below; Nelson, below: 93; Bennett, below: 138).

We thus have a choice. Either we make it clear whether we are using
'feud' in its medieval or its modern sense, or (probably preferably) we
should banish the word 'feud' from our discussions of early medieval
violence, except in the handful of instances where it is justified, keep it
as a separate category of violence, and use 'customary vengeance'
instead to describe instances where, after a violent attack the aggrieved
party uses, or threatens to use, retaliatory violence to bring about an
end to a dispute (through compensation, where violence is not actually
employed). If we choose it we do no more than remove a term which
has become unhelpful, and unhelpfully value-laden, and replace it with

---

24. In Britain, perhaps this was related to its use in Scottish law (cp. Wormald 1983)
    and, specifically, its use to describe the 'true' feuds which existed in the stateless
    border regions between England and Scotland (or the Scottish Highlands,
    similarly removed from effective state control).

25. The idea that 'feud' was a right has a long pedigree, going back to Brunner
    1906: 221 and beyond.

26. This is clear from *Ed. Roth.* 74: *Faida quod est inimicitia.*

one which fits the data exactly.

Another related type of violence which must be discussed in this section is larger-scale tactical violence used to obtain a political advantage over rivals. A wide range of actions could be included under this heading, from raids, the ravaging of lands, estates or settlements, the destruction of homesteads or castles, to pitched battles. At lower levels (attacks, murders), this violence could be regulated by the usual mechanisms of customary vengeance; in certain political circumstances it might even escalate into feud. Distinction becomes necessary with larger-scale action: attacks, involving sometimes significant numbers of armed men, directed towards higher level political and territorial advancement. In certain political formations, it might lead to tit-for-tat reprisals carried out over a long period of time. If that were the case the word feud might well describe it. Often, however, this is tactical violence, and, in Coser's terms, 'reasonable' conflict with a specific goal in mind. Although the violence may be carried out by both sides, these episodes are discrete, limited in time, ending either with victory for one side or with a negotiated peace. This kind of violence is described in Bennett's paper, and by contemporaries, as war (*werra*, sometimes distinguished from *bellum*, external war; Nelson, below: 93), and the same types of violence feature both in several of the Tourangeaux cases cited by Stephen White (1986), and in Timothy Reuter's (1991b) study of Salian political violence.

That this warfare took place within early medieval polities, rather than between them, has led to the use of the term 'private war' to describe it. This raises all the difficulties of distinguishing too readily between private and public, and impinges on the issue of the legitimacy or illegitimacy of violent action, already discussed (above: 10; see also Bennett, below: 138). Nevertheless, it is important to distinguish between warfare within and warfare between polities. This distinction lies at the root of the differences between the practice of warfare against rebels and that against 'foreign' enemies. It might explain some of the observable contrasts between Norman and French warfare and that amongst the Celtic princes noted by Gillingham (1991; 1994). Early medieval internal warfare seems distinct from external in that it is almost invariably both 'tactical' and (in Coser's terms) 'reasonable'. Contemporaries used the term civil war (*bellum civile*) to describe this kind of conflict. Although in modern times it has gained the sense of a general war involving the whole of a polity, reaching down through all levels of society, it might yet be more satisfactory than 'private war', but it is not unproblematic. Is warfare between the count of Maine and the duke of Normandy civil (in that both were nominally at least subjects of the king of France) or external (in that the county of Maine and the duchy of Normandy could in many ways be seen as independent polities)? It may be simplest to use the fairly neutral terms 'internal' and 'external' to distinguish between these kinds of warfare.

VIOLENCE AND THE SOCIAL ORDER: CHANGE AND STABILITY

It has become apparent in the previous sections that violence and violent relationships, and their legitimation, play an important part in social organization. In particular, it is a commonplace that violence has a role in state formation (e.g. Hindess and Hirst 1975: 34–35; Runciman 1989, esp. 12–20; Keane 1996: 26–28) Diverse local societies can be bound into a unified polity by a government's ability to arbitrate in violent disputes and to defend the interests of one social group against another, especially by the legitimation of certain types of violence and the outlawing of others (see García Moreno, below: 52–57; Fouracre, below: 71–73). However, it is difficult to establish a close link between the state and 'class interests' in this period; indeed there was quite often conflict between 'governmental' interests and those of the aristocracy (e.g. Wickham 1981: 131, 192; Heather 1995b for a recent statement of these problems in Theoderic's Italy). Contrary to much theorization of state formation, the rise of increasingly stable local hierarchies very frequently led to the weakening of states, and strong states could coincide with local instability and the absence of a pronounced hierarchy (Halsall 1995a: 259–61).

In this period, however, just about every dimension of the social order was in some way dependent upon violence. The role of suppressing or limiting violence and keeping the peace in concepts of rulership is well known, as is the common function of the king as war-leader.[27] We have already noted the historiographic attention lavished upon the military specialization of the aristocracy. The right to participate in particular types of violent activity was very important in defining a social group. The military function of the 'barbarians' in post-Roman Europe helped to define Frank or Burgundian from Gallo-Roman (Amory 1993: 24–25; Halsall 1995a: 27–29, 258), Goth from Italian (Moorhead 1992: 71–75), possibly Anglo-Saxon from Briton (Härke 1992), Lombard from Italian, and so on. This identity was proclaimed by attendance at the assembly of the army. That the army was the *de facto* assembly of the powerful is recognized by numerous law-codes and by the rituals of victory and triumph (e.g. McCormick 1986: 315–16). Thus the right to participate in warfare, as opposed to other kinds of lower-order violence, which might involve household servants and even slaves (*LH* X.5; Valerian of Cimiez, *Homily* 20.iii), was an important marker of social standing. Although the view has recently been cogently questioned by Reuter (1990: 395–401), it still seems true that as the period progressed the requirements of participation in warfare became heavier, in terms of specialized equipment, training and tactics. The

---

27. E.g. Chaney 1971 (with care); McCormick 1986; Wallace-Hadrill 1971. Aitchison, below: 115, raises again the association between Irish kingship and warfare.

frequency with which weapons are deposited in Frankish burials, especially of young adults, and the levels of 'military hardware' involved, seem to attest a widely distributed right, and possibility, of participation in organized violence, and contrasts significantly with the specialist military equipment of even the impoverished knight of the central Middle Ages; in the earlier period it may well be that involvement in higher-level violence was related to the life-cycle and a career path based upon it (Charles-Edwards 1976; Halsall 1995a: 255) rather than upon birth or position in a 'vertical' hierarchy of ranks (even if this was moderated by age too). At the other end of the social scale, the distinctions between free and unfree were delineated in violent terms (e.g. Fouracre, below: 72; García Moreno, below: 55–56).

If position in the male life-cycle could be symbolized by weaponry and the right of participation in certain types of violence, so gender was also commonly delineated by the same rights and symbolism. Across the so-called *Reihengräberzivilisation* it is common for weapons to be the standard masculine grave-goods (although at what ages weapons were buried with the dead varies from place to place), whilst jewellery is the classic female signifier (again moderated variously by age in different regions and periods; Halsall 1995b). Although attitudes, as usual, were not uniform (cp. *Ed. Roth.* 378 and *LC* 92; early Frankish law has nothing to say about female violence), the right, even the ability, to participate in violence was commonly seen as an index of masculinity (Balzaretti, ch. 9).

Violence was very important in maintaining social distinctions of all kinds. This was so not primarily in the use of violence by one social group against others; force and coercion alone are unlikely to maintain social stability. Rather, stability was maintained by the existence of types of violence which served the interests of particular groups. Thus warfare, rather than bringing about social change, very frequently served, via the distribution and redistribution of booty in endemic small-scale raiding, to maintain the socio-political status quo. The existence of such warfare also proclaimed the social divisions discussed above. Fouracre (below: 71–72) plausibly suggests further ways in which violence could maintain the status quo. Thus legislation, notably that of the early eleventh-century peace councils, rarely aimed to eliminate violence entirely, but rather sought to define more clearly when and where it could take place and who was permitted to participate in it (Goetz 1992; Bennett, below: 137–39).

This is not, however, the only side of the story. García Moreno (below: 57–58) shows how, in different socio-political circumstances, the use of similar kinds of violence could have a quite different effect, and produce significant socio-political instability. The difference between Fouracre's Merovingian state of affairs and the Visigothic situation discussed by García Moreno probably hinges upon different relationships between the central government or monarchy and regional or local elites. Merovingian aristocrats, at least until the eighth century, needed the legitimation and patronage of the royal court to maintain their position, so their sometimes violent factional rivalries were fought out for control of the court, and thus conserved the political system for most of the seventh century (although there are some changes perceptible even within this period). The more independently powerful Visigothic magnates similarly fought for control of the whole kingdom yet, whereas Merovingian politics aimed at legitimation sought from a single royal dynasty and an established political system, Gothic rivalries produced repeated changes of dynasty, and consequent changes in the legitimacy of power and status at lower levels. García Moreno (below: 58) notes (as, for example, does Collins 1983: 115) that this could lead to much higher stakes and potentially spiralling violence.

Violence could also produce social change. Speight (ch. 8) discusses the ways in which violence, not always physical or indeed on a particularly large scale was used to create the new Norman order in Yorkshire. Guy Morris (ch. 7) shows how social and political change was effected in the emergent eleventh-century Scandinavian kingdoms in the course of warfare between Norway and Denmark; again, high stakes were played for and violence could spiral dangerously.

RITUAL VIOLENCE

Violence at all levels was surrounded by ritual, from the public display of the legitimately slain, through the elaborate processes associated with ordeals, including trial by combat (on which see Bloomfield 1969), up to the complex rituals associated with major warlike expeditions. Executions were important foci of ritual.

Ritual's importance in violent relationships is best understood by a brief consideration of the general role of ritual in society. Ritual can most easily be understood as a performed restatement of cosmology, broadly defined as including man's relations with man and with the environment, as well as with the supernatural (Tambiah 1985: 130). As such it is performed to an audience according to a generally understood script governing procedure, location and language, including material cultural symbolism. The norms making up this script are shared by all involved in the ritual, actively or otherwise. Two features emerge. The first is that ritual is often a unifying force, bringing a community together. This might simply be the community of the politically powerful, but it might also be a wider social community including all groups within it. Shared participation in the ritual, or witnessing of it, can smooth over tensions or stress between the different elements by the emphasis laid upon common cultural inheritance and belief. The second feature is directly related to the first. The importance placed upon shared belief and the standardized procedure and symbolism produce an effect of normality. Rituals build a 'scene' consciously recreating in the minds of the participants and observers the last time such a ritual was performed, telescoping time. The effect may, again, be to reassure and unify by stressing normality and 'how things ought to be', smoothing over tensions which have arisen since the last performance of the ritual. Rituals, of course, can and do change, they may be subverted, and they may fail to achieve their intended aim. Nevertheless, these general points can be seen to apply to most ritual behaviour from that associated with royal inauguration (Nelson 1986) through those associated with the human life-cycle (e.g. Lynch 1986), to the rituals of death and burial (Halsall, forthcoming a), and especially, peace-making.

We can thus better understand the rituals of violence. They can work towards its legitimation by proclaiming to third parties the normality and correctness of the violence. This can be seen in the publication of legitimate killing, and is especially visible in executions, where the degree of ritual performance is probably commensurate with the political importance of the victim and the political sensitivity of the killing (Aitchison, ch. 5; Nelson 1992: 139-40). Nelson (below: 99-100) takes us through the elaborate rituals performed by Carolingian rulers during the similarly sensitive and difficult events of civil war. Speight, on the other hand (below: 166), graphically illustrates how certain kinds of legal ritual could be forcibly appropriated to legitimize violent seizure and expropriation.

Although this ritual speaks to third parties, in the cases just cited it also justifies violence to the participants in it. The followers of warring Carolingians needed to know that their cause was just, as they had been told in the days of wars against foreign peoples. Complicated rituals accompanying the departure of kings on campaign (McCormick 1986: 308-12) served not only to legitimize but also to normalize always risky and potentially abnormal events. Ceremonial homecomings and the rituals associated with the distribution of booty are the correlate of this.

The rituals performed during the ninth-century Frankish civil wars spoke, of course, to the enemy as well as to followers and bystanders. This is particularly true of the rigmarole before Fontenoy (Nelson, below: 99-100). Ritual was the medium of much of the communicative element in violent relationships, particularly warfare. This can be seen in the rituals of challenges. Once again, Fontenoy stands as an example, but so too, do the challenges which brought about the battle of Maldon (on which see Scragg (ed.) 1991; Cooper (ed.) 1993). Another good example can be found in the Viking army's occupation of Cwichelmslow Barrow (Berks) in 1006 (*ASC*), playing on an English tradition that no invader who reached the barrow would see the sea again. The same points can be made of early Merovingian challenges (e.g. *LH* V.17). If violent relationships can be seen as discourses, with statements and responses based upon shared norms, then they were usually carried on in the 'heightened language' of ritual. The performance of challenges are also potent means of demonstrating legitimacy to one's own side and to potential third parties (Bourdieu 1977: 11–12 for the social practice in the challenge).

From here it is not difficult to progress to what we might call acts of ritual violence, that is to say violent (or at least ostensibly violent) acts which constitute a ritual in themselves. The importance of the military assembly in underlining the social status of various classes, age-groups or genders, meant that such gatherings had to take place quite frequently. This in turn led to frequent situations where armies were gathered together but little or no violent activity ensued (Leyser 1994a: 50; *LH* VI.41). In addition to these 'warlike' gatherings – with no war – the clearest examples of ritual violence come from early medieval Ireland (e.g. Mac Niocaill 1972: 47).

Even if they are never articulated as such, some military actions may become, to all practical intents, ritual by their repeated performance. Under this heading we could include invasions following a usual route, or repeatedly opening hostilities by attacking a particular enemy stronghold. Both 'moves' would have many of the effects of ritual action, both on one's followers and in making a fairly formal communication to the enemy of one's aims, intentions and the means by which they were to be achieved. The ritual aspects of early medieval warfare still need fuller treatment (Halsall forthcoming b).

Similar ritual violence can be seen at lower levels, and, as with that at a higher level, is often strategic, drawing attention to the dispute. This includes formal declarations of enmity – *inimicitia*, *odium* or *ira* – noted above. Some of these rituals are known, such as the breaking and casting down of twigs to signify *diffidatio* ('defiance'; Bloch 1962: 228; Bennett, below: 136–37), stemming ultimately from the breaking of twigs to symbolize the casting off of a kinsman (*PLS* 60; Callendar Murray 1983: 150–55). Other examples of ritual violence, again strategic, are cited in Wickham's (unpublished) study of Tuscan violence. Perhaps the clearest examples of ritual violence are those associated with the 'humiliation' of the saints (Geary 1994a; 1994b).

Attacks deliberately limited to the destruction of buildings or property, in order to avoid the escalation of conflict (as Gillingham 1994: 36; Bennett, below: 137–39), might also be seen as a form of ritual violence. The rituals of violence thus bind many of the issues discussed throughout this volume: legitimacy of violence; violence as discourse; the relationships involved in violence; and the strategic or tactical nature of violence.

NON-PHYSICAL VIOLENCE

It is important to remember that not all violence is physical. The issue of psychological violence is very important. Speight (below: 166) discusses the ways in which the English of Yorkshire were forced to participate in the legitimation of their own violent dispossession, and raises (below: 168–70) the extremely interesting issue of the forcible superimposition of new cultural forms on the old; the implanting in the centre of a community of a dominating symbol of its defeat and subjugation, a symbol which the locals may well have been violently compelled to help construct. Miller has recently (1993: 60–65) pointed out how psychological violence is often far more effective in keeping the peace and social order than is physical violence, though he also (*ibid.*: 67) correctly draws attention to the fact that many post-modernist literary critics have trivialized non-physical violence.

Under the heading of non-physical violence we might include the effects on people other than the victims of violent attacks. Julie Coleman (ch. 10), in the only paper in this collection to tackle issues from a literary perspective, highlights the psychological effects of a rape on the victim's guardian. We might imagine the act envisaged by Wulfstan (*Sermo Lupi*, ll. 113–17; Coleman, below: 199–200) as psychological violence against the guardian at the same time as physical violence (with, of course, enormous psychological effects) upon the woman herself. In these cultures, shaming in general (see Balzaretti, below: 179) might usefully be seen as a form of psychological violence (Miller 1993: 83–87). The acute psychological pressures upon the practitioners of infanticide are brought out in Wicker's paper (ch. 11).

Other non-physical forms of violence include verbal violence (see Lesnick 1991 for a later period) and witchcraft. It is not surprising, given the usually masculine associations of armed violence (above: 31; Balzaretti, below: 187–89) that such kinds of violence are often the only ones where active female participation is envisaged (*PLS* 19.iv; Bald's Leechbook III. 57 seems to refer to verbal violence). Some forms of strategic and ritual violence discussed above are obviously non-physical, but produce effects just as powerfully. These forms of violence need much more attention.

CONCLUSIONS AND LACUNAE

In this introduction I have attempted to outline the historiographical significance of early medieval violence, provide a very basic bibliographical orientation, and sketch what seem to be key issues in the study of violence in western Europe between c. 500 and c. 1100. The following essays examine a variety of issues raised under the general heading of 'violence in early medieval society'. They are diverse in approach, in the period and place under study, in the evidence adduced, and in the types of violence examined.[28] They do not, however, pretend to offer a com-

---

28. Other essays originally offered on Anglo-Saxon, Viking Age Northumbrian and central medieval Spanish violence were never submitted.

prehensive coverage of the diverse types of violence encountered in the early Middle Ages, or indeed of the whole period in every region.

A number of important lacunae, thematic, geographical and chronological, ought to be acknowledged. On the thematic side, archaeological approaches to violence are under-represented. There is much work to be done on material cultural approaches to the subject. Key ways are through the study of violent symbolism, such as in the use of weaponry and its associations with gender, age, ethnicity or rank, or fortification (e.g. Samson 1987; 1992); and the violent superimposition of one cultural identity upon another (see Speight, below: 168–70; Tarlow 1997). Nancy Wicker's chapter shows how demographic and other data from cemetery sites can be used to examine the sort of intra-household violence which rarely intrudes into literary sources.

Another area which requires work is that of piracy and brigandage. Haywood (1991) offers a study of pre-Viking naval activity, to complement the work done on Viking seaborne violence, and Pryor (1988) has studied such activity in the Mediterranean. Land-based brigandage is a neglected area, and concepts of the legitimacy or otherwise of violence could still be profitably applied to ship-borne activities.

The role of violence in the construction of social age is another field which would repay work (see above, and Halsall 1995a: 255), and non-physical violence could do with detailed contextualized study. Religious violence, against heretics and infidels (e.g. Brown 1963; 1964), or against violators of ecclesiastical norms and regulations, is another area which could profitably have been included in this survey but which has, alas, had to be side-stepped.

This volume leaves certain periods and places uncovered. The absence of specific treatment of early Merovingian Gaul has, it is hoped, been made up for by the heavy use of examples from this era in this introduction. The book's failure to deal with Germany is perhaps compensated for by the works of the late Karl Leyser (1963; 1984; 1994a) and Timothy Reuter (1985; 1990; 1991b; 1996); pre-Carolingian German violence, however, will remain an archaeological field of research. Spain in the later part of the early Middle Ages, in the Islamic and Christian realms, has sadly had to be ignored, and here there is much interesting work to be done on violence and the clash of cultures, and the roles of violence in the establishment of new socio-political orders. Anglo-Saxon England, especially its early period, has also had to be ignored; again I have made some use of earlier Anglo-Saxon examples in this introduction, but the subject has been far from neglected. [29]

Admitting these lacunae, this introduction has aimed to serve as a

29. There is a huge bibliography. Most recently, see Abels 1987; Chadwick-Hawkes (ed.) 1989; Scragg (ed.) 1991; Cooper (ed.) 1993.

core around which the following more detailed and specific case studies can be brought together. It should perhaps be read in conjunction with William Ian Miller's (1993) recent thoughtful consideration of the issues involved in the study of violence.[30] The place of violence in early medieval society was an important one, yet still needs careful and contextualized study. It is hoped that the essays collected here will help provide a way into that study.[31]

BIBLIOGRAPHY

Primary Sources

Æthelberht's laws: See Anglo-Saxon Law.

Alfred's laws: See Anglo-Saxon Law.

Ammianus Marcellinus, *Res Gestae*: J. C. Rolfe (ed. & trans.), *Ammianus Marcellinus* 3 vols (London, 1935–52).

Anglo-Saxon Chronicle: D. Whitelock, D. Douglas & S. Tucker (trans.) *The Anglo-Saxon Chronicle: A Revised Translation* (London, 1961).

Anglo-Saxon Law: F. Liebermann (ed.), *Die Gesetze der Angelsachsen* vol. I (Aalen, 1960); D. Whitelock (trans.) *EHD* 1, c. 500–1042, pp. 391–478.

Armes Prydein: I. Williams & R. Bromwich (eds & trans.), *Armes Prydein. The Prophecy of Britain, from the Book of Taleisin* (Dublin, 1982).

Augustine, *Questiones in Heptateuchum*: *PL* 34, col. 547–824.

Bald, Leechbook: Selection: M. Swanton (trans.), *Anglo-Saxon Prose* (London, 1975), pp. 180–85.

Beowulf: S. A. J. Bradley (trans.), *Anglo-Saxon Poetry* (London, 1982), pp. 407–94.

Capitularia Regum Francorum, A. Boretius (ed.), *MGH Capitularia Regum Francorum* I (Hanover, 1883); Selection: P. D. King (trans.), *Charlemagne. Translated Sources* (Lambrigg, 1987), pp. 202–68.

Childebert's Decrees: K.-A. Eckhardt (ed.), *MGH Legum* I, 4.1 *Pactus Legis Salicae* (Hanover, 1962), pp. 267–69; K. F. Drew (trans.), *The Laws of the Salian Franks* (Philadelphia, 1990), pp. 156–59.

Dream of the Rood: S. A. J. Bradley (trans.), *Anglo-Saxon Poetry* (London, 1982), pp. 158–63.

Edictum Rothari: See Lombard Law.

Edmund's laws: See Anglo-Saxon Law.

---

30. See also Keane 1996, who, alas, has a rather odd view of the Middle Ages.

31. I should like to thank the contributors to this volume, firstly for the stimulation which their papers has provided, and secondly, for the patience which they have shown during the excessively long time which it has taken to collect the chapters together. I am most grateful to Timothy Reuter and Chris Wickham for kindly sending me copies of articles in advance of publication. I must also express a great debt of thanks to Matt Bennett, Paul Fouracre, John Gillingham, Paul Kershaw, Jinty Nelson, Alan Thacker, Andrew Wareham and Geoff West, for many informal but interesting and enjoyable discussions of feud and violence. Finally my thanks go to Jo Simmons for reading through this introduction.

The *Fortunes of Men*: S. A. J. Bradley (trans.), *Anglo-Saxon Poetry* (London, 1982), pp. 341–43.

The *Gifts of Men*: S. A. J. Bradley (trans.), *Anglo-Saxon Poetry* (London, 1982), pp. 325–28.

Gregory of Tours, *Ten Books of Histories*: B. Krusch & W. Levison (eds), *MGH SRM* 1.1 (Hanover, 1951); L. Thorpe (trans.), *Gregory of Tours. History of the Franks* (Harmondsworth, 1974).

Gregory of Tours, *Vita Patrum*: B. Krusch & W. Levison (eds), *MGH SRM* 1.2 (Hanover, 1969), pp. 211–94; E. James (trans.), *Gregory of Tours. Life of the Fathers* 2nd edition (Liverpool, 1991).

Historia Wambae: J. N. Hillgarth (ed.), *Corpus Christianorum Series Latina* 115 *Sancti Juliani Toletanae Sedis Opera Pars I* (Turnhout, 1976), pp. 213–55.

Hlothhere & Eadric's laws: See Anglo-Saxon Law.

Hywel Dda, Laws: D. Jenkyns (trans.), *The Law of Hywel Dda* (Llandysul, 1986).

Ine's laws: See Anglo-Saxon Law.

Leges Visigothorum: Zeumer, K. (ed.), *MGH Leges* I, 1 *Leges Visigothorum* (Berlin, 1902).

Lex Baiuariorum: E. de Schwind (ed.), *MGH Leges* I, 5.2 *Lex Baiwariorum* (Hanover, 1926).

Lex Ribuaria: F. Beyerle & R. Buchner (eds), *MGH Leges* I, 3 *Lex Ribuaria*. (Hanover, 1951); Rivers, T. J., (trans.), *The Laws of the Salian and Ripuarian Franks* (New York, 1987), pp. 165–214.

Lex Romana Burgundionum: L. De Salis (ed.), *MGH Leges* I, 2.1 *Leges Burgundionum* (Hanover, 1892), pp. 123–63.

Liber Constitutionum: L. De Salis (ed.), *MGH Leges* I, 2.1 *Leges Burgundionum* (Hanover, 1892), pp. 29–122; K. F. Drew (trans.), *The Burgundian Code* (Philadelphia, 1972).

Liber Historiae Francorum: B. Krusch (ed.), *MGH SRM* 2, pp. 215–328; cc. 43–53 trans. in Fouracre & Gerberding 1996: 87–96.

Liutprandi Leges: See Lombard Law.

Lombard Law: F. Beyerle (ed.), *Leges Langobardorum 643–866* 2nd edition (Witzenhausen, 1962); Bluhme, F. (ed.), *Leges Langobardorum, MGH Leges* 4 (Hanover, 1868); K. F. Drew (trans.), *The Lombard Laws* (Philadelphia, 1973).

Maxims I & II: S. A. J. Bradley (trans.), *Anglo-Saxon Poetry* (London, 1982), pp. 344–50, 512–15.

Njál's Saga: M. Magnusson & H. Pálsson (trans.), *Njal's Saga* (Harmondsworth).

Pactus Legis Salicae: K.-A. Eckhardt (ed.), *MGH Legum* I, 4.1 *Pactus Legis Salicae* (Hanover, 1962); K. F. Drew (trans.), *The Laws of the Salian Franks* (Philadelphia, 1990).

Ratchis' laws: See Lombard Law.

Revised Annals: F. Kurze (ed.), *MGH SRG* 6 (Hanover, 1895); P. D. King (trans.), *Charlemagne. Translated Sources* (Lambrigg, 1987), pp. 108–31.

Royal Frankish Annals: F. Kurze (ed.), *MGH SRG* 6 (Hanover, 1895); P. D. King (trans.), *Charlemagne. Translated Sources* (Lambrigg, 1987), pp. 74–107; B. Scholz (trans.), *Carolingian Chronicles* (Ann Arbor, 1972), pp. 37–125.

Sidonius Apollinaris, *Epistolae*: Anderson, W. B. (ed. & trans.), 1936–65. *Sidonius. Poems and Letters*, 2 vols (London, 1936–65).

Valerian of Cimiez, *Homilies*: G. E. Ganss (trans.), *Saint Peter Chrysologus, Selected Sermons, and Saint Valerian, Homilies* (New York, 1953), pp. 291–436.

Venantius Fortunatus, *Carmina*: C. Nisard, & E. Rittier (eds & trans.), *Venance Fortunat: Poésies Mêlées Traduites en Français* (Paris, 1887).

Vita Desiderii: B. Krusch & W. Levison (eds), *MGH SRM* 4 (Hanover, 1902), pp. 547–602.

Vita Faronis: B. Krusch & W. Levison (eds), *MGH SRM* 5 (Hanover, 1910), pp. 171–206.

Wihtred's laws: See Anglo-Saxon Law.

Wulfstan, *Sermo Lupi ad Anglos*: D. Bethurum (ed.), *The Homilies of Wulfstan* (Oxford, 1958); M. Swanton (trans.), *Anglo-Saxon Prose* (London, 1979), pp. 116–25.

Secondary bibliography

Abels, R., 1988. *Lordship and Military Obligation in Anglo-Saxon England* (London).

Althoff, G., 1982. 'Zur Frage nach der Organisation sächsicher Coniurationes in der Ottonenzeit', *Frühmittelalterliche Studien* 16: 129–42.

Amory, P., 1993. 'The meaning and purpose of ethnic terminology in the Burgundian laws', *Early Medieval Europe* 2.1: 1–28.

Andersson, T. A., 1984. 'The thief in Beowulf', *Speculum* 59: 493–508.

Auerbach, E., 1953. *Mimesis. The Representation of Reality in Western Literature* (Princeton).

Bachrach, B. S., 1970. 'Charles Martel, mounted shock combat, the stirrup and feudalism', *Studies in Medieval and Renaissance History* 7: 49–75.

—— 1983. 'Charlemagne's cavalry: myth and reality', *Military Affairs* 47: 181–87.

Barthélemy, D., 1992. 'La mutation féodale a-t-elle eu lieu?', *Annales* 47: 767–77.

Beeler, J., 1971. *Warfare in Feudal Europe, 730–1200* (Ithaca).

Bisson, T., 1994. 'The feudal revolution', *Past and Present* 142: 6–42.

Black-Michaud, J., 1975. *Feuding Societies* (Oxford) [also published in the same year as *Cohesive Force*].

Bloch, M., 1962., *Feudal Society* 2 vols 2nd English edition (L. A. Manyon, trans.) (London).

Bloomfield, M. W., 1969. 'Beowulf, Byrtnoth and the judgement of God: trial by battle in Anglo-Saxon England', *Speculum* 44: 545–59.

Boehm, C., 1984. *Blood Revenge: The Anthropology of Feuding in Montenegro and Other Tribal Societies* (Lawrence, Kansas).

Bois, G., 1992. *The Transformation of the Year 1000. The Village of Lournand from Antiquity to Feudalism* (J. Birrell, trans.) (Manchester).

Bonnassie, P., 1991. 'The survival and extinction of the slave system in the early medieval West', in *id.*, *From Slavery to Feudalism in South-Western Europe* (Cambridge), pp. 1–59.

Bossy, J. (ed.), 1983. *Disputes and Settlements. Law and Human Relations in the West* (Cambridge).

Bourdieu, P., 1977. *Outline of a Theory of Practice* (R. Nice, trans.) (Cambridge).

Brown, P. R. L., 1963. 'Religious coercion in the later Roman empire: the case of Africa', *History* 48: 283–305.

40   Halsall

—— 1964. 'St. Augustine's attitude to religious coercion', *Journal of Roman Studies* 54: 107–16.

Brunner, H., 1887. 'Der Reiterdienst und die Anfänge des Lehnwesens', *Zeitschrift der Savigny Stiftung für Rechtsgeschichte, Germanisches Abteilung* 8: 1–38.

—— 1906. *Deutsche Rechtsgeschichte* 2nd edition (Leipzig).

Brunner, K., 1979. *Oppositionelle Gruppen im Karolingerreich* (Vienna).

Byock, J., 1982. *Feud in the Icelandic Saga* (Berkeley).

Byrne, F. J., 1973. *Irish Kings and High Kings* (London).

Callendar Murray, A., 1983. *Germanic Kinship Structure: Studies in Law and Society in Antiquity and the Early Middle Ages* (Toronto).

—— 1988. 'From Roman to Frankish Gaul: "centenarii" and "centenae" in the administration of the Merovingian kingdom', *Traditio* 44: 59–100.

—— 1994. 'Immunity, nobility and the Edict of Paris', *Speculum* 69: 18–39.

Campbell, J., 1975. 'Observations on English government from the tenth to the twelfth century', *Transactions of the Royal Historical Society*, 5th ser., 25: 39–54.

Caplan, P. (ed.), 1995. *Understanding Disputes. The Politics of Argument* (Oxford).

Chadwick-Hawkes, S. (ed.), 1989. *Weapons and Warfare in Anglo-Saxon England* (OUCA Monograph 21) (Oxford).

Chaney, W. A., 1970. *The Cult of Kingship in Anglo-Saxon England* (Manchester).

Charles-Edwards, T., 1976. 'The distinction between land and moveable wealth in Anglo-Saxon England', in P. H. Sawyer (ed.), *Medieval Settlement. Continuity and Change* (London), pp. 180–87.

Collins, R. J. H., 1983. *Early Medieval Spain. Unity in Diversity, 400–1000* (London).

Cooper, J. (ed.), 1993. *The Battle of Maldon: Fiction and Fact* (London).

Coser, L. A., 1965. *The Functions of Social Conflict* (London).

Cross, J. E., 1971. 'The ethic of war in Old English', in P. Clemoes & K. Hughes (eds), *England Before the Conquest. Studies in primary Sources presented to Dorothy Whitelock* (Cambridge), pp. 269–82.

Davies, R. R., 1969. 'The survival of the bloodfeud in medieval Wales', *History* 64: 338–57.

Davies, W., & Fouracre, P. (eds), 1986. *The Settlement of Disputes in Early Medieval Europe* (Cambridge).

—— (ed.) 1995. *Property and Power in the Early Middle Ages* (Cambridge).

Debord, A., 1992. 'The Castellan revolution and the Peace of God', in Head & Landes (eds) 1992: 135–64.

Dill, S., 1926. *Roman Society in Gaul in the Merovingian Age* (London).

Farrell, R. T. (ed.), 1982. *The Vikings* (Chichester).

Foot, S., 1991. 'Violence against Christians? The Vikings and the church in ninth-century England', *Medieval History* 1.3: 3–16.

Fouracre, P., 1984. 'Merovingians, mayors of the palace and the notion of a low-born Ebroin', *Bulletin of the Institute of Historical Research* 57: 1–14.

—— 1990. 'Merovingian history and Merovingian hagiography', *Past & Present* 127: 3–38.

—— 1995. 'Carolingian justice: the rhetoric of improvement and contexts of abuse', *La Giustizia nell'Alto Medioevo, Secoli V-VIII (Settimane di Studi 42)*: 771–803.

Fouracre, P. & Gerberding, R., 1996. *Late Merovingian France. History and Hagiography, 640-720* (Mancherster).

Frase, M., 1989. *Friede und Königsherrschaft. Quellenkritik und Interpretation der Continuatio Reginonis* (Studia Irenica 35) (Frankfurt).

Fried, J. (ed.), 1996. *Träger und Instrumentarien des Friedens im Hohen und Späten Mittelalter* (Vorträge und Forschungen 43) (Sigmaringen).

Fustel de Coulanges, N., 1890. *Les Origines du Système Féodale. La Bénéfice et le Patronat pendant l'Epoque Mérovingienne* (Histoire des Institutions Politiques de l'Ancienne France 5) (Paris).

Ganshof, F. L., 1964. *Feudalism* 3rd edition (London).

García-Moreno, L. A., 1994. 'Gothic survivals in the Visigothic kingdoms of Toulouse and Toledo', *Francia* 21.1: 1-15.

Garnett, G., & Hudson, J. (eds), 1994. *Law and Government in Medieval England and Normandy. Essays in Honour of Sir James Holt* (Cambridge).

Geary, P., 1994a. 'Humiliation of saints', in Geary 1994d: 95-115.

―――― 1994b. 'Coercion of saints in medieval religious practice', in Geary 1994d: 116-24.

―――― 1994c. 'Living with conflicts in stateless France: a typology of conflict management systems, 1050-1200', in Geary 1994d: 125-60.

―――― 1994d. *Living with the Dead in the Middle Ages* (Ithaca).

Gillingham, J., 1992. 'Conquering the barbarians: war and chivalry in twelfth-century Britain', *Haskins Society Journal* 4: 67-84.

―――― 1994. '1066 and the introduction of chivalry into England', in Garnett & Hudson (eds) 1994: 31-55.

Gluckman, M., 1962. 'The peace in the feud', *Past and Present*; reprinted in *id. Custom and Conflict in Africa* (Oxford, 1965).

Goebel, J., 1976. *Felony and Misdemeanour. A Study in the History of Criminal Law* (Philadelphia).

Goetz, H.-W., 1992. 'Protection of the church, defense of the law and reform: On the purposes and character of the Peace of God, 989-1038', in Head & Landes (eds) 1992: 239-58.

―――― 1995. 'Social and military institutions', in McKitterick (ed.) 1995: 451-80.

Goffart, W., 1988. *The Narrators of Barbarian History, AD 550-800. Jordanes, Gregory of Tours, Bede, Paul the Deacon* (Princeton).

―――― 1989. 'Foreigners in the *Histories* of Gregory of Tours', in *id. Rome's Fall and After* (London, 1989), no. 11; originally *Florilegium* 4 (1982), pp. 80-99.

Guerreau, A., 1990. 'Lournand au Xe siècle: histoire et fiction', *Le Moyen Age* 5th ser., 4: 519-37.

Halsall, G., 1992. 'Playing by whose rules? A further look at Viking atrocity in the ninth century', *Medieval History* 2.2: 2-12.

―――― 1995a. *Settlement and Social Organization. The Merovingian Region of Metz* (Cambridge).

―――― 1995b. *Early Medieval Cemeteries. An Introduction to Burial Archaeology in the Post-Roman West* (Glasgow).

―――― 1996. 'Female status and power in early Merovingian northern Gaul: the burial evidence', *Early Medieval Europe* 5.1: 1-24.

―――― forthcoming a. 'Burial, ritual and early Merovingian society', in J. Hill & M. Swan (eds), *The Community, the Family and the Saint: Patterns of Power in Early Medieval Europe* (Leeds).

——— forthcoming b. *Warfare and Society in the Barbarian West, 450-900* (London).

Härke, H., 1992. 'Changing symbols in a changing society: the Anglo-Saxon weapon rite', in M. O. H. Carver (ed.), *The Age of Sutton Hoo. The Seventh Century in North-Western Europe* (Woodbridge), pp. 149-65.

Harrison, D., 1993. *The Early State and the Towns. Forms of Integration in Lombard Italy, 568-774* (Lund).

Haywood, J., 1991. *Dark Age Naval Power* (London).

Head, T., & Landes, R. (eds), 1992. *The Peace of God. Social Violence and Religious response in France around the Year 1000* (Ithaca).

Heather P., 1995a. 'The Huns and the end of the Roman empire in western Europe', *English Historical Review* 110: 4-41.

——— 1995b. 'Theoderic, king of the Goths', *Early Medieval Europe* 4.2: 145-73.

Hilton, R., 1971. 'A comment', in *id.* (ed.), *The Transition from Feudalism to Capitalism* (London), pp. 109-17.

Hindess, B., & Hurst, P. Q., 1975. *Pre-Capitalist Modes of Production* (London).

Hoffmann, H., 1964. *Gottesfriede und Treuga Dei* (MGH Schriften 20) (Stuttgart).

Hughes, K., 1972. *Early Christian Ireland: Introduction to the Sources* (London).

James, E., 1983. '*Beati pacifici*: bishops and the law in sixth-century Gaul', in Bossy (ed.) 1983: 25-46.

Jarnut, J., Nonn, U. & Richter, M. (eds), 1994. *Karl Martell in seiner Zeit* (Beihefte der Francia 37) (Sigmaringen).

John, E., 1966. 'English feudalism and the structure of Anglo-Saxon society', in *id.*, *Orbis Britanniae and Other Studies* (Leicester), pp. 128-53.

Kaiser, R., 1983. 'Selbsthilfe und Gewaltsmonopol. Königliche Friedenswahrung in Deutschland und Frankreich im Mittelalter', *Frühmittelalterliche Studien* 17: 55-72.

Keane, J., 1996. *Reflections on Violence* (London).

Kershaw, P., forthcoming. '*Rex Pacificus*: Studies in Royal Peacemaking and the Image of the Peacemaking King in the Early Medieval West', University of London PhD thesis.

Keynes, S., 1995. 'England, 700-900', in McKitterick (ed.) 1995: 18-42.

Koziol, G., 1992. 'Monks, feuds and the making of peace in eleventh-century Flanders', in Head & Landes (eds) 1992: 239-58.

Lesnick, D. R., 1991. 'Insults and threats in medieval Todi', *Journal of Medieval History* 17: 71-89.

Leyser, K., 1963. 'The battle of the Lech, 955. A study in tenth-century warfare', *History* 50: 1-25.

——— 1984. 'Early medieval canon law and the beginning of knighthood', in L. Fenske, W. Rösener & T. Zotz (eds), *Institutionen, Kultur und Gesellschaft. Festschrift für Josef Fleckenstein zu seinem 65. Geburtstag* (Sigmaringen), pp. 549-66, reprinted in Leyser 1994b: 51-71.

——— 1994a. 'Early medieval warfare', in Leyser 1994b, pp. 29-50.

——— 1994b. *Communications and Power in Medieval Europe. The Carolingian and Ottonian Centuries* (T. Reuter, ed.) (London).

Liebeschuetz, J. H. G. W., 1990. *Barbarians and Bishops. Army, Church and State in the Age of Arcadius and Chrysostom* (Oxford).

——— 1992. 'Alaric's Goths: nation or army?', in J. F. Drinkwater & H. Elton (eds), *Fifth-Century Gaul: A Crisis of Identity?* (Cambridge), pp. 75-83.

Loseby, S. T., 1995. Review of Mathisen 1993, *Journal of Roman Studies* 85: 335–36.

Lynch, J. H., 1986. *Godparents and Kinship in Early Medieval Europe* (Princeton).

MacNiocaill, G., 1972. *Ireland before the Vikings* (Dublin).

Magnou-Nortier, E., 1992. 'The enemies of the peace: reflections on a vocabulary', in Head & Landes (eds) 1992: 58–79.

Markus, R., 1983. 'Saint Augustine's views on the "just war"', *Studies in Church History* 20: 1–14.

Marx, E., 1972. 'Some social contexts of personal violence', in M. Gluckman, (ed.), *The Allocation of Responsibility* (Manchester), pp. 281–321.

Mathisen, R. W., 1993. *Roman Aristocrats in Barbarian Gaul. Strategies for Survival in an Age of Transition* (Austin).

McCormick, M., 1986. *Eternal Victory. Triumphal Rulership in Late Antiquity, Byzantium and the Early Medieval West* (Cambridge).

McKitterick, R. (ed.), 1995. *The New Cambridge Medieval History* vol. 2, c. 700 – c. 900 (Cambridge).

Miller, W. I., 1983a. 'Choosing the avenger: some aspects of the bloodfeud in medieval iceland and England', *Law and History Review* 1: 159–204.

—— 1983b. 'Justifying Skarpheðin: of pretext and politics in the Icelandic bloodfeud', *Scandinavian Studies* 55: 316–44.

—— 1986. 'Gift, sale, payment, raid: case studies in the negotiation and classification of exchange in medieval Iceland', *Speculum* 61: 18–50.

—— 1990. *Bloodtaking and Peacemaking. Feud, Law and Society in Saga Iceland* (Chicago).

—— 1993. 'Getting a fix on violence', in *id.*, *Humiliation and Other essays on Honor, Social Discomfort, and Violence* (Ithaca), pp. 53–92.

Moorhead, J., 1992. *Theoderic in Italy* (Oxford).

Nelson, J. L., 1986. *Politics and Ritual in Early Medieval Europe* (London).

—— 1989. 'Ninth-century knighthood: the evidence of Nithard', in C. Harper-Bill, C. J. Holdsworth, & J. L. Nelson (eds), *Studies in Medieval History Presented to R. Allen Brown* (Woodbridge), pp. 255–66.

—— 1992. *Charles the Bald* (London).

—— 1994. Review of Head & Landes (eds) 1992, *Speculum* 69: 163–69.

—— 1996. 'The quest for peace in a time of war', in J. Fried (ed.) 1996: 87–114.

O'Brien, B. R., 1996. 'From *mordor* to *murdrum*: the pre-conquest origin and Norman revival of the murder fine', *Speculum* 71: 321–57.

Peters, E., 1975. 'Foreword', in Black-Michaud 1975: ix–xxvii.

Poly, J.-P., & Bournazel, E., 1991. *The Feudal Transformation* (C. Higgett, trans.) (New York).

Prinz, F., 1971. *Klerus und Krieg im früheren Mittelalter. Untersuchungen zur Rolle der Kirche beim Aufbau der Königsherrschaft* (Monographien zur Geschichte des Mittelalters 2) (Stuttgart).

Pryor, J. H., 1988. *Geography, Technology and War. Studies in the Maritime History of the Mediterranean, 649–1571* (Cambridge).

Renna, T., 1980. 'The idea of peace in the West, c. 500–1150', *Journal of Medieval History* 6: 143–67.

Reuter, T., 1985. 'Plunder and tribute in the Carolingian empire', *Transactions of the Royal Historical Society* 5th series, 35: 75–94.

—— 1990. 'The end of Carolingian military expansion', in P. Godman & R. Collins (eds), *Charlemagne's Heir. New perspectives on the Reign of Louis the Pious* (Oxford), pp. 391–405.

—— 1991a. *Germany in the Early Middle Ages, 800–1056* (London).

—— 1991b. 'Unruhestiftung, Fehde, Rebellion, Widerstand: Gewalt und Frieden in der Politik der Salierzeit', in S. Weinfurter (ed.), *Die Salier und das Reich* Band 3, *Gesellschaftlicher und ideengeschichtlicher Wandel im Reich der Salier* (Sigmaringen), pp. 297–325.

—— 1996. 'Die Unsicherheit auf den Strassen im europäischen Früh- und Hochmittelalter: Täter, Opfer und ihre mittlelalterlichen und Modernen Betrachter', in Fried (ed.) 1996: 169–201.

Reuter, T., & Wickham, C. J., 1995. 'Introduction', in Davies & Fouracre (eds) 1995: 1–16.

Reynolds, B., 1987. 'The mind of Baddo. Assassination in Merovingian politics', *Journal of Medieval History* 11: 117–24.

Reynolds, S., 1994. *Fiefs and Vassals. The Medieval Evidence Reinterpreted* (Oxford).

Roberts, S., 1983. 'The study of dispute: anthropological perspectives', in Bossy (ed.) 1983: 1–24.

Rosenwein, B., 1994. Review of Bois 1992, *Speculum* 69: 749–51.

Roy, B., 1994. *Some Trouble with Cows. Making Sense of Social Conflict* (Berkeley).

Runciman, W. G., 1989. *A Treatise on Social Theory* vol. 2, *Substantive Social Theory* (Cambridge).

Samson, R., 1987. 'The Merovingian nobleman's home: castle or villa?', *Journal of Medieval History* 13: 287–315.

—— 1992. 'Knowledge, constraint and power in inaction: the defenseless medieval wall', *Historical Archaeology* 26: 26–44.

Sawyer, P., 1962. *The Age of the Vikings* 1st edition (London; 2nd edition 1971).

—— 1982a. *Kings and Vikings. Scandinavia and Europe AD 700–1100* (London).

—— 1982b. 'The causes of the Viking age', in Farrell (ed.) 1982: 1–7.

—— 1987. 'The bloodfeud in fact and fiction', *Tradition og Historieskrivining* (Acta Jutlandica 63.2) (Humanistik serie 61) (Aarhus), pp. 27–38.

Scragg, D. (ed.), 1991. *The Battle of Maldon, A.D. 991* (Oxford).

Shaw, B., 1984. 'Bandits in the Roman empire', *Past and Present* 105: 4–52.

Smail, D. L., 1996. 'Common violence: vengeance and inquisition in fourteenth-century Marseille', *Past and Present* 151: 28–59.

Strickland, M., 1994. 'Against the Lord's anointed: aspects of warfare and baronial rebellion in England and Normandy', in Garnett & Hudson (eds) 1994: 56–79.

Sutherland, J. N., 1975. 'The idea of revenge in Lombard society in the eighth and tenth centuries: the cases of Paul the Deacon and Liutprand of Cremona', *Speculum* 50: 391–410.

Tambiah, S. J., 1985. *Culture, Thought and Social Action. An Anthropological Perspective* (Cambridge, Mass.).

Tarlow, S., 1997. 'The dread of something after death, violation and desecration on the Isle of Man in the tenth century', in J. Carman (ed.), *Material Harm. Archaeological studies of war and violence* (Glasgow), pp. 133–42.

Van Dam, R., 1985. *Leadership and Community in Late Antique Gaul* (Berkeley).

Wallace-Hadrill, J. M., 1962. 'The bloodfeud of the Franks', in *id., The Long-Haired Kings* (London, 1962), pp. 121–47, originally in *Bulletin of the John Rylands Library* 41, no. 2, (1959).

—— 1971. *Early Germanic Kingship in England and on the Continent* (Oxford).

White, L., 1962. *Medieval Technology and Social Change* (Oxford).

White, S. D., 1986. 'Feuding and peace-making in the Touraine around the year 1000', *Traditio* 42: 195–263.

Wickham, C. J., 1981. *Early Medieval Italy. Central Power and Local Society, 400–1000* (London).

—— unpublished. 'Violence and the settling of disputes in the Tuscan country-side in the twelfth century.'

Wood, I. N., 1994. *The Merovingian Kingdoms, 450–751* (London).

—— 1995. 'Teutsind, Witlac and the history of Merovingian *precaria*', in Davies & Fouracre (eds) 1995: 31–52.

Wormald, J., 1983. 'The blood feud in early modern Scotland', in Bossy (ed.) 1983: 101–44.

Wormald, P., 1982. 'Viking studies: whence and whither?', in Farrell (ed.) 1982: 128–53.

CHAPTER 1

Legitimate and illegitimate violence in Visigothic law

Luis A. García Moreno

The Visigothic kingdom saw itself as a state ruled by law in the best late Roman tradition. For this the hegemony of law, and of written law in particular, was essential. Yet the dominance of the law contradicted another late Roman tradition, the explicit affirmation of an absolute monarchy of divine right, and a clear tendency towards theocratic models (King 1972: 23ff.; Reydellet 1981: 554 ff.). Although, in line with this imperial tradition, royal power attempted to impose the exclusiveness of the king's courts and judges, this only served to collide with an increasingly 'feudalized' socio-political reality, wherein a whole new system of lay and ecclesiastical immunities was beginning to flourish (Petit 1985; 1986; García Moreno 1992).

Visigothic legal history has its principal memorial in the so-called 'Book of Judges or Judgements'. This code, in proto-Byzantine style, monopolized judicial practice in the Gothic kingdom after its promulgation by King Reccesvinth in 654, following a long process of elaboration and important legislative action by his father and predecessor, King Chindasvinth.[1] In it is pointed out that the triumph of the law would

---

1. I, nevertheless, do not believe that we can accept the idea that a legal code was previously issued by Chindasvinth in 643 as King (1980: 131–37) claims, because, amongst other things, as K. Zeumer pointed out, a retroactive interpretation of the sense of *LV* II.1.v seems unlikely. Besides which, I believe that many years before Chindasvinth, Gothic monarchs had been issuing laws of a territorial character (doubtless true of Reccared, to judge by *LV* III.5.ii, not to mention the famous procedural law of Theudis examined by Zeumer).

also mean victory over any internal or external violence directed against the kingdom's stability, given that 'from the good-will of princes legislation is born; from legislation the strengthening of behaviour; from the strengthening of behaviour, harmony among the citizens; and from harmony amongst the citizens, victory over enemies' (*LV* I.2.vi).

Inevitably, the legislation contained in the *Liber Iudicum* showed especial interest in illegitimizing violent actions carried out outside the ambit of the state's coercive powers. Therefore, amongst other things, the mere inference, or threat, of the use of violence would nullify any obligation expressed in a written document obtained by such means (*LV* II.5.ix, *antiqua*), in spite of the value of the written document in Visigothic law. In particular, Visigothic law revoked any purchase or sale in which the buyer had used or threatened violence (*LV* V.4.iii = *Codex Eurici* 286). By highlighting this particular circumstance, the Gothic legislator no more than echoed a recent concern of imperial legislation.[2] This recurrent concern is understandable in the light of the frequency of such violent actions and threats in a society undergoing an accelerated process of socio-economic differentiation, where the more powerful attempted, through any means at their disposal, to accumulate the greatest amount of land and servile manpower. [3]

The royal interest in maintaining the monopoly on violence also explains a Eurician *antiqua*, according to which attempts to recover land through the use of force would illegitimize any right to the property, however sound the basis of the claim; otherwise the invader would not only lose the land occupied by force, but would also have to give its owner another piece of his landed property, equal in value to that seized (*LV* VIII.1.ii; cp. D'Ors 1960: 191 ff.). Such legal precepts certainly had many imperial precedents and doubtless reflected a frequent practice in Euric's day, with a large number of properties occupied and an irrepressible tendency on the magnates' part to use force to increase their landholdings. Nevertheless, more than a century and a half later, King Chindasvinth was forced to issue a very similar law (*LV* VIII.1.v), surely indicating that such abuses by the powerful, outside the exercise of royal justice, were still common, if not increasing, in spite of the ending of the exceptional historical circumstances produced by the barbarian invasions and the Gothic *Landnahme* of the fifth century. [4]

---

2. *Novella Valentiniani* 32, also included in the *Breviarium Alarici* 10. Cp. D'Ors 1960: 213.

3. Of which there is evidence from the mid-fifth century, both in the complaints of Salvian of Marseille and the portrait which Sidonius Apollinaris (*Epistolae* V.13) has left us of the powerful Seronatus. Cp. García Moreno 1975: 129ff.; Bruguière 1974: 380 ff.

4. See the important observations of Petit (1986: 57 ff.) regarding these two laws. It

The resort to violence to acquire property was certainly not limited to land and other real estate. It is very possible that the appropriation, without a prior court ruling, of any other disputed goods had already been strictly prohibited by a Eurician or Leuvigildan law, later substituted by *LV* VIII.1.v, of Chindasvinth (Zeumer (ed.) 1902: 314, n. 1; D'Ors 1960: 191 ff.). What is remarkable about it is that the legislator explicitly mentions, amongst those who habitually took such a course of action, government representatives, such as the count or his deputy, and others including dependants of a great landlord, such as the manager of his properties, who could even comprise people of servile origin. This doubtless illustrates the extent to which royal jurisdiction had been 'seigneurialized' by the nobility, to the point where great landlords, holding positions of power within the royal justicial system, often proceeded to take justice into their own hands, executing sentences which they issued themselves, for themselves, outside the formalities of the royal justice in whose name they were said to be acting.[5]

The frequency and continuity of such violence related to landownership, and the diminishing importance of royal justice in the many lawsuits brought about for this very reason, are best explained by the increase in the importance of patronage networks in Visigothic society.[6] An *antiqua* (*LV* II.2.viii: D'Ors 1960: 57) had already prohibited the transfer of someone's case to a powerful *patronus*, such action being considered an offence which could produce a judgement inclining towards the patron's client. The transgression of such a rule implied automatic

---

is unnecessary to explain the occupation of a property by its legitimate owner as stemming from the latter's lack of confidence in a royal justice dominated by magnates, since any violent invasion of property presupposes that its leader was a magnate, or at least someone more powerful than the property's occupier. It would be better to consider such invasion as further proof of the contempt in which such magnates held royal justice, and of their tendency to extend private seigneurial justice over people who somehow or other lived in the territory under their socio-economic, if not political, control. Unfortunately, in this respect, it is not imperative for the legislator to use the term *possidentem* when referring to the occupant evicted by force, since in Visigothic legal vocabulary *possessio* and *proprietas* are used indistinctly (cp. Levy 1951: 19 ff.). Hence, in this case, it could refer to a free small landowner or a tenant dependent upon a large landowner.

5. Petit 1986: 58–60. Such appropriations were carried out, according to the law, *post nomen regie potestatis vel dominorum suorum aut suum*. The second alternative assumes, on the other hand, the tacit recognition of a seigneurial jurisdiction with immunity exercised by great landowners over their dependants, or inhabitants of the lands where they were socio-economic overlords. See, further, below.

6. The classic study of Hispano-Visigothic *patrocinium* with special reference to the lower social groups is that of Sanchez Albornoz (1924: 179–95), which can be updated, in particular, with King 1972: 187 ff., and also Diesner 1977: 20 ff.; Barbero & Vigil 1978: 22 ff.; and García Moreno 1991: 335 ff.

loss of the case, and in the, often frequent, event that the magnate refused to give up the case, he was fined two pounds of gold. Nevertheless, it does not seem that either threat was enough to prevent this
practice, to the extent that Ervig thought it necessary to introduce a
small, but significant, amendment to the old law. Instead of the fine
going to the public treasury, it was to be shared equally between the
judge and the adversary of the person supported by the magnate. This
Ervigian amendment was no less than a failure of the very principle of
the exclusivity and equity of royal justice. Since it recognized implicitly
the venality of judges and continued to feed the patronage networks, it
is very possible that the hope of obtaining a pound of gold would allow
the other party to buy the support of another magnate to defend its
rights. The Ervigian amendment proves in itself that the circumstances
foreseen in *antiqua* II.ii.28 remained in force to the end of the seventh
century. Some decades earlier, Chindasvinth (642–53) had similarly been
forced to prohibit the commendation of a lawsuit to a magnate, except
where the other party had done the same (*LV* II.3.ix), tacitly admitting
that royal justice would only be impartial, and not meet with violence, if
both litigants had similar socio-political influence and power.[7]

There were undoubtedly other ways, probably less drastic than the
translatio ad potentiores, through which relations of patronage could
violently influence the outcome of a judicial process. Even Visigothic
legislation showed how a trial's outcome was frequently affected by the
mere presence in the court room of a magnate, and his skill in influenc-
ing the judge by applying more or less violent pressure. Here it will not
be superfluous to recall that the Ervigian law-maker broke the general
rule by which a slave could not represent another person in a judicial
process, and that of the desired equality between litigious parties, by
allowing slaves to represent their masters, whether private individuals,
the church or the state (*LV* II.3.iii; cp. Petit 1985: 237). Furthermore, the
legislator assumed that, in certain ways, this inferior representation
balanced the two sides in a case.[8] Thus a king like Chindasvinth, so
jealous of royal power vis-à-vis the nobility (García Moreno 1991: 232 ff.;
Diesner 1979: 8 ff.), decreed the general principle that in court rooms
the only people who should be present were those directly involved in
the proceedings, placing special emphasis on prohibiting the presence
of powerful patrons of litigants, who, no doubt frequently at the head of

---

7. Petit 1985: 230 ff. The same purpose encouraged another law of Chindasvinth:
LV II.2.iv (Petit 1985: 47–48).

8. It was decreed compulsory that the king (CVIII Toledo, 'Decretum iudicii uni-
versalis') as well as the bishops (*LV* II.3.i) get others to represent them in trials in
which they were involved, since, after Chindasvinth, both bishops (Martinez Díez
1960: 586 ff.) and king received petitions for appeals and could thus overrule
other judges. Cp. Petit 1985: 238–40.

their clients and vassals, could disrupt the proceedings with shouts and violent armed action (*tumultus*), thus breaching the king's justice. The patron's contempt in those cases would be severely punished with a fine of ten pounds of gold. As in the Ervigian amendment mentioned above, Chindasvinth also decreed that in this case the sum would be given to the judge rather than to the public treasury, as an incentive to increase compliance with the law.[9] Once again this demonstrates how contradictory such legal measures were in the face of the court-room violence stemming from powerful ties of patronage; in the end they countered them by creating other such links in favour of the king's judicial representatives. All this fits in well with Chindasvinth's well-known pragmatism, always ready to strengthen his relationships of dependence, and those of his *fideles principis*, at the expense of those other nobles (García Moreno 1975: 166–70; Diesner 1979: 12 ff.).

It does not require too much imagination to conceive that the groups of armed retainers at the magnates' disposal would have participated actively in the court-room commotions created by such people in defence of their interests or those of people commended to them. These armed bands included slaves as well as freemen in relationships of patronage. Within this latter group there were also truly professional warriors whose service was rewarded with conditional grants of land as *beneficium*, and who bore the Roman title *bucellarii* or the Gothic name *saiones*. Unlike contemporary Roman emperors, Visigothic monarchs, from Euric at least, allowed and legitimized the existence of such bands in magnate service, which fitted in with other Gothic realities grounded in Germanic *Hausherrschaft*, to the extent that by the second half of the seventh century they had become the main component of Visigothic royal armies.[10]

It is clear that these groups of warriors were not maintained solely with the resources that came from the important landed estates of their patrons. Their violent actions doubtless also constituted an important source of income. Booty made up, according to a famous *antiqua*, a very important part of the profits of the *leudes* or young aristocrats with a special bond of loyalty to the king, who, as their *patronus*, could also grant them fiscal land in benefice.[11]

---

9. *LV* II.2.ii. Cp. Petit (1985: 234; 1986: 72-74) who demonstrates very solidly that the legal norm bore no relationship to a supposed popular judicial element of Germanic origin.

10. On all this, see García Moreno 1992: 24 ff; Diesner 1978a: 4 ff.; 1970: 183 ff.; with previous references (one can dispense with R. Sanz (1986: 261-64) who, apart from ignoring the most elementary *germanische Altertumskunde*, does not place the phenomenon in the context of early Visigothic 'feudalism').

11. *LV* IV.5.v for *leudes* and the problems caused by the legal disposition regarding the booty obtained. See García Moreno 1974b: 106-09. The legal principle stated that booty acquired justly by freemen in war was the property of the

Like armed groups throughout history, it was common for these Visigothic magnates' bands to carry out thefts and other abuses against the population that they were supposedly defending. A Eurician *antiqua* took into account the frequency of violent actions carried out by groups of slaves accompanying their master to war, and for which he was held responsible.[12] That this norm persisted, with certain modifications, in Leuvigild's *Codex Revisus* and in Reccesvinth's later code (*LV* IV.2.xv; cp. Merêa 1948: 52ff. & 59) would be proof enough of the continuity and frequency of such actions, to the point that Reccesvinth himself would be forced to legislate specifically against them (*LV* VIII.1.ix). Plunder and illegal confiscations must have been a daily event along the route of a Visigothic army; another Eurician *antiqua* punished such excesses where committed by freemen.[13]

Visigothic law inherited from Roman law the rule that the owner was totally responsible for any crimes committed by slaves acting on his orders. Furthermore, Visigothic law tended to widen the slaves' lack of responsibility in such cases; public authorities would only punish them for those crimes which the state pursued particularly severely, as threats to its security and basic moral principles.[14] Visigothic law had a clear tendency to unify the status of slaves with that of freemen or freedmen still under obligation to a *patronus* (García Moreno 1975: 127–29), and thus extended the same lack of responsibility to people in relationships of dependence upon a patron.

Two *antiquae* demonstrate that it was quite common for slaves and armed retainers to join forces when carrying out violent actions on their owner or patron's orders, such as armed raids on an estate to rob and kill its owner, or to kidnap him (*LV* VI.4.ii; VII.3.v). The frequency of such violent crimes forced Chindasvinth and Reccesvinth, in the mid-seventh century, to legislate on this matter yet again. Reccesvinth's ruling sanctioned the lack of civil responsibility of slaves and retainers for crimes committed on their owner or patron's orders. The latter, in turn, was then forced to repair any damage caused. All this was done in the context of legislation which tried to equate the legal situation of freedmen *in patrocinio* with that of slaves (*LV* VIII.1.i. cp. Nehlsen 1972:

---

person who obtained it (Reccesvinth's *LV* IV.2.xvi). The importance of booty is well documented in other literary records of war (Diesner 1978b: 138 ff.).

12. *Codex Eurici* 323, which establishes a specific solution for goods acquired in war by a husband with the help of his wife's slaves; they would be the husband's exclusive property.

13. *LV* VIII.1.viii, related to *Lex Baiuariorum* II.5. Cp. Stroheker 1937: 114, n. 105; D'Ors 1960: 104, 190 & n. 601.

14. Nehlsen 1972: 218 ff., & 228 ff. The exceptions are pointed out by the possibly Leuvigildian *antiqua* VI.1.iv, (D'Ors 1960: 76): cooperation in crimes such as adultery, homicide, witchcraft, treason and counterfeiting (also in *LV* VII.6.i).

218-22, 247). For its part, Chindasvinth's earlier law lists, in all sorts of detail, two violent crimes whose increase demanded a new, specific ruling. The first of these was the forced entry by an armed group of slaves and freedmen into a magnate's house (*domus*) or farm (*curtis*) with the intention of holding him by force. The other criminal act considered was the kidnapping of a person away from his home or farm with the intention of keeping him away from his lands, belongings and dependants (*LV* VIII.1.iv). These last two legal norms undoubtedly reveal one of the main sources of illegitimate violence in the Visigothic kingdom in the second half of the seventh century, and the extent to which legal measures against it could be effective.

Violence arose from ruthless competition between *potentes* as they tried to gain for themselves the greatest amount of material resources, and the highest number of dependants. This usually implied an increase in their landholdings and in the number of peasants necessary to exploit them, whether slaves or free or freed tenants *in patrocinio cum obsequio*. Given the limited mobility of the ownership of land and men, the most important tool to achieve this goal was the use of violence against third parties, and especially against other *potentes*. For this it was essential to have armed clients and a core of elite warriors; this last group were tied to their *patronus* through a special oath of fealty, and were rewarded with conditional grants of land. [15]

In such circumstances, the only possible legal measure to stop such violent actions would have been to illegitimize these vertical social groupings, and the clientage of professional warriors in particular. The Visigothic monarchy could do no such thing because, ever since the *Landnahme* which enabled the birth of the Kingdom of Toulouse at the beginning of the fifth century, a great part of its own strength was based upon such armed clients, its own and those of other *potentes* tied to the reigning monarch by a special bond of fealty. This 'feudalizing' state of affairs only grew and consolidated in later centuries, so that by the second half of the seventh century it has been possible to speak of a Visigothic state based upon a sort of 'proto-feudal' *Lehnshierarchie* at whose summit was the king, and whose most distinctive characteristic was a very strong tendency, on the part of the monarch's noble *fideles*, to turn *honores* or high positions in the administration into parts of their own patrimonies.

In the event, Visigothic royal legislation not only did not ban such social vertical solidarities, but helped them with other measures. In con-

---

15. The best example of the workings of these offences, and of the necessary means to succeed through them is given by the former Ostrogothic general Theudis, who managed to take the Visigothic throne thanks to the support of 2,000 *bucellarii* dependent upon him and maintained at the expense of the wealth and extensive landholdings of his wife, a Hispano-Roman noblewoman (Procopius, *Wars* V.12.1-li).

junction with its extension of the slaves' traditional lack of civil and criminal responsibility to other dependants acting *iubenti domino*, as mentioned above, Visigothic legislation did the same for everything related to the capacity to testify or litigate. If an *antiqua* (V.7.xi) forbade freedmen to testify against their former owner, now landlord, or all his descendants, a later law of Reccesvinth (*LVV.*7.xvii) forbade freedmen and their descendants to litigate against any of their former owners or their offspring, who were their *patroni*. To understand the social consequences of such rulings, one must remember that from the middle of the fifth century the position of tenants had been fused with that of slaves, and that, if manumissions were certainly frequent, particularly, since Ervig at least (*LV* V.7.xii), through wills, they could not be granted except by maintaining the freedman and all his progeny *in obsequio* of the previous owner's family, as had been instituted much earlier (633) for slaves freed by the church (Claude 1980: 159–87).

The only exceptions to these rules are expressed in a well-known *antiqua* (VI.1.iv), according to which, besides being held penally responsible in cases of collaboration or concealment, slaves could testify under torture against their owners in crimes of adultery, homicide, witchcraft, treason and counterfeiting. If some of these exceptions could be explained by the traditions of Roman law, other additions (witchcraft, counterfeiting and homicide) refer to crimes committed by magnates for which the cooperation of their dependants was most necessary, particularly in the case of rebellions and usurpations (Petit 1986: 97 ff.).[16] According to a law of the tireless Chindasvinth (*LV* VI.1.ii), to solve certain crimes such as homicide, adultery and treason, freemen and even the high palatine nobility could be subject to torture, although a later and much weaker monarch like Ervig was forced to exclude the lay and ecclesiastical nobility from such proceedings, in what is known as the '*Habeas Corpus* of the Goths'.[17]

Some of these crimes, on the other hand, were included in the situations where Visigothic law legitimized the use of violence. A series of *antiquae* left unpunished a freeman who murdered his adulterous wife (*LV* III.4.i; this was further decreed by Chindasvinth, who also considered adultery a cause for divorce; *LV* III.6.ii) and her lover (III.4.iv). The tendency of Roman vulgar law (Petit 1984: 217–22) to treat marriage and betrothal equally also led to legitimation for the killing of a

---

16. Witchcraft was partly related to homicide. It was very frequently used to make an attempt on the king's life in an active way (black magic) or in a prospective way (in foretelling the king's future): VII Toledo, 5; *iudicium inter Martianum et Habentium episcopos* D.2 & F.1 (Dahn, ed. 1885: 615–20).

17. XIII Toledo, 2, although the more energetic Egica tried to revoke such privilege, taking advantage of a favourable opportunity, the failure of the rebellion of Sisibert in 693 (Petit 1986: 17, 129).

betrothed woman by her fiancé if she became another man's lover (*LV* III.4.ii). Even parents and brothers were entitled to kill an adulterous daughter or sister (III.4.iv). Eventually a woman was also allowed to kill her husband's lover if the latter was proven to have encouraged the adulterous liaison (III.4.ix).

These legitimate violent acts can all doubtless easily be explained as following well established traditions of Roman vulgar law (D'Ors 1960: 144 ff.). Christian doctrine, moreover, eased the way for legislators to take a firm stance in situations concerning transgresssions of conjugal sexual morals. A whole series of Visigothic laws is based upon this point of view, laws which severely punished sexual crimes such as the abduction or rape of a free woman (III.3.i, v & viii) or the mere collaboration in such acts (III.3.v); even the abduction of a slave or freedwoman by another slave was pursued by royal justice, and not left to the owner's discretion (III.3.ix & x). Furthermore, the murder of a woman's abductor was not punishable if it was carried out to safeguard her honour (III.3.vi). It would be inaccurate, nevertheless, to say that Visigothic legislation faithfully followed the church's dictates in these matters of sexual morals. In this respect we can point to two particularly significant discrepancies, one regarding the freedom of a woman to marry, and the other regarding the punishment of adulterous slaves.

The Visigothic church's doctrine regarding the freedom of the sacrament of matrimony was firm, following a line well defined by the Holy Fathers, limiting the father's authority inherent in Roman law (Gaudemet 1958: 537 ff.). Conciliar canons and hagiographic anecdotes clearly demonstrate that to the Visigothic church a woman had the right to oppose a marriage enforced by her parents or even by the king (III Toledo 10; García Moreno 1974a: nos 27 & 177). On other hand, Visigothic legislation is clear cut. The father's will regarding to whom his daughter was to be betrothed and married was to be enforced by any means possible (*LV* III.1.ii, *antiqua*). Although Chindasvinth later prohibited the use of violence to force a young woman to marry against her will, he nevertheless allowed two exceptions: the father's will and the king's (III.3.xi). This last royal right, decreed by a king so interested in reinforcing his position vis-à-vis the powerful nobility, reveals the reason behind the legitimation of the violent imposition of a husband upon a woman. Marriage was one of the preferred and more powerful tools used to bind clients and friendly relationships amongst the nobles; it was also the favourite weapon used by magnates to increase the number of their clients and wealth in the constant competition that existed among them and between them and the monarch and his *fideles*. To this end, Visigothic legislation did not hesitate to transgress other basic Christian sexual mores, such as the second marriage of widows or the higher age of a husband in relation to his wife (García Moreno 1986: 421–25).

We have seen how Visigothic legislation legitimized private violence if the husband's honour was at stake as a result of a wife's infidelity. The situation was nevertheless not the same at all levels of society. It was valid for those placed at the higher end of the scale but not for those at the bottom. Two *antiquae* (*LV* III.4.xv & xvi) deal with adultery or the violent rape of a slave by another slave or freedman. In both cases the Visigothic legislator, following Roman legal principles (D'Ors 1960: 149), attempted to protect the honour of the slave's owner more than that of the adulterer's family, to the extent that he distinguished between cases where the actions were carried out in the slave-owner's home and those where they were not. Only in the first instance was public justice interested in intervening and punishing the adulterer, a punishment far from the possibility of receiving death with impunity at the hands of the slave-owner. Whether or not to punish the female slave was a different matter, and one of no interest to the state. It was left to her owner's discretion; he could do whatever he chose to her, even kill her (*LV* III.4.xv).

These last cases bring us to a different sphere of violence legitimized by Visigothic law: that related to seigneurial jurisdiction. This is, of course, a subject which is difficult to study, in the first place because it lies outside the public domain and thus did not interest the king's justice, that reflected in the *Liber Iudicum*,[18] but also because seigneurial jurisdiction implied a fissure in the principle of the universality of royal justice, for which the more energetic monarchs fought so hard (Petit 1984: 249; 1986: 154). Nevertheless, the existence, consolidation and extent of seigneurial jurisdiction remains an extremely significant issue when attempting to explain the development of Visigothic 'proto-feudalism' and demonstrate how the type of violence legitimized by Visigothic law also favoured the consolidation of vertical social groups headed by members of the lay and ecclesiastical nobility.

It was precisely the energetic and jealous Chindasvinth who issued a well-known law (*LV* II.1.xviii) prohibiting judicial action by anyone not administering royal justice. This meant, in principle, the prohibition of any private jurisdiction. A previous, apparently Leovigildan, *antiqua* (VI. 1.i; D'Ors 1960: 76)[19] had ordered large landowners immediately to hand over to the judge those of their slaves who were accused of a crime. At the same time, the law demonstrates that it was not uncommon for magnates (*seniores loci*) to refuse to hand their slaves over to

---

18. There are not many studies of Visigothic seigneurial jurisdiction. The salient aspects can be found in Petit 1984: 249–52; 1985: 223; García Moreno 1992: 32, 40.

19. Leovigild (569–586) was also an energetic monarch who tried to reinforce his position vis-à-vis the nobility, attempting thus to imitate the emperor Justinian's stand (Stroheker 1965: 135 ff.; García Moreno 1991: 179 ff.).

royal justice,[20] allowing judges in all cases to enter their property and arrest the accused slaves. Another law of Chindasvinth (*LV* VI.5.xii), altering a well-established tradition of Roman law (Nehlsen 1972: 172 ff), strictly prohibited owners from killing their slaves, a custom which the same monarch recognized was very widespread and which affected not only slaves but freemen too. His son, Reccesvinth, later also attempted to limit the *ius puniendi* of the great landowners further when he forbade them to mutilate their slaves in any way (*LV* VI.5.xiii). Nevertheless, Chindasvinth himself allowed a series of exceptions to his prohibition: the death of a slave at the hands of his owner when acting in self-defence; in the case of a revolt by the slave (the owner's oath and the affidavit of some of the participating slaves would be proof enough); through unintentionally excessive punishment, to prove which the owner's oath was enough; finally, a capital sentence decreed by the royal judge could be executed by the slave's owner. Besides, neither Chindasvinth nor Reccesvinth had withdrawn from the *Codex* an *antiqua* (VII.2.xxi) allowing the owner to impose any punishment, including death, on a slave who had stolen something either from him or from another of his slaves; in such a case it is specifically pointed out that the royal judge should not interfere at all.

In spite of such contradictions and escape-clauses, it does not seem that the powerful Visigothic nobles of the second half of the seventh century were disposed to allow royal legislation which illegitimized the extremes of jurisdictional violence necessary to maintain the cohesion and reality of the vertical social groupings which they headed. Some decades after the issue of Chindasvinth's and Reccesvinth's laws, King Ervig (680–87), much weaker and more in need of the support of the lay and ecclesiastical nobility (García Moreno 1991: 248–52), proceeded to reform his predecessors' laws in a way more favourable to seigneurial jurisdiction. *LV* VI.5.xii was reformed to allow slave-owners to sentence and execute capital punishment of their slaves, their only duty being to appear in front of a judge *a posteriori* and swear that the slave had committed a crime deserving such a sentence. Ervig was even more drastic with regard to the explicit *LV* VI.5.xiii; he simply removed it from the *Codex*.[21]

---

20. Other laws also allow us to surmise how common was the reluctance of magnates to hand their dependants over to royal justice. See Petit 1985: 236, which must be complemented with XVI Toledo 2, indicating that magnates could shelter from justice not only their slaves but all peasants within their areas of influence.

21. Nevertheless I disagree with Petit (1984: 251), who believes that in Ervig's *LV* IX.2.ix 'the figure of the *dominus* who beats multitudes of slaves is presented as something natural'. The sentence referred to is *cum quidam illorum laborandis agris studentes servorum multitudines cedunt* and should be translated thus: 'when a multitude of slaves is withdrawn to work on the fields [the nobles who with their slaves should join the royal armies]'.

This last action would be regretted by his successor Egica (687–702), who reintroduced the law (*LV* VI.5.xiii*). Egica was an energetic monarch who tried, by all the means at his disposal, to weaken the cohesion of those vertical groups not controlled by his own *fideles* (García Moreno 1991: 256–59). In spite of this, he kept in force a law of Reccesvinth (*LV* VI.5.viii) which exempted a master, owner or patron from any responsibility for the homicide, through excessive punishment, of an apprentice, slave or dependant; he apparently did not even have to prove that it had been done without malice. Reccesvinth justified this with a sentence from the Holy Scriptures, although not all Visigothic churchmen would have agreed with such a statement (Isidore, *Sententiae* II.18.ii).

Finally, the most terrible and extreme kind of violence illegitimized by Visigothic law: rebellions and attempts to usurp the throne made by groups of nobles at the head of their vertical social groupings, and especially their military clients. Laws of both Chindasvinth (*LV* II.1.viii) and Reccesvinth (*LV* II.1.ix) punished such acts of violence with the severest penalties. Royal legislation did no more than summarize a rich earlier, and subsequent, conciliar legislation.[22] Later, King Wamba (672–80) in his famous military law (IX.2.viii) would also sanction passivity, the failure to help the monarch when this type of violence took place. Nevertheless, anyone knowledgeable about Visigothic history, and about its last century in particular, will be well aware that if these violent crimes succeeded in placing somebody on the throne, they were immediately legitimized. What is more, they helped to strengthen and consolidate further the vertical groupings headed by the triumphant nobles (García Moreno 1975: 47–51).

But this dynamic of violence and its treatment in the Visigothic state's legislation led to an impasse: from loss of the ability to testify, widened to all those involved in rebellions, actively or passively, to a social confrontation which endangered the whole system. This fed from the harshness of the growing seigneurial jurisdiction and the discrimination and incapacity of royal justice, but it was made possible particularly by the spread of military skill and weaponry amongst retainers (García Moreno 1975: 64–82; Claude 1978: 311–25). Some of the laws examined above allow us to see how certain crimes committed by slaves or retainers were not always carried out on behalf of their owner or patron (VII.1.iv & viii); it does not seem to have been abnormal for bands of slaves and retainers to be established with such criminal ends in mind, and with people other than their owners and patrons at their heads (*antiquae* VIII.1.iii & vi). There is no doubt that in most cases these bands were made up of runaway slaves and thieves, but they also comprised runaway nobles, punished by royal authority, or who had failed in at-

---

22. IV Toledo 75; V Toledo 4 & 6; VI Toledo 17; VII Toledo 1; VIII Toledo 2 & 10; XVI Toledo 10. Cp. Iglesia 1971: 21–81.

tempted rebellions or usurpations. The latter could be in touch with out-side powers, and thus be ready to head or join a new rebellion (Diesner 1978b: 129–42). In short, some vertical groups could be destroyed by, and others be born from, any such violent action.

This socio-political dynamic was certainly a dangerous game, especi-ally for the survival of a state ruled by law such as the Gothic kingdom claimed to be. Some members of the powerful and influential ecclesiast-ical intelligentsia were doubtless aware of the danger. With their patron-age of the *pauperes* (Diesner 1977: 7–25) and their attempt to organize royal succession, people like Isidore of Seville, with his condemnation of all violence, including that exercised by the powers of the state, tried to dispel or diminish such risks (García Moreno 1975: 210–12). The end of the Visigothic kingdom and its ideological restoration between the beginning and the end of the eighth century demonstrate the successes and failures of such attempts.

(Translated by Theresa Lindquist and Guy Halsall)

BIBLIOGRAPHY

Primary Sources

Breviarium Alarici: G. Haenel (ed.), *Lex Romana Visigothorum* (Aalen, 1962).

Church Councils: J. Vives (ed.), *Concilios Visigóticos e Hispano-Romanos* (Barce-lona, 1963).

Isidore, *Sententiae*: J. Campos & I. Roca, *Santos Padres Españoles* II (Madrid, 1971).

Leges Visigothorum: K. Zeumer (ed.), *MGH Leges* I.1 *Leges Visigothorum* (Berlin, 1902).

Lex Baiuariorum: E. de Schwind (ed.), *M.G.H. Legum* Sect. I vol. V, part 2, *Lex Baiwariorum* (Hanover, 1926).

Novellae Valentiniani: C. Pharr *et al.* (eds & trans.), *The Theodosian Code and Novels and the Sirmondian Constitutions* (Princeton, 1952).

Procopius, *Wars*: H. B. Dewing (ed. & trans.), *Procopius* vols 1–5 (London, 1914–28).

Sidonius Apollinaris, *Epistolae*: W. B. Anderson (ed. & trans.), *Sidonius. Poems and Letters*, 2 vols (London, 1936–65).

Secondary Bibliography

Barbero, A. & Vigil, M., 1978. *La formación del feudalismo en la Península Ibérica* (Barcelona).

Bruguière, M. B., 1974. *Littérature et Droit dans la Gaule du V* siècle* (Paris).

Claude, D., 1978. 'Soziale Spannungen im Westgotenreich', *Klio* 60, II: 311–25.

——— 1980. 'Freedmen in the Visigothic kingdom', in James (ed.) 1980: 159–88.

D'Ors, A., 1960. *El Código de Eurico* (Estudios Visigóticos II) (Rome-Madrid).

Dahn, F., 1885. *Die Könige der Germanen VI* 2nd edition (Leipzig).

Diesner, H.-J., 1970. 'Sklaven, Untertanen und Untertanenverbände im West-gotenreich', *Jahrbuch für Wirtschaftsgeschichte* 2: 173–92.

—— 1977. *Isidor von Sevilla und das westgotische Spanien* (Abhandlungen der sächsischen Akad. der Wissenschaften zu Leipzig, Phil.-hist. Kl. 67.3) (Berlin).

—— 1978a. *Westgotische und langobardische Gefolgschaften und Untertanenverbände* (Abhandlungen der sächsischen Akademie der Wissenschaften zu Leipzig, Phil.-hist. Klasse 120,2) (Berlin).

—— 1978b. 'Bandas de criminales, bandidos y usurpadores en la España visigoda', *Hispania Antiqua* 8: 129–42.

—— 1979. *Politik und Ideologie im Westgotenreich von Toledo: Chindasvind* (Sitzungsberichte der sächsischen Akademie der Wissenschaften zu Leipzig. Phil.-hist. Klasse 121.2) (Berlin).

García Moreno, L. A., 1974a. *Prosopografía del Reino visigodo de Toledo* (Salamanca).

—— 1974b. 'Estudios sobre la organización administrativa del Reino visigodo de Toledo', *Anuario de Historia del Derecho Español* 44: 5–155.

—— 1975. *El fin del Reino visigodo de Toledo* (Madrid).

—— 1986. 'La mujer visigoda entre la represión sexual y el poder político', in E. Garrido (ed.), *La mujer en el Mundo antiguo* (Madrid), pp. 415–25.

—— 1991. *Historia de España Menéndez Pidal. España Visigoda*, III,1 (Madrid).

—— 1992. 'El estado protofeudal visigodo: precedente y modelo para la Europa carolingia', in J. Fontaine & C. Pellistrandi (eds), *L'Europe héritière de l'Espagne wisigothique* (Madrid), pp. 17–43.

Gaudemet, J., 1958. *L'Eglise dans l'Empire Romain (IVe-Ve siècles)* (Paris).

Iglesia, A., 1971. *Historia de la Traición. La Traición regia en León y Castilla* (Santiago de Compostela).

James, E., (ed.), 1980. *Visigothic Spain: New Approaches* (Oxford).

King, P. D., 1972. *Law and Society in the Visigothic Kingdom* (Cambridge).

—— 1980. 'King Chindasvind and the first territorial law-code of the Visigothic kingdom', in James (ed.) 1980: 131–57.

Levy, E., 1951. *West Roman Vulgar Law. The Law of Property* (Philadelphia).

Martínez Díez, G., 1960. 'Función de inspección y vigilancia del episcopado sobre las autoridades seculares en el periodo visigodo-católico', *Revista Española de Derecho Canónico* 15: 579–89.

Merêa, P., 1948. *Estudos de Direito visigótico* (Coimbra).

Nehlsen, H., 1972. *Sklavenrecht zwischen Antike und Mittelalter. Germanisches und römisches Recht in den germanischen Rechtsaufzeichnungen I. Ostgoten, Westgoten, Franken, Langobarden* (Göttingen-Frankfurt-Zürich).

Petit, C., 1984. 'Consuetudo y Mos en la Lex Visigothorum', *Anuario de Historia del Derecho Español* 54: 209–52.

—— 1985. 'De negotiis causarum I', *Anuario de Historia del Derecho Español* 55: 151–251.

—— 1986. 'De negotiis causarum II', *Anuario de Historia del Derecho Español* 56: 5–165.

Reydellet, M., 1981. *La royauté dans la littérature latine de Sidoine Apollinaire à Isidore de Séville* (Rome).

Sánchez Albornoz, C., 1924. 'Las Behetrías. La Encomendación en Asturias, León y Castilla', *Anuario de Historia del Derecho Español* 1: 179–95.

Sanz, R., 1986. 'Aproximación al estudio de los ejércitos privados en Hispania durante la Antigüedad tardía', *Gerión* 4: 225–64.

Stroheker, K.-F., 1937. *Eurich, König der Westgoten* (Stuttgart).

—— 1965. *Germanentum und Spätantike* (Zürich).

CHAPTER 2

Attitudes towards violence in seventh- and eighth-century Francia[1]

Paul Fouracre

In a celebrated essay Wallace-Hadrill showed how, amongst the Franks from Clovis to Charlemagne and beyond, the feud remained as an ultimate coercive sanction, underpinning rather than undermining, the formal legal process (Wallace-Hadrill 1962: 121–47). Here, he challenged the common assumption that the elimination of feud was the necessary, even moral, duty of early medieval rulers. Yet Wallace-Hadrill may actually have exaggerated the importance of feud by being rather too ready to classify as feud violence of other kinds, despite initially warning of precisely this danger. 'To work through the seven volumes of the *Scriptores Rerum Merowingicarum*', he wrote, 'is to be made aware that feuds are like volcanoes. A few are in eruption, others are extinct, but most are content to rumble now and again leaving us guessing' (*ibid.*: 143). He thus implied that feuds are to be found throughout the Merovingian narrative sources, nearly all of which are contained in these seven volumes, and his typically brilliant metaphor evokes the sense that amongst the Franks violence could erupt at almost any time. Unfortunately, this impression is untestable. We have so few examples, taken from narratives of such variable quality, that we can neither tell whether Merovingian Francia was becoming more or less violent, nor say whether it was more or less violent than any other early medieval society. What can be done, as

---

1. The term 'Francia' is used here to refer to territory subject to Frankish rulers before AD 751 and is of cultural rather than ethnic significance. The work 'Frankish' suggests a certain ethnic identity, but the importance of such an identity is questionable (Ewig 1958: 587–648; Geary 1985: 101–12). I am grateful to Janet Nelson and Chris Wickham for commenting on a preliminary draft of this paper.

Wallace-Hadrill demonstrated, is to comment on specific instances of violence in relation to other available information about conflict and its resolution. We can also focus on the particular sources which talk about violence, in order to examine how, and why, they discuss it. By thus putting the narratives into context, we may say something about changing attitudes towards violence. These are the aims of the present chapter, which concentrates on the later Merovingian period and attempts to show how the discussion of violence, like almost every aspect of human behaviour, was drawn into the language of Christian culture. The effect of this Christianization of language upon the attitudes towards violence expressed in early Carolingian narratives will also be examined. The question here is why the Carolingian régime appears to have been less violent than its Merovingian predecessor. Was this apparent difference a trick of the sources, or do they reflect real differences between Merovingian and Carolingian levels of violence? We must, therefore, consider the relationship between literary convention and social reality, although, as in nearly every other area, we know more about preaching than practice.

Almost all we can read about later Merovingian violence relates to that small elite whose actions are the primary focus of the narratives. Chronicles and saints' lives had a marked political content, for their subjects were people invariably involved in high politics. Violence is thus often presented to us in the form of political behaviour, above all in the context of struggles for power. Most of Wallace-Hadrill's volcanic eruptions therefore turn out to have been of a more limited political nature, although feud and politics are not always separable categories of behaviour (Black-Michaud 1975: 26–27; Bennett, below: 129–36). Furthermore, the authors' predilection for spectacular stories may have led them to accentuate the violence of Merovingian politics, leaving us with the false impression that Frankish political life was typically violent. This certainly seems true of Gregory of Tours' work. Gregory narrated history in more detail than anyone else in western Europe in the sixth century, or indeed for centuries after. He is similarly one of the few sources with enough detail to allow one to observe protracted political enmity.[2] As a result it

---

2. In early medieval sources generally the sparsity of background information on acts of violence makes it usually impossible to distinguish between vengeance-killing and feud. To identify feud we must have some indication the killing took place against a background of collective group solidarity, although Black-Michaud's (1975: 27–30) distinction between vengeance and feud may be over-schematic. The small quantity and variable quality of narrative material means that it is unusual to be able to follow any conflict for more than two rounds. Confidence that apparently isolated incidents of violence do relate to feud otherwise hidden from us relies upon assumptions about kinship solidarity and ethnically determined social structure which are increasingly under fire (Murray 1983: *passim*). Sawyer's (1987) extreme, but in some ways cogent, view is that it is impossible to identify a single feud from the early medieval period. He thus rejects the Sichar-Chramnesind affair as an example (see also the introduction, p. 24).

has been used as a source for comment on the quality of political life, which it presents as unpredictable, and governed by short-sighted greed and violence. In more recent thinking the reliability of Gregory as a witness in these matters has been called into question (Goffart 1988: 153–226). It has been reasoned that Gregory highlighted incidents of violence and emphasized the chaotic behaviour of powerful persons as a means of demonstrating the hopelessness of acting without submission to the will of God. Spectacular violence was for Gregory a way of driving home the point that those who did not act in a Christian manner would invariably come to a sticky end, just as he used endless miracle stories to show how those who kept faith would be rewarded (Van Dam 1993: 82–149). What Gregory's world-view lacked in subtlety it gained in conviction, and one cannot read any early medieval accounts of violence without being aware that they are predicated upon the same theological certainties.

The mid-seventh-century work known as the *Chronicle of Fredegar* is clearly more secular in tone than Gregory's history. Its focus is also more narrowly political, for the narrative radiates outwards from the various royal courts and is largely concerned with kings, queens and their immediate associates. *Fredegar*'s portrayal of violence, unlike Gregory's, does not serve the purpose of contrasting good and bad behaviour; violence is seen within Christian culture, rather than as opposed to it. The violence of rulers and their opponents takes place in a plainly Christian context. For example, when, c. 626, one Godinus married his step-mother, King Clothar II resolved to kill him unless he gave up his new wife whom he had married 'against canon law'. Godinus did give her up, but remained a threat, and Clothar sent him on a tour of the premier saints shrines in order to arrange his murder. Eventually Godinus was caught unawares and killed, along with some of his followers (*Fredegar* IV.54). Here, outrage at the man's technical incest was doubtless only one element in a power struggle in which Godinus intended to step into his father's shoes as leader of Burgundy as well as (or, rather, by way of) climbing into his bed. Family affairs and high politics were bound up together: Clothar's initial move had been to order Godinus's own brother-in-law to kill him, possibly, one imagines, on the basis that the family's honour had been compromised. When Godinus was finally put to death, it was at the hands of other magnates, and this involvement of leaders in face-to-face violence is a common feature in *Fredegar*'s narrative. Unlike Gregory, *Fredegar* does not seem to have been of a mind, or perhaps was not in a position, to censure the behaviour of leaders. In this story, the only hint of criticism was of Godinus himself.

For *Fredegar*, therefore, violence does not seem to have been a moral issue. The points of censure in the work are largely concerned with taking church property, breaking canon law, betrayal, perjury, and sacrilege, or, more comprehensively and more simply, 'injustice'. One of the chronicle's most colourful stories will serve as illustration: *Fredegar* closes with an account of a long-running dispute between two magnates, Willebad and Flaochad (*Fredegar* IV.90). It is a story which Wallace-Hadrill quoted as an example of feud, but it is more clearly a political narrative related to the Godinus episode, because the context is again the struggle for power in Burgundy. The story's climax comes with a pitched battle between the two men and their respective supporters. The description of the fighting is perhaps the liveliest piece of writing in all of *Fredegar*, and contains invaluable details. In particular this striking picture of Frankish magnates in furious personal combat is a key source for impressions about aristocratic behaviour, not least for the idea that they were the sort of hot-heads who would get involved in 'feuds'. *Fredegar* finally winds down the excitement with an ending worthy of Gregory: Willebad having been killed in the fight, Flaochad was struck down by divine vengeance and died of fever eleven days later. God killed both men because they had made false oaths of friendship in holy places, because they had oppressed and robbed the people under their rule, and generally because of their perfidy and lying. On the fight itself, *Fredegar* makes no comment.

The Willebad/Flaochad narrative shows how *Fredegar* liked a good story, and the quality of writing may suggest that the story was well rehearsed before it was set down in this Latin chronicle. There are several other excursus in which the work's compiler seems to have appropriated narrative from elsewhere. Most obviously, *Fredegar* borrowed wholesale from the *Lives* of Columbanus and Desiderius of Vienne. Both works were used to provide material on Queen Brunichildis and her grandsons, who were of great interest to this chronicler. *Fredegar* took from these sources his hostile portrayal of Brunichildis and embellished the *Vita Columbani*'s detail in order to stress the violence of the campaign to dislodge the queen from power in Burgundy and to highlight her gruesome death (*Fredegar* IV.42; *Vita Columbani* I.27). Far from restraining him from spicing the narrative with talk of violence, the author's use of hagiographic material may actually have encouraged him to do so. As we shall see, in saints' lives violence was a common feature, and Christian culture was attuned to violence, both through the suffering of the saints and via the manifestly vigorous execution of divine judgement. *Fredegar*'s portrayal of Brunhild's death drew on both streams.

The *Liber Historiae Francorum*, which provides the main political narrative for the period between the end of *Fredegar* (c. 642) and the year 727, shows a similar attitude towards violence. This chronicle, completed in 727, is much more terse than *Fredegar*, covering the period 614 to 727 in a mere twelve chapters, whereas *Fredegar* took forty-seven chapters of roughly comparable length to describe the events of the years 614–642. Nevertheless, the author of the *LHF* shared *Fredegar*'s penchant for dwelling on the more colourful epsiodes of Merovingian politics. He (or, just possibly, she[3]) went into detail on two seventh-century subjects: King Clothar II's campaign against the Saxons, and the politics of the period 673–687 (*LHF* 41, 45–48). The former, set some-time towards the close of Clothar's reign in 628, included a legendary account of the king's personal combat against the Saxon leader, and the latter was action-packed with three changes of leadership, the deposition of one king, the murders of two others, incipient civil war and two big battles between the kingdoms of Neustria and Austrasia. Nevertheless, if we take the dramatic but probably fictitious account of Clothar's slaying of his Saxon adversary out of the picture, then, according to the *LHF*'s narrative as a whole, for most of the seventh century Francia was rather quiet and peaceful. Yet a casual reading of the chronicle leaves one with the contrary impression that kings, like Clothar, were active warriors in the van of the carnage, and that politics, as in the 670s and 680s, were characterized by betrayal and slaughter.

The picture of Clothar's combat may have been poetically inspired, but the events of 673–687 were not far beyond the living memory of an author writing in 727. They were, moreover, recorded in contemporary hagiography, and may have stood out precisely because they followed a prolonged period of peace and stability. The author's attitude here is complex. He favoured peace and political consensus, but applauded the violent actions of leaders when they reflected the cunning and prowess of his own people, the Neustrian Franks (Gerberding 1987: 159–72). For instance, he disliked King Childeric II for being too frivolous, breaking consensus, and humiliating the Franks. Childeric's murder by these same Franks in 675 is not condemned in the chronicle, although the author regretted the fact that Queen Bilichildis was killed alongside him, particularly because she was pregnant, although this, presumably, was one reason for killing her. Interestingly, Childeric's assassination is re-ferred to in contemporary hagiography as the 'sentence of God'; the same source does not mention Bilichildis's death. Here is a partisan view of both peace and violence. It is visible in later seventh-century hagiography and becomes more marked in eighth-century narratives, be-ginning with the *LHF* and developing in the course of the century in-to strongly pro-Carolingian versions of events. Its effect is to accentu-ate later Merovingian violence and to play down the violence of the following Carolingian regime. This requires more detailed considera-tion.

---

3. Gerberding (1987: 146–59) assumed that the author of the *LHF* was male. J. L. Nelson (1991) has argued that we should not discount the possibility of a female author. Of the other sources discussed here, a female author is also a possibility for the *Annals of Metz*, and that a woman composed the *Passio Praejecti* is a fairly strong possibility (Fouracre and Gerberding 1996). If these authors were women, we should note that their attitudes towards violence were no different from those of their male counterparts.

Merovingian politics undoubtedly contained a violent element, for the organization of political power depended largely on rivalry between different factions of nobles, each of which could wield military force. Competitive nobles were, however, generally keen to do the bidding of the kings and 'mayors of the palace', so that rivalry mostly worked to keep the peace and to enhance rather than to weaken the rulers' authority (Fouracre 1984: 3–10). Indeed, especially, perhaps, in the earlier part of the century, seventh-century rulers could occasionally exercise a power of command which was as absolute, and as violent, as that of the Roman Emperors. Godinus, as we have seen, was one unfortunate victim of such power. On the other hand, factional rivalry could get out of hand if the palace lost the political initiative and if no leader was strong enough to control the different noble groups. This seems to have happened in 673–676 and again in 680–687. The result, as the *LHF* reported it, was an increase in political violence as the different factions fought for control. Church leaders were also involved in political violence because they were usually great nobles whose status and power meant that they were active in high politics. At the same time there was also a strong demand for new saints' cults as the church expanded into areas relatively untouched by the Roman martyr cults which had been the focal points of a burgeoning culture of sanctity, and in response to the invention of cults in new areas, traditional ecclesiastical centres, such as Clermont, Lyons and Autun, also set up cults. Because of the demand for new saints, several Merovingian church leaders at this time of political crisis were acclaimed saints, and if they died violent deaths, they were hailed as martyrs (Fouracre and Gerberding 1996). There is in the hagiography of the period a consequent reflowering of the martyr genre as several leaders who became casualties of violent later seventh-century politics were quickly honoured as saints. The result was hagiography produced close in time and place to the events it described, in which the conventional aspects of sanctity were placed in a political context, and in which violence was the key which unlocked the hero's sanctity (*ibid.*).

In these rather unusual circumstances five new martyrs were created: Aunemund, bishop of Lyons (killed c. 660); Germanus, abbot of Grandivalle in the Sornegau (murdered c. 675); Praejectus, bishop of Clermont (killed 676); Leudegar, bishop of Autun (executed probably in 677); and finally, Landibert, bishop of Tongres-Maastricht (slain 705–707). With the possible exception of Aunemund (Fouracre and Gerberding 1996), all five had accounts of their careers and deaths written up soon after their deaths. In these works the saint's violent end was portrayed as his crowning moment of glory. Incidents of violence were thus highlighted and placed in a strongly Christian framework, the ultimate inspiration for which was Christ's own suffering. In earlier Christian tradition martyrs had died at the hands of the Roman state (Delehaye 1966:

171-218); in Merovingian hagiography contexts of martyrdom were much more complex, as all the parties involved were part of the same Christian community. Aunemund and Leudegar were killed on the orders of rulers, but elements in their own religious communities contributed to their downfall. Praejectus was more or less lynched by the Auvergnat nobility, Germanus was killed by an aggressive duke's henchmen, and Landibert's killing was an act of vengeance. In each case the hagiographer carefully explained the background to the violence in order to show why the hero had been attacked and why the killing was unjust. There was in these explanations a degree of equivocation which, initially, looks rather surprising in a hagiographical context. Authors pulled their punches because the perpetrators of violence were otherwise respected members of the ecclesiastical and political establishment. Both Praejectus' and Leudegar's antagonists actually succeeded them as bishop. The ruler associated with Aunemund's death became a saint herself. Germanus's persecutor, duke Eticho, was in other contexts a church patron, and one of the family who took revenge on Landibert later became abbot of the all-important abbey of St-Denis. Equivocation may also have been a by-product of a peace-making function in the writing of these saints lives, as in the case of the *Passio Praejecti*. Here, the hagiographer showed that Praejectus died unjustly but also indicated that those responsible for his death had earned a measure of forgiveness by recognizing their victim as a martyr and by giving property to a monastery which honoured his cult. This donation could be interpreted as an act of compensation, in order to make peace with Praejectus's family, one of whom had charge of the monastery which received these gifts of land and movable wealth (*Passio Praejecti* 31-39). On the other hand, authors also stressed the violent power of divine retribution. It was conventional for the lowly executioners, rather than the masters who gave the orders, to die in agony as a result of killing the saint. Landibert went further: the entire family of his killers all perished (*Vita Landiberti* 24), save Godobald, who repented and became abbot of St-Denis. In short, those who refused to recognize the saint's powers were in mortal danger.

The adaptation of the martyr genre to the particular conditions in which the later Merovingian church operated reflects the further development of that pragmatic attitude towards violence seen in *Fredegar*. In a given conflict both sides were Christian, but one side was just, the other unjust. The devil (Satan himself rather than the annoying little demons which afflicted earlier saints; Graus 1989) returned to hagiographical centre-stage as the agent of provocation, dividing communities, fostering injustice and leading men into violent action. The violence between the different magnate factions was thus inspired by the devil. What they fought for was 'power', that is, for that control of the palace which would give them the right to issue legally binding commands and through which they could coerce others. According to the *Passio Leude-garii*, when in 676 the old leader Ebroin had fought his way back to the palace, he then formally resumed office as 'mayor of the palace'. He thus 'obtained the rights of power' (i.e. power vested in legal right and supported by all of the available government machinery) and this greatly increased the amount of force at his disposal (*Passio Leudegarii* 28). The author firmly associated violence with power. 'If God gives him the power', he wrote, 'man on earth takes vengeance, he seizes, he plunders, he burns, he kills' (*ibid*.: 22). But power could be used for good, in which case the associated violence was less objectionable. There are in the work examples of violence being used to express God's will, and of force used on behalf of, or even by, the saint. That the author saw King Childeric II's murder as 'God's sentence' has already been mentioned. Leudegar himself had been 'a judge to be feared' and the *Passio Leude-garii* implies that he used force to bring order to Autun when he became the town's bishop (*Passio Leudegarii* 2). His associate, Hector, ruler of Marseilles, was painted in saintly terms in this work, but in the *Passio Praejecti* the same man appears as violent and evil (*Passio Praejecti* 23). In the *Passio Leudegarii*, Hector, 'Godwilling, defended himself manfully' when arrested on the charge of treason (*Passio Leudegarii* 11). Violent resistance was thus condoned, even though it meant that Hector's companions were killed with him. Leudegar himself was reported to have urged the people of Autun to 'fortify their souls and the town's defences' when Ebroin sent a force against him, and the citizens fought 'bravely' on his behalf before handing the bishop over to his persecutors (*Passio Leudegarii* 22-23). Bishop Landibert, *proeliator fortissimus* ('the fiercest of fighters'), first seized his sword when he heard his enemies coming, and it took *altissimum consilium* ('the very highest advice') to persuade him not to resist violence with violence (*Vita Landi-berti* 14).

In all of these texts we see a discriminatory attitude towards violence: in some circumstances it was condoned, in others it was condemned. Hagiographers had to interpret recent conflicts over power according to religious convention, and in relation to the part their particular subject had played in events. Not surprisingly, authors tended to use language which had meaning in both religious and secular terms as they sought to imbue all sorts of behaviour with religious significance. It is across this bridge between the secular and the religious that we see religious morality advancing into law and politics through such terms as 'justice/injustice', 'right/wrong', 'punishment', 'sentence' and 'law'. Even the phrase *fortissimus proeliator*, which seems to conjure up the image of a warrior bishop, has, in fact, a particular biblical reson-ance (Isaiah 42; 13). The elision between the mundane and the divine in both subject matter and language reflects the degree to which writ-ten culture had become Christianized by the end of the seventh century.[4] Saints' lives were the most widespread form of narrative writing and because they focussed upon violence, they were important in the formation of other writers' attitudes towards it. Writing about martyrs not only gave the discussion of violence a key position in the narrative, the careful and equivocal treatment of violence within the Christian community made these works uniquely rich in historical detail. It is that detail which has so often given modern historians the impression that the later seventh and early eighth centuries in Francia were a time of widespread violence and disorder. By contrast, the following period looks calmer, even though there are good reasons for doubting this impression.

We have already seen how the *LHF*'s author wrote history from the Neustrian elite's point of view. In the course of the eighth century history-writing increasingly favoured a single camp, that of the Carolingian family and its regime (Innes and McKitterick 1994: 202–03). The *Continuations* of the *Chronicle of Fredegar*, forming the central narrative from 727 to 768, were written at the behest, first, of Charles Martel's half-brother, and then of the latter's son (Collins 1994: 224–26). The *Royal Frankish Annals*, which furnish the most detailed continuous narrative for Charlemagne's reign (768–814), can be described as a 'court-production', and the first section of the *Annals of Metz*, completed around 806, is an impressively crafted laudatory account of the Carolingian family's rise to supreme power (Haselbach 1970; Fouracre and Gerberding 1996). History written in this vein showed the Carolingians from the 730s onwards as leaders of all the Franks, and it concentrated on their success in wars against peoples outside the Frankish community. At the same time the sequence of hagiographies focussed on conflict within the Christian community came to an end. As a result, although we are relatively well informed about the violence the Franks did to other peoples, we hear almost nothing in such texts about local conflict, or rivalry between different magnate factions. In other ways, history now took up where hagiography left off, for the Carolingian histories were much less secular in tone than either *Fredegar* or the *LHF* and some hagiographical characteristics began to appear in writing about Carolingian regimes, portrayed as God-guided and ineffably just in their actions. Their victories were God's judgement; that is, the violence they wielded was divinely sanctioned, and their kings were increasingly cast in a biblical mould. There was, however, no equivocation in this writing, for the Carolingians were not presented as seeking peace and consensus within the community, but as leading an already united people against outsiders (Nelson, below: 90–92). Satan could return to the wings, for

---

4. This phenomenon is equally visible in the writing of charters, in which divine sanction is given to the protection of property (Davies and Fouracre (eds) 1995: 266–68).

once again there were non-Christians to aim at.

The focus on wars rather than politics, the lack of any narrative in opposition to the rulers after Charles Martel (d. 741), and the disappearance of that element of local history which hagiography had earlier provided, combine to make the eighth-century Franks look more stable and less endemically violent than their seventh-century predecessors. But for the peoples on the periphery of, and outside, Francia the eighth-century was clearly a much more violent period, as almost every year warfare was directed at them. There are some hints that the campaigns involved much brutality; in Alemannia in the 740s (Reuter 1991: 59-60), in Aquitaine in the 760s (*Fredegar, Continuations* 41-52) and, most notoriously, in Saxony for most of the last third of the century. On the other hand, the Carolingians appear to have been less brutal towards their enemies within the Frankish elite, and within their own family. Is there a real contrast here with the behaviour of the Merovingians?

The impression that the Carolingians eschewed violence in their treatment of opponents may in part stem from deliberate silence and it may consequently be a misleading one. For example, whereas a late Merovingian hagiography, the *Life of Eucherius*, complained bitterly about Charles Martel's treatment of the family of Eucherius, bishop of Orleans in the 730s (*Vita Eucherii* 7-9), the same action appears in the *Continuations of Fredegar* in the following terms: 'Prince Charles swiftly penetrated into the land of Burgundy and established men of well-proven ability and valour within the boundaries of that kingdom, to curb disaffection as well as pagan penetration amongst the people' (*Continuations of Fredegar* 14). Without the help of the *Life of St Eucherius* we could not see that this involved driving out a bishop who had formerly been a firm ally. There are, moreover, hints that the rulers did occasionally kill and mutilate opponents. The curiously pessimistic revised version of the *Royal Frankish Annals* tells of two conspiracies against Charlemagne, about which the original source was silent. After the first, in 785, Charlemagne had some of the ringleaders exiled and others blinded. The second, more dangerous, plot had formed around the king's son Pippin in 792. The conspirators were hanged, beheaded or exiled. Pippin was sent to a monastery. Commenting on these events in his *Life of Charlemagne*, Einhard (once regarded as the author of the revised annals) wrote that Charlemagne's actions were, 'fundamentally opposed to his normal kindliness and good nature' (Einhard, *Vita Caroli* III.20). Never again was he so cruel. It would be tempting to dismiss Einhard's jejune comment out of hand, but for the fact that it is very hard to find other examples of the killing of opponents. There are also instances in which Charlemagne, and other Carolingians, actually spared the kind of rival whom in a Merovingian context we might have been expected to see killed. Pippin's survival in 792 is a case in point. Another case is that of Grifo, son of Charles Martel, who was still offered terms after taking up arms against his half-brothers in the early 740s. Or, in 788, Charlemagne cornered his cousin Tassilo, duke of Bavaria, but despite finding him guilty of a series of capital crimes, incarcerated him in a monastery. A further example might be Wala, again a cousin of Charlemagne, whom Louis the Pious seems to have seen as a rival for power in 814, and who was exiled to the monastery of Corbie. In each case, there may have been special circumstances which made mercy not only expedient but essential. Nevertheless, it is possible to relate the 'normal kindliness' of the Carolingians to a lingering precariousness in their position as kings. Raising the family to royal status had broken with Frankish custom and needed careful justification in terms of moral imperative. Violence within the family might compromise that special morality. Louis the Pious, who used a measure of violence (including killing) in stamping his authority on the palace in 814 and in slashing back a rival branch of the family in Merovingian style in 817, publicly repented his deeds in 821, an action which reflects the moral climate which the Carolingians had engendered. Whether the same morality and insecurity really did work to limit violence against the nobilty in general is ultimately impossible to assess, but if the reactions to the conspiracies of 785 and 792 are anything to go by, it did not.

So far we have seen how later Merovingian writers tended to highlight violence, both as chroniclers interested in the spectacular, and as hagiographers fashioning martyrs out of the casualties of conflict. Their efforts revealed the continuing advance of Christian language into the arena of power and law in which violence operated. A further step in this direction in the eighth century saw the writing of history which emphasized the role of the Carolingian rulers as defenders of the faith, and to this end largely excluded talk of violence within the Frankish community. As a result our impression is of a decline in violence, or the growth of an inner peace, in Francia and we have just discussed whether this mirrors a real change in behaviour, or is a misleading effect produced by the shift in orientation of the source material. About increased levels of violence towards peoples construed as enemies of the Franks, there can be no doubt.

Having now pointed out the danger of taking the sources too literally when they mention violence, let us now try to draw from them a more realistic impression of the place of violence in Frankish life. As we have seen, occasional violence was undoubtedly part of the political process in later Merovingian Francia. In a political structure organized around rivalry between different factions of magnates, violence was sometimes the means by which power was redistributed when one faction was seen to have dominated the palace and to have been exclusive in their control of the resources of royal authority. In this situation, the palace, and the king, were in the eye of the storm when fighting broke out. When political tension erupted into violence, fighting was often to the death, and kings too could be killed, as in 675 and 679. Magnates clearly took the field themselves, as seen in the combat between Flaochad and Willebad's factions. In the years 673–676, about which we are best informed, disorder was obviously widespread as the magnates fought each other throughout the regions once subject to Neustria. The scale of killing then, and during other outbursts of political violence, is impossible to estimate. We know, of course, of some famous casualties, like Germanus, Praejectus and Leudegar, and very often when we hear of the violent death of important people it is clear that others died with them. When Godinus was murdered, or when Hector was killed in 675, a number of unnamed companions died with them. But this violent political behaviour seems to have been exceptional, and stands out precisely because it was perceived as shocking. It is important to note that even when violence reached exceptionally high levels (the highest level probably being in the period 714–740 during which the Carolingians forcibly established themselves in power), it never compromised social stability. Violence could reinforce rather than weaken the social order. We must, finally, consider the relationship between violence and stability and put the whole issue of violence into a wider social context.

In Francia, as in every early medieval kingdom, rulers exercised authority over a limited range of issues, and in many areas the intervention of the ruler was by invitation rather than by right. Custom rather than law defined acceptable social practice, and violence was one means of safeguarding custom. Since it was necessary to defend honour and social status at all costs, violence in this sphere was recognized as legitimate (Sawyer 1987: 31), and there are examples of people who exercised public power using violence in a private capacity to avenge insults or injury to self or family. Such a case is that of Landibert's killer, Dodo (*Vita Landiberti* 11). The public courts also used violence to maintain social order by dealing very harshly with those who threatened property. How much criminal violence (that is, murder, rape, robbery and arson) there was across Francia is impossible to say because no later Merovingian legislation survives, and it is legislation against such crimes which is the main source of information about them. Given their rudimentary police mechanisms, there is no reason to doubt that the Merovingian rulers found brigandage as hard to deal with as their Roman predecessors or Carolingian, and even Norman, successors (Shaw 1984: 8–10; Murray 1988: 90; Reuter 1996). Apprehended criminals could be dealt with very violently, but punishment had to fit status as well as crime. One of the reasons Childeric II was killed was that he had outraged custom by ordering two noble Franks to be bound and beaten. Hanging and torture were for criminals of lower status; that this cruelty of treatment was referred to in several hagiographies of the period suggests that it was seen as commonplace. In these cases violence in its different forms helped to maintain the social hierarchy (García Moreno, above: 53–56).

Defence of honour by violence protected noble status, and the punishment of theft by death protected those with property against those without. But the social distinction drawn with greatest violence was that
between the free and the unfree. According to Salic Law (*Pactus Legis
Salicae* 40), slaves were flogged or put to death for thefts for which free
persons could make compensation, and sexual intercourse between free
and unfree was discouraged with threats of extreme violence (Bonnassie
1991: 19–22).

Where violence worked to protect social status, it mattered little
whether it was exercised privately or through the public courts. Violence
exercised independently of royal authority usually did not, in Francia,
threaten the stability of important dimensions of social organization.
Nor was it exercised in opposition to those public insitutions which local
people also used to protect their status and property. As Wallace-Hadrill
emphasized in his discussion of feud, rulers worked with custom in
order to keep the peace. The fact that, at least at important levels,
Frankish social structure and custom, as well as political organization,
remained unchanged for centuries suggests that over the longer term
violence could have had a basically conservative effect.

The intention of this chapter has been to reveal the complexities
which underlie the question of how violent late Merovingian and early
Carolingian Francia were. We have seen that seventh-century narrative
sources concentrated on political violence and that in all probability
they exaggerated both its level and its effect. In the eighth century, levels
of violence may have risen as the incidence of warfare increased, but as
the century progressed, inter-magnate rivalry within Francia may have
become less violent. In the locality, at all times, violence seems to have
been readily used against those without property. The violence of
masters towards servants and slaves may have been routine. The mid-
eighth-century *Life of Pardulf*, an Aquitanian source from the eve of
Frankish conquest, tells of how the *praepositus* (head) of a monastery intended to flog two carpenters who had got their measurements wrong.
The same source mentions the arbitrary and forceful expropriation of
foodstuffs from the poor by the powerful; in passing, the way in which
the Arabs killed and burned as they retreated through Aquitaine after
their defeat at Poitiers in 733; and, finally, that after the Franks burned
Bourges in 742 only one house remained standing (*Vita Pardulfi* 9, 15,
18, 20). This source shows the two basic kinds of violence to which
people were subject: first, the ubiquitous violence against those without
property, which underpinned the social order, and, second, the exceptional violence which in the eighth century came in the form of fighting
over territory, or which in the seventh century had been the result of
political conflict. It is specific instances of the second, exceptional, kind
which figure in contemporary narratives, and which, paradoxically, is the
source for impressions about normal Frankish behaviour. The present

argument is that when we look more carefully at how and why the narratives relate violent episodes, we find that Francia was rather less exotically violent than Wallace-Hadrill's picture of the feud imagined, and that, overall, violence amongst the elite worked to let off political steam rather than to destroy political stability. We have also seen how Christian writing dealt with violence in essentially pragmatic terms when explaining violent behaviour within the Christian community. As important was the way the church condemned excessive cruelty towards the defenceless, including criminals, but nevertheless condoned the more measured violence which was necessary to maintain social discipline. The difficulties we face in understanding the place of violence in Frankish life stem in large measure from the church's success in recasting discussion about violence in a religious mould and in privileging the religious over the social significance of violence. According to this view, it was not the feud which was bubbling away beneath the surface, but the law of Talion, sanctioned by a God deemed willing to let violence play a part in the pursuit of justice and in the protection of the faith.

BIBLIOGRAPHY

Primary Sources

Annals of Metz: B. von Simson (ed.), *MGH SRG* 10 (Hanover, 1905); trans. (to A.D. 724) in Fouracre & Gerberding 1996: 350–70.

Einhard, *Vita Caroli:* G. Waitz (ed.), *MGH, SRG* 25 (Hanover, 1880); L. Thorpe (trans.), *Einhard and Notker the Stammerer. Two Lives of Charlemagne* (Harmondsworth, 1969).

Fredegar's Chronicle and its *Continuations:* B. Krusch (ed.), *MGH SRM* 2 (Hanover, 1888), pp. 1–193; J. M. Wallace-Hadrill (trans.), *The Fourth Book of the Chronicle of Fredegar with its Continuations* (London, 1960).

Gregory of Tours, *Ten Books of Histories:* B. Krusch and W. Levison (eds), *MGH SRM* 1, part 1 (Hanover, 1951); L. Thorpe (trans.), *Gregory of Tours. History of the Franks* (Harmondsworth, 1974).

Liber Historiae Francorum: B. Krusch (ed.), *MGH SRM* 2, pp. 215–328; cc. 43–53 trans. in Fouracre & Gerberding 1996: 87–96.

Life of Columbanus (Vita Columbani): B. Krusch (ed.), *MGH SRM* 4 (Hanover, 1902), pp. 61–152.

Life of Eucherius (Vita Eucherii): W. Levison (ed.), *MGH SRM* 7 (Hanover, 1920), pp. 41–53.

Life of Landbert (Vita Landiberti vetustissima): B. Krusch (ed.), *MGH SRM* 6 (Hanover, 1913), pp. 353–84.

Life of Pardulf (Vita Pardulfi): W. Levison (ed.), *MGH SRM* 7, pp. 24–40.

Pactus Legis Salicae: K.-A. Eckhardt, (ed.), *MGH Legum* Sect. 1 vol. 4 part 1 *Pactus Legis Salicae* (Hanover, 1962); K. F. Drew (trans.), *The Laws of the Salian Franks* (Philadelphia, 1990).

Passio Leudegarii: B. Krusch (ed.), *MGH SRM* 5 (Hanover, 1919), pp. 249–362; trans. in Fouracre & Gerberding 1996: 215–53.

Passio Praejecti: B. Krusch (ed.), *MGH SRM* 5, pp. 225–48; trans. Fouracre & Gerberding 1996: 271–300.

Royal Frankish Annals: F. Kurze (ed.), *MGH SRG* 6 (Hanover, 1895); P. D. King (trans.), *Charlemagne. Translated Sources* (Lambrigg, 1987), pp. 74–107; B. Scholz (trans.), *Carolingian Chronicles* (Ann Arbor, 1972), pp. 37–125.

Secondary Bibliography

Black-Michaud, J., 1975. *Cohesive Force. Feud in the Mediterranean and the Middle East* (Oxford).

Bonnassie, P., 1991. *From Slavery to Feudalism in South-Western Europe* (Cambridge).

Collins, R., 1994. 'Deception and misrepresentation in early eighth-century Frankish historiography: two case studies', in J. Jarnut, U. Nonn & M. Richter (eds), *Karl Martell in seiner Zeit* (Beihefte der Francia, 37) (Sigmaringen).

Davies, W., & Fouracre, P. (eds), 1995. *Property and Power in the Early Middle Ages* (Cambridge).

Delehaye, H., 1966. *Les Passions des Martyrs et les Genres Littéraires* 2nd edition (Brussels).

Ewig, E., 1958. 'Volkstum und Volksbewusstsein im Frankenreich des 7. Jahrhunderts', *Settimane di Spoleto* 5: 587–648.

Fouracre, P., 1984. 'Merovingians, mayors of the palace, and the notion of a "low-born" Ebroin', *Bulletin of the Institute of Historical Research* 57: 1–14.

Fouracre, P., & Gerberding, R., 1996. *Late Merovingian France. History and Hagiography, 640–720* (Manchester).

Geary, P., 1985. *Aristocracy in Provence. The Rhône Basin at the Dawn of the Carolingian Age* (Stuttgart).

Gerberding, R., 1987. *The Liber Historiae Francorum and the Rise of the Carolingians* (Oxford).

Goffart, W., 1988. *The Narrators of Barbarian History (A.D. 550–800)* (Princeton).

Graus, F., 1989. 'Hagiographie und Dämonenglauben', *Settimane di Spoleto* 36: 93–120.

Haselbach, I., 1970. 'Aufstieg und Herrschaft der Karolinger in der Darstellung der sogenannten Annalen Mettenses priores', *Historische Studien* 412: 1–208.

Innes, M., & McKitterick, R., 1994. 'The writing of history', in R. McKitterick (ed.), *Carolingian Culture: Innovation and Emulation* (Cambridge), pp. 193–220.

Murray, A. C., 1983. *Germanic Kinship Structure. Studies in Law and Society in Antiquity and the Early Middle Ages* (Toronto).

—— 1988. 'From Roman to Frankish Gaul: "centenarii" and "centenae" in the administration of the Frankish kingdom', *Traditio* 44: 59–100.

Nelson, J. L., 1991. 'Gender and genre in women historians of the early Middle Ages', in J.-P. Genet (ed.), *L'Historiographie médiévale en Europe: Actes du Colloque organisé par la Fondation Européenne de la Science au Centre de Recherches Historiques et Juridiques de l'Université Paris du 29 mars au 1er avril 1989* (Paris), pp. 149–63.

Reuter, T., 1991. *Germany in the Early Middle Ages c. 800–1056* (London).

—— 1996. 'Die Unsicherheit auf den Strassen im europäischen Früh- und Hochmittelalter: Täter, Opfer und ihre mittelalterlichen und modernen Betrachter', in J. Fried (ed.), *Träger und Instrumentarien des Friedens im Hohen und Späten Mittelalter* (Vorträge und Forschungen 43) (Sigmaringen), pp. 169–201.

Sawyer, P., 1987. 'The bloodfeud in fact and fiction', *Tradition og Historieskrivining* (Acta Jutlandica 63.2) (Humanistik serie 61) (Aarhus), pp. 27–38.

Shaw, B., 1984. 'Bandits in the Roman empire', *Past and Present* 105: 3–52.

Van Dam, R., 1993. *Saints and Their Miracles in Late Antique Gaul* (Princeton).

Wallace-Hadrill, J. M., 1962. 'The bloodfeud of the Franks', in *ibid.*, *Long Haired Kings and Other Studies in Frankish History* (London).

CHAPTER 3

Urban violence in early medieval Italy: the cases of Rome and Ravenna

T. S. Brown

One of the most striking images of urban violence in the Middle Ages can found in the Sala della Pace of the Palazzo Pubblico in Siena. There the vices depicted in Lorenzetti's fresco of Mal Governo include *furor*, *divisio* and *guerra*, and constitute a vivid reminder of the disorder, or at least fear of it, which dominated central and later medieval Italian city life (Frugoni 1991: 120). Outbreaks of violence are frequent in literary sources as well and the subject has not surprisingly received considerable scholarly attention.[1] Urban violence in other areas, especially France, in the central and later Middle Ages, has been the subject of numerous studies, pointing to such factors as the pressures of rapid growth, immigration and feelings of *déracinement*.[2] On the other hand there have been few studies of violence in a specifically urban context in early medieval Italy. This is especially surprising in view of the considerable attention paid to urban violence in the classical world (Africa 1971/2; Brunt 1966; Lintott 1968; 1982) and in the 'sibling' societies of the early Byzantine East.[3]

One explanation for this is the intense continuing debate about the

---

1. E.g. Heers 1977a; 1977b; Hughes 1975; Martines (ed.) 1972; Ruggiero 1980: Zorzi 1990; and on a more general level Waley 1988: ch. 6 and Hyde 1973: 104–11.

2. Österberg and Linström (eds) 1986; Raynaud 1991; Gonthier 1992a; 1992b; Gauvard 1993.

3. Cameron 1975: ch. 10 especially; Patlagean 1977: 203–32; Gregory 1979; Liebeschuetz 1992.

nature and extent of urban continuity in the peninsula.[4] Proponents of wholesale discontinuity and impoverishment would reject the existence of specifically urban violence of the scale and types common in later cities. Where violence is recorded in cities, this would be seen as an extension of the usual rural and aristocratic forms of violence. Violent episodes within cities, like King Alboin's murder in the *palatium* of Verona, have even been seen as a reflection of 'the Lombards' misgivings about the city', a deliberate thumbing of noses at Roman *civilitas* (La Rocca 1992: 168). Other scholars have played down urban violence for a diametrically opposite reason, namely an idealizing of the city as a peaceful and integrating force in society as 'the dominant expression of civilized order'.[5] A more convincing expanation can be found in the belief that urban conflicts did not exist in early medieval Italy, or if they did the records are too sketchy to enable the historian to reconstruct their origin and nature. The first proposition does not stand up: Wickham's study of early medieval Italy lists a number of ninth-century uprisings in cities such as Cremona, Milan, Parma, Pavia and Ravenna, usually against the imperially appointed bishop.[6] Nor was such unrest unknown in the south. Violence and revolts, often apparently arising from tension between local families and factions, are recorded in the three surviving chronicles from tenth- and eleventh-century Bari (Von Falkenhausen 1986: 208). The 'lack of evidence' argument has greater validity. In general we have only the barest references to such unrest, until the better-documented revolt of the Pataria in mid-eleventh-century Milan. Also, although Wickham (1981: 190) rightly pointed out that these uprisings display the strength of civic identity and involved ordinary people as well as the elite, they can be seen as distinct from other forms of urban violence in that they represent a struggle against what is perceived as an outside power and may be regarded as precursors of the struggles for communal independence from the late eleventh century on. The question remains whether early medieval Italy offers cases of the intense violence between families, factions and parties within cities familiar from the later Middle Ages.

The cities of Romano-Byzantine Italy, i.e. those remaining under the Byzantine emperor's increasingly nominal authority, offer more promising scope for investigation. The four most important, Rome, Ravenna, Venice and Naples, have left useful narrative sources, and each city suffered outbreaks of unrest. This may well have been aggravated for

---

4. Wickham 1988. Much of the bibliography is listed in La Rocca 1992.
5. Thrupp 1963: 121. Cf. Capogrossi Colognesi 1995: 32 and Harrison 1993: 229 especially.
6. Wickham 1981 records revolts in Cremona in 852 and 1037 (pp. 90, 191), Verona in 968 (p. 190), Milan in 983 and 1037 (pp. 190, 191). In 897 the citizens of Turin attacked their bishop (Niccolai 1941: 18).

much of the seventh and eighth centuries by a crisis of legitimacy, as
the government in Constantinople became increasingly unpopular,
imperially appointed officials lost much of their authority and local
groups, clerical and lay, struggled for power.[7] In Venice there were
numerous eighth- and ninth-century outbreaks of strife, but those cannot be examined in detail here, because the sources do not throw clear
light on the family and regional rivalries involved and because it is argu-
able whether the collection of settlements which constitute Venetia at
this stage constitute a city in any meaningful sense (Brown 1995a: 338–
41). For Naples we have records of late sixth-century disputes over
episcopal elections[8] and of highly obscure conflicts over iconoclasm in
the eighth (Bertolini, P., 1974). However, the main source for Neapoli-
tan history, the *Gesta Episcoporum Neapolitanorum*, is surprisingly reticent
on internal tensions, perhaps because relative peace was maintained by
powerful rulers, some of whom combined the offices of *dux* and bishop.

The city which has left the most numerous and detailed records of
conflicts is Rome. In the sixth century these appear have to followed a
common late Roman model and involved rivalry between circus and
theatre partisans, senatorial factions which mobilized crowds, food
shortages and, increasingly, tension over papal elections; the Laurentian
schism of 498 provoked such violent strife that Theoderic had to intervene.[9] Seventh- and early eighth-century references to conflicts are
sporadic and lacking in detail. While disputed papal elections did occur
– in 686 'as is the customary practice, the populace of the city of Rome
was divided into two parties' (*LP* I: 371) – conflicts were apparently not
very violent, perhaps because continuing external threats, especially
from the Lombards, served as a unifying influence. Imperial authority
was generally accepted, and the most prominent violent episodes involved repression by the state, such as Pope Martin I's arrest and trial
for treason in 651 (Llewellyn 1993: 152–55). Change is evident from
c. 680, however, with the establishment of peace with the Lombard
kingdom and a possible grant of a measure of autonomy to the duchy of
Rome.[10] Certainly the papal bureaucracy attempted to build up its
authority by the division of social groups into a precise hierarchy in
official documents from c. 684 and the assumption of terms such as
proceres and *optimates*, previously the preserve of the military elite. A new
balance of power was evident in 693 when the resistance of Italian

---

7. The governors (*duces*) of most areas of Roman Italy were 'elected' locally from c.
   727 onwards. On all this, see Brown 1984.

8. Gregory the Great, *Epp.*, IX.47, X.19, XII.14. For other disputes over elections,
   e.g. in Syracuse, see Brown 1984: 100.

9. Llewellyn 1995: 41–42, 328 and references; Moorhead 1993: 118–27, 146 and
   239; Piétri 1996.

10. See the slightly differing views of Noble 1984 and Llewellyn 1986.

troops prevented an imperial official, Zacharias, from arresting Pope Sergius I, and forced him into hiding under the pontiff's bed (*LP* I: 373). Internal tensions became more acute in the eighth century with the complete collapse of Byzantine authority in northern and central Italy and an ensuing power struggle between powerful lay elements in the city and its hinterland and the clerical bureaucracy. These continued at a serious level throughout much of the ninth century, despite the increased power of the clerical hierarchy within the Lateran palace and the *entente cordiale* which the papacy established from the 750s onwards and cemented with Charlemagne's imperial coronation in 800.[11]

These conflicts frequently took the form of mob violence and resulted in some grisly episodes, including actual and attempted blindings, the murder of Pope John VIII, and most bizarrely of all, the exhumation and trial of the body of Pope Formosus by his opponents in 897. It is not intended to survey these complex events here; they are the subject of numerous general studies (e.g. Zimmermann 1968; Partner 1972; Noble 1984 and 1995; Llewellyn 1993). It is often difficult to reconstruct the factors and forces at work because of the circumspection shown by the main Roman account, the *Liber Pontificalis*. However, for two episodes of unrest we have relatively detailed evidence from more than one source.

The first period covers the pontificate of Stephen III (768–772). The violent episodes of this troubled reign are recorded not only in the pope's unusually detailed *Life*, but also in letters sent by the pope himself and his anti-pope predecessor Constantine II, the Roman council of 769 and a lost Bavarian source which can be reconstructed from a later text.[12] On the death of Paul I (767) a representative of the military aristocracy, Duke Toto of Nepi, had his brother, a layman named Constantine, forcibly consecrated as pope and murdered a leading opponent, the Campanian *dux* Gregory. In July 769 Constantine was deposed with the armed support of the Lombard duke of Spoleto and later blinded. Toto, the power behind the papal throne, was killed by two of his accomplices. A party sympathetic to the Lombard king, Desiderius, replaced him with another anti-pope, Philip, who only ruled for a day, before being replaced by Stephen III, the choice of the main power in the Lateran bureaucracy, the *primicerius* Christopher. A vicious purge then followed, with mutilation, blinding or death being meted out

---

11. Tenth-century Rome, which has had a bad press because of the partisan writings of Liuptrand of Cremona, was comparatively peaceful for much of the time and especially under the principate of Alberic (932–954): Partner 1972; Llewellyn 1993: 304–12.

12. This helpful but problematic source, usually known as Creontius, is discussed in Bertolini, O., 1968, who also published a Latin text. Its authenticity has not been universally accepted. For further discussion and an English translation, King 1987: 41, 340–43.

to Constantine and Philip's supporters. A council held the same year condemned Constantine and excluded the laity from involvement in future elections. There then developed a rift between Christopher and his appointee, Stephen, who resented the former's intimidatory tactics and allied himself with the ambitious pro-Lombard papal chamberlain, Paul Afiarta. Both camps built up armed followings and tried to attract popular support. With Lombard support Paul got the better of Christopher, who was soon blinded and killed along with his son. However, Paul's weak position crumbled when his ally Pope Stephen died a few days later. His successor, Hadrian I, abandoned the pro-Lombard policy for a Frankish alliance, and had Paul's accomplices arrested and sent for trial in Ravenna, while Paul was detained and executed by the archbishop of Ravenna. [13]

These turbulent events have been intensively studied by a number of scholars, but their results have remained inconclusive (e.g. Bertolini 1968; Hallenbeck 1974 a & b; Noble 1984; Llewellyn 1993, together with relevant bibliography). It has been pointed out that a clear struggle was under way between the secular military aristocracy and the clerical elite based in the Lateran palace, but the picture is complicated by individual ambitions and conflicts, and by factional divides within each group. Peace was restored in Hadrian I's pontificate because that pope was a strong figure with firm backing from a cooperative Frankish monarchy, which controlled Lombard Italy from 774 onwards, but also because he represented a compromise between the military elite, to which his family belonged, and the clerical bureaucracy. Certain points can also be made about the conflicts of 767-772. The first is that the there was no armed popular militia in Rome (Patlagean 1974: 45-46), and that we do not find the populace acting *en masse* in support of one or other faction. The armed forces involved seem to have been small bands of retainers, or forces of troops or rustics from the countryside. That the numbers involved were small is confirmed by the key role played by Lombard intervention in 768 and 771. Secondly recurrent preoccupations emerge from the sources, all produced in, or influenced by, clerical circles, although not always identical factions. One is a fear of armed intervention by laymen, which led to the Roman Council of 769's exclusion of secular involvement in papal elections, and ultimately to the building up of an armed force under direct papal control, of the *militia sancti Petri* based on the papal estates known as *domuscultae* (Christie 1991, introduction). Another, connected, reaction is evident in the papal biographies of this period – increased concern with proper procedures in papal elections and emphasis on the supposed unity and concord reflected by the ultimate choice (Daileader 1993). Finally our clerical sources display a close

---

13. Noble 1984: 112-37, Llewellyn 1993: 221-28, who wrongly post-dates the events of 767 and 768 by one year.

identification with the city of Rome itself and an antagonism to outsiders, whether Lombards, rural warlords such as Duke Toto, or the
'bands of rustics' (*catervae rusticorum: Concilium Romanum* a. 769: 84)
who were their main weapon in Roman politics. An impression is given
of a close alliance between the Roman *populus* and the dominant clerical
faction. The *populus* is depicted as assenting to rightful elections and
supporting the 'good' party, such as that of Christopher, who in turn
protects it and defends its interests. [14]

Our second episode of violence is an obscure one but one with
immense consquences. On 25 April 799 a mob led by two papal officials,
the *primicerius* Paschal and the *sacellarius* Campulus, attacked Hadrian's
successor Pope Leo III, attempted to blind him and confined him in the
monastery of S. Erasmo. Leo was rescued the same day by his chamberlain, given protection by the Frankish duke of Spoleto and then escorted
to Paderborn to see Charlemagne. The visit of the Frankish king to
Rome the following year to investigate the affair culminated in his
coronation as emperor. Although the events of 799–800 are recorded in
a number of Frankish sources as well as the Roman *Liber Pontificalis* and
have probably received more scholarly attention than any other episode
in the early Middle Ages, the precise causes of the conflict remain un-
knowable (Noble 1994: 568; for a detailed account Mohr 1960). However, we can point to the likelihood that the ringleaders, nephews of the
aristocratic Hadrian I, represented noble resentment against the par-
venu Leo, and that the support they received from a commander from
Nepi, Maurus, reflected the antagonism of a country party of 'outs'
against the clerical establishment of Rome evident from the rising of
Toto. As with the strife of 767–772, the violence occurred during a
period of acute political uncertainty. The duchy of Rome's vestigial links
with the Byzantine empire had been thrown into crisis by the blinding
of the emperor Constantine VI by his mother in 797. Leo III's flair
for public relations and ambitious building programme, including the fit-
ting out of an imperial-style *triclinium*, may well have given rise to fears
that he was aiming to establish a monarchical position (Llewellyn 1990).
The plot had some bizarre aspects: the conspirators appear half-hearted
in trying to incapacitate Leo, did not install an anti-pope, did not
attempt to whip up support and did not flee when their victim was
rescued. This suggests that, as a group who had held power in Hadrian's
pontificate, they made a miscalculation and bargained on getting Frankish support.

The failure of the crowd to rush to the pope's defence in a crowded
location during a procession is also striking. It is possible that Leo

---

14. The attitudes reflected in the use of the term *populus* is at times ambiguous. For
example, a letter of the anti-pope Constantine II implies a fear of the *populus*:
populorum proclamitionibus atque lacrimosis ululationibus percutior: CC 98 (AD 767).

lacked wide popular support because of his fiscality and oppressive tendencies. There was another revolt against him after Charles' death led by those who claimed he had confiscated their lands (Llewellyn 1993: 252).

Outbreaks of violence remained frequent throughout ninth-century Rome. Do these represent widespread urban violence by the Roman people? The exact causes and circumstances are usually unclear, but one can point to certain familiar features, such as an uprising in 816, Paschal I's bloody massacre of opponents in 824, opposition by an armed gang of rustics to the election of Sergius II in 846 and a possible Byzantine conspiracy in 854 (Noble 1995: 568–69; 1984: 248; Llewellyn 1993: 259–60, 267). The basic conflict appears to have been between a pro-Frankish 'imperial party', led by figures such as Anastasius the Librarian and later Bishop Formosus of Porto, and the more inward-looking clerical elements of the Lateran bureaucracy. As always the parties and alliances were very fluid, and Noble has rightly pointed to other factors, such as struggles for family aggrandizement and the need for lay families to gain access to the increasingly important clerical powers of jurisdiction and patronage (Noble 1995: 571). Interestingly the *Liber Pontificalis* emphasized the support which some pontiffs had from the *populus* because of their concern for the poor (e.g. *LP* II: 52, 142–43, 173). It has been concluded that some clerical circles opposed to the aristocratic 'imperial' party sought and obtained support from the populace of Rome (Noble 1995: 570). This is possible but unlikely because it is difficult to find evidence of the Roman population behaving as an active and coherent unit, and we have already seen that earlier invocations of the *populus* can be seen as ideological moves stressing the unifying, peace-making intentions of a particular faction. In a similar vein the (supposedly pro-aristocratic) Frankish sources accused 'certain popes' of harming the Roman people (e.g. *ARF s.a.* 824: *statum populi Romani iam dudum quorundam presulum perversitate depravatum*[15]). The most likely conclusion is that, although violence was common and intense in Rome throughout much of the late eighth and ninth centuries, it was the work of particular factions and their armed retainers, often from the countryside. The populace of the city as a whole seems to have remained fairly passive, although its support could be courted for political reasons, and some factions made a point of stressing their appeal to the whole *populus Romanus* as an ideological platform.

The other main city of Byzantine Italy, Ravenna, also had its share of outbreaks of violence. There were occasional poorly documented con-

---

15. Similar criticism of Leo III was made by the biographer of Louis the Pious known as the Astronomer: Llewellyn 1993: 252. It may also be significant that the *Constitutio Romana* imposed by the Franks in 824 provided for the election of popes by all the Romans.

flicts in the sixth century, involving a riot against the Jews in 519 (Moorhead 1993: 98–99; Brown 1991) and strong opposition to the emperor Justinian's imposition of the outsider Maximian as archbishop (Agnellus, 71–72). From the seventh century occurrences became more numerous and more fully recorded. These have been the subject of studies by Guillou (1969: 162–63, 203–32) and Brown (1984: 100–01, 159–63). In both cases, however, the emphasis has been on autonomous movements and their resistance to outsiders, especially the repression of imperially appointed exarchs or punitive expeditions sent out by Constantinople. These studies have emphasized the aggressive sense of local identity from the early seventh century onwards and the city's role as a focus for the resistance of the surrounding areas: for example the inhabitants of nearby Sarsina, Cervia, Forlimpopoli, Forlì, Faenza, Imola and Bologna joined the Ravennati in resisting a Byzantine invasion in the early eighth century (Agnellus, 140). Our main source for these episodes is a series of biographies of the city's bishops, composed by the local cleric Agnellus in the 840s. Sometimes the accounts given are relatively detailed, as in the case of the resistance to the oppression of the Emperor Justinian II. Agnellus' version of events has to be used with caution because of his highly stylized literary approach, and because of his partisanship; the Greeks are viewed as vicious serpents, while every effort is made to exalt the role of his own ancestors, the scribe Iohannicius and his son, the military leader (*dux*) Georgius (Brown 1995b; Pizarro 1995: 171–88). More relevant to our concerns is the information Agnellus also gives on internal strife in the city. Often these references are short and it is foolhardy to attempt precise interpretations. For example he states that the Ravennati drove one of their archbishops, John VI (c. 720 – c. 742), into exile in Venice until a local official arranged his recall through the exarch (Agnellus, 152). Since the ringleaders of this revolt were powerful lay tenants of the church, the cause of this obscure conflict may have been arguments over the conditions of emphyteutic grants of land (Brown 1984: 187–88, 208); what emerges most clearly from the account, however, is Agnellus' stress on the rightful authority of the archbishop as unifying leader of his community, *pater patriae*. Elsewhere the author confines himself to vague mentions of strife (*dissensiones*) or deals with conflicts within the church, most usually between bishops and their clergy over the sharing of episcopal revenues (e.g. Agnellus, 121–22; cf. Pizarro 1995: 52–60). Nor can Agnellus be relied on as a full and trustworthy guide: we happen to know of one serious outbreak of strife in 769 from the Roman *Liber Pontificalis*, when the *dux* of Rimini tried to impose his own lay candidate as archbishop of Ravenna, but Agnellus' text, patchy for this period, fails to mention the episode (*LP* I: 477).

The most detailed piece of evidence to be garnered from Agnellus is a remarkable account of bloody conflicts between neighbourhood factions in Ravenna in the late seventh century.[16] The historian (c. 126) records that it is a custom of long standing 'which has lasted until today' for citizens of all ages and backgrounds to engage in open brawls on Sunday afternoons. During the pontificate of Archbishop Damian the tension between the factions of the Porta Teguriensis and the Porta Posterulensis, both on the west side of the city, degenerated into a vendetta culminating in the wholesale slaughter of the former faction by the other. As a consequence 'there was great mourning, and lamentation everywhere. . . . The baths were closed, public theatricals ceased, merchants retraced their steps and went home, publicans kept their taverns closed. tradesmen abandoned their shops . . . [and] all souls were drowned in bitterness' (c. 128).

Historians' interpretations of this astonishing passage have varied wildly. Some have accepted it completely, one going so far as to conclude from it that the city was divided into quarters whose inhabitants were organized into armed militias on the supposed model of the *demoi* in Eastern cities.[17] Others, perhaps understandably, have rejected the story as a work of fiction.[18] It has to be admitted that there are unlikely and inconsistent elements, as well as obvious literary exaggeration, in Agnellus' account and some aspects do give grounds for suspicion, such as the complete lack of proper names, apart from that of the bishop. It is unlikely that groups covering the whole social spectrum would have been permitted to bear weapons such as swords, lances and arrows in the seventh century, when the military elite of landholding *milites* still had a monopoly of armed force, but there is evidence for a more general arming of the populace in Ravenna in response to external threats from the early eighth century onwards.[19] The association of clearly defined neighbourhood quarters (*vicinanze*) with gates is attested in other Italian cities in the early Middle Ages and later (Wickham 1981: 85; Pini 1986: 22–29). What has to be borne in mind is that Agnellus, who delivered his work in the form of lectures to clerics of his see (Brown 1986; Pizarro 1995: 1–2, 27–28), can hardly have manufactured such a dramatic episode *ex nihilo*, and the likeliest explanation is that he was building on an existing oral tradition. What Agnellus may be offering is his highly coloured version of a popular explanation of *contemporary* military institutions, quarters and tensions, based on a remote event

16. The date of the episode cannot be determined with precision but is recorded during the episcopate of Damian (c. 692–708).
17. Gulliou 1969: 162–63. This interpretation reads too much into certain terms best explained on other grounds and is based on a view of city faction in the east which is no longer generally accepted: see Brown 1984: 101 and n. 18.
18. Reservations, to my mind excessive, are expressed by Ward-Perkins 1984: 109, who identifies similarities between Agnellus' passage and Eusebius' *Vita Constantini*.
19. The question is discussed in Brown 1984: 82–108. Particularly significant is Agnellus' use of the term *bandus* (military unit) for quarters in his own time.

which had assumed mythic proportions. An analogous case from early thirteenth-century Florence would be the Buondelmonte murder (Larner 1980: 106). In any case what is important about such traditions is less the literal truth of the events described but the social memory, the ideological agenda, involved. If we examine Agnellus's interpretation of the story, we can gain an impression of the social function of the past in contemporaries' eyes (Fentress and Wickham 1992: especially 144–72). Viewed in this light, this and other passages in Agnellus' text display recurring preoccupations. The most obvious is the author's concern with the irrationality of the mobs involved and the violence which they inflict (Pizarro 1995: 53). Although such crowd trouble is a recurrent theme of late antique, Byzantine and early medieval authors, some aspects of Agnellus's treatment are conspicuously original (Pizarro 1995: 146–55). In particular the acceptance of violence almost as incidental suggests that violence was an integral part of the urban scene. There is also a constant emphasis on the random, confused and highly diverse nature of the warring factions and this is contrasted with the unifying, peace-making role of the archbishop, who organizes an elaborate series of liturgical ceremonies performed by the whole city and aimed at reconciling the warring groups and securing God's favour. By their very nature these rites involve each social group (*ordo*) and emphasizes the rightful hierarchy and essential unity of the entire Christian community (*congregatio*) of the city of Ravenna. There are echoes here of the elaborate liturgical ceremonies developed in Rome from the late seventh century onwards preserved in the *Ordines Romani* which emphasize the pope's position of authority over the papal court and the city as a whole and which were focused on its seven ecclesiastical regions. These have been described as 'in effect a state function of the city' (Llewellyn 1993: 124), and involved the various ranks of lay aristocrats and soldiers, as well as clergy. Pizarro has viewed Agnellus' portrayal of these events as part of his general 'clericalist' critique of secular society: the innate vices and divisions of lay society are contrasted with the unity and benign leadership exercised by the ideal bishop as shepherd of his flock.[20] These high ecclesiological ideals did exist, but in practice the church cooperated closely with secular government, its personnel was largely drawn from leading lay families and its concerns were often worldly.[21] What is more our immediate concern is that churchmen's own political and ideological interests focus on the city, and that their lay congregations were receptive

20. Pizarro 1995: 155, developing themes he discussed earlier (pp. 36–52). Agnellus of course recognized that many bishops failed to live up to such ideals.

21. Agnellus himself shows a recurring interest in wealth and 'the sensual diversity of life' (Pizarro 1995: 155). Unlike Pizarro, I do not find a sharp secular/'clericalist' dichotomy helpful for Italy before the Gregorian reform period: Brown 1984: 175–89 and references and Brown 1986.

to the leadership and strong sense of urban identity which it (and notably its saints and rituals) offered. The corollary of this of course also applied, as when Agnellus admitted that in the time of Archbishop Sergius (744–769) 'the priests were envious and quarrelsome, divided in spirit, so that the people too were at odds' (c. 154). In Ravenna, as in Rome, a struggle for authority followed the weakening of imperial power in the seventh and eighth centuries and appeals to urban unity (centred on the church and its symbols) and the church's claims to be an effective counter to the real and recurring threat of urban violence proved key weapons in this struggle.

Various conclusions can be reached on the basis of these case studies. Italian cities, especially those from the Romano-Byzantine area, offer promising scope for further investigation of the neglected topic of urban violence in the early Middle Ages. The evidence, while relatively varied and plentiful, does not enable us to identify all the factors involved or to attempt the kind of conclusions about levels of demographic pressure, criminality, alienation, repression and solidarity, and so forth reached in recent studies of later medieval cities. Unrest does not appear to follow certain models put forward for other periods, such as that of the 'symbiotic mob' manipulated by court factions in pre-1900 capitals such as Vienna and Naples (Hobsbawm 1973) or pressure created by food shortages (Rudé 1964). The picture that emerges is sometimes ambiguous, with territorial divisions appearing as a factor in urban unrest in Ravenna, but not apparently elsewhere. On the other hand, some of the factors involved, such as individual ambition, family rivalries, and tensions between urban and country groups or between clerical and lay elites are reminiscent of some of the complex divisions found in later medieval Italian cities (Heers 1977b). Studies of violence in Rome and the Romagna in the later Middle Ages have pointed to analogous phenomena, including the widespread involvement of individuals and groups from the countryside and the positive social function which violence could have (Brentano 1972; Larner 1972). There is no clear evidence of purely popular groups resorting to violence on their own; while concern at the destructive tendencies of 'mobs' is expressed, most crowds appear to have been led or manipulated by elite interests. Violence, mostly of a political nature, was a widespread and serious phenomenon, and was largely the result of a power vacuum and general crisis of legitimacy. At the same time the ideal of unity and concord in towns seems to have been remarkably resilient, and the dangers of violence could be exploited by particular groups, most notably the church, as a means of reinforcing their leadership as advocates of peace and harmony. Finally, and perhaps most significantly, the saga of *furor*, *divisio* and *guerra* in the early medieval Italian cities confirms their strong sense of identity and their role as centres, not only of residence, but of political activity, and supports the case for a high level of urban continuity.

BIBLIOGRAPHY

Primary Sources

Agnellus, *Liber Pontificalis Ecclesiae Ravennatis:* O. Holder-Egger (ed.), *MGH Scriptores Rerum Langobardorum et Italicarum* (Hanover, 1878), pp. 273–391. Extracts translated in Pizarro 1995.

Andrieu 1971: M. Andrieu (ed.), *Les Ordines Romani du Haut Moyen Age,* ii. *Les Textes (Ordines I-XIII)* (Louvain).

Codex Carolinus: W. Gundlach (ed.), in *MGH, Epistolae* 3 (Berlin, 1892), pp. 496–657.

Concilium Romanum a. 769: A. Werminghoff (ed.), *MGH Concilia* 2, *Concilia Aevi Karolini* 1 (Hanover-Leipzig, 1906), pp. 74–92.

'Creontius': ed. in Bertolini, O., 1968: 616–20; also L. Duchesne, *Le Liber Pontificalis* 3 vols (Paris, 1886–1957) I, p. 484, n. 58; P. D. King (trans.), *Charlemagne. Translated Sources* (Lambrigg, 1987), pp. 340–43.

Gesta Episcoporum Neapolitanorum: G. Waitz (ed.), *MGH, Scriptores Rerum Langobardorum et Italicarum* (Hanover, 1878), pp. 398–46.

Gregory the Great, *Epistolae:* P. Ewald (ed.), *MGH Epp.* I *Gregorii I Papae Registrum Epistolarum* I (Berlin 1887); L. Hartmann (ed.), *MGH Epp.* II *Gregorii I Papae Registrum Epistolarum* II (Berlin 1899); J. Barmby (trans.), *Nicene & Post-Nicene Fathers* 2nd series vol. 12–13 (reprinted Grand Rapids, Michigan, 1989).

Liber Pontificalis: L. Duchesne (ed.), *Le Liber Pontificalis,* 3 vols (Paris, 1886–1957); R. Davis (trans.), *The Book of the Pontiffs (Liber Pontificalis to A.D. 715)* (Liverpool, 1989); *The Lives of the Eighth-Century Popes (Liber Pontificalis)* (Liverpool, 1992); *The Lives of the Ninth-Century Popes (Liber Pontificalis)* (Liverpool, 1995).

Royal Frankish Annals: F. Kurze (ed.), *MGH SRG* 6 (Hanover, 1895); P. D. King (trans.), *Charlemagne. Translated Sources* (Lambrigg, 1987), pp. 74–107; B. Scholz (trans.), *Carolingian Chronicles* (Ann Arbor, 1972), pp. 37–125.

Secondary Bibliography

Africa, T. W., 1971/2. 'Urban violence in imperial Rome', *Journal of Interdisciplinary History* 11: 3–22.

Bertolini, O., 1968. 'La caduta del primicerio Cristoforo (771) nelle versioni dei contemporanei, e le correnti antilongobarde e filolangobarde in Roma alla fine del pontificato di Stefano III (771–2)', in *Studi Storici* (Livorno), pp. 613–75.

Bertolini, P., 1974. 'La chiesa di Napoli durante la crisi iconoclasta. Appunti sul codice Vaticano Latino 5007', *Studi sul medioevo cristiano offerti a Raffaello Morghen,* i (Rome), pp. 101–27.

Brentano, R., 1972. 'Violence, disorder and order in thirteenth-century Rome', in Martines (ed.) 1972: 308–30.

Brown, T. S., 1984. *Gentlemen and Officers. Imperial Administration and Aristocratic Power in Byzantine Italy, A.D. 554–800* (London).

—— 1986. '*Romanitas* and *Campanilismo:* Agnellus of Ravenna's view of the past', in C. Holdsworth & T. Wiseman (eds), *The Inheritance of Historiography, 350–900* (Exeter), pp. 107–14.

—— 1991. 'Ebrei ed orientali a Ravenna' in A. Carile (ed.), *Storia di Ravenna* II (Ravenna), pp. 135–49.

——— 1995a. 'Byzantine Italy, 680–876', in McKitterick (ed.) 1995: 320–49.

——— 1995b. 'Justinian II and Ravenna', *Byzantinoslavica* 56: 29–36.

Brunt, P., 1966. 'The Roman mob', *Past and Present* 35: 3–23.

Cameron, A., 1975. *Circus Factions* (Oxford).

Capogrossi Colognesi, L., 1995. 'Limits of the ancient city and evolution of the medieval city in the thought of Max Weber', in T. Cornell & K. Lomas (eds), *Urban Society in Roman Italy* (London), pp. 27–37.

Christie, N. (ed.), 1991. *Three South Etrurian Churches. Santa Cornelia, Santa Rufina and San Liberato* (London).

Daileader, P., 1993. 'One will, one voice and equal love. Papal elections and the *Liber Pontificalis* in the early Middle Ages', *Archivum Historiae Pontificiae* 31: 11–31.

Fentress, J., and Wickham, C., 1992. *Social Memory* (Oxford).

Frugoni, C., 1991. *A Distant Landscape. Images of Urban Experience in the Medieval World* (Princeton).

Gauvard, C., 1993. 'Violence citadine et résaux de solidarité: l'exemple française aux XIVe et XVe siècles', *Annales* 48: 1113–26.

Gonthier, N., 1992a. *Cris de haine et rites de l'unité. La violence dans les villes, XIIIe-XVI siècles* (Paris).

——— 1992b. 'La contrôle de la violence dans les villes au moyen age', in B. Garnot & R. Fry (eds), *Histoire et criminalité de l'antiquité au XXe siècle. Nouvelles approches* (Dijon), pp. 431–37.

Gregory, T. E., 1979. *Vox Populi. Popular Opinion and Violence in the Religious Controversies of the Fifth Century A.D.* (Columbus, Ohio).

Guillou, A., 1969. *Régionalisme et indépendance dans l'empire byzantin au VII siècle: l'exemple de l'Exarchat et de la Pentapole d'Italie* (Rome).

Hallenbeck, J., 1974a. 'Paul Afiarta and the papacy: an analysis of politics in eighth-century Rome', *Archivum Historiae Pontificiae* 12: 722–54.

——— 1974b. 'Pope Stephen II: why was he elected?', *Archivum Historiae Pontificiae*, 12: 287–99.

Harrison, D., 1993. *The Early State and the Towns. Forms of Integration in Lombard Italy, A.D. 568–774* (Lund).

Heers, J., 1977a. *Family Clans in the Middle Ages* (Amsterdam-New York-Oxford).

——— 1977b. *Parties and Political Life in the Medieval West* (Amsterdam-New York-Oxford).

Hobsbawm, E., 1973. *Primitive Rebels. Archaic Forms of Social Movement in the Nineteenth and Twentieth Centuries* (London).

Hughes, D., 1975. 'Urban growth and family structure in medieval Genoa', *Past and Present*, 66: 3–28.

Hyde, J. K., 1973. *Society and Politics in Medieval Italy* (London).

Larner, J., 1972. 'Order and disorder in Romagna 1450–1500', in Martines (ed.) 1972: 38–71.

——— 1980. *Italy in the Age of Dante and Petrarch* (London).

La Rocca, C., 1992. 'Public buildings and urban change in northern Italy in the early mediaeval period', in Rich (ed.) 1992: 161–80.

Liebeschuetz, W., 1992. 'The end of the ancient city', in Rich (ed.) 1992: 1–49.

Lintott, A. 1968. *Violence in Republican Rome* (Oxford).

——— 1982. *Violence, Civil Strife and Revolution in the Classical City, 750–350 B.C.* (Oxford).

Llewellyn, P., 1986. 'The popes and the constitution in the eighth century', *English Historical Review* 101: 42–67.

—— 1990. 'Le contexte romain du couronnement de Charlemagne. Le temps de l'Avent de l'année 800', *Le Moyen Age* 96: 209–28.

—— 1993. *Rome in the Dark Ages* (reprint with afterword of 1971 edition, London).

McKitterick, R. (ed.), 1995. *New Cambridge Medieval History* vol. 2 (Cambridge).

Martines, L. (ed.), 1992. *Violence and Civil Disorder in Italian Cities, 1200–1500* (Berkeley, London, Los Angeles).

Mohr, W., 1960. 'Karl der Grosse, Leo III und der römische Aufstand von 799', *Bulletin Du Cange. Archivum Latinitatis Medii Aevi*, 30: 39–98.

Moorhead, J., 1993. *Theoderic in Italy* (Oxford).

Niccolai, F., 1941. *Città e signori* (Bologna).

Noble, T. F. X., 1984. *The Republic of Saint Peter* (Philadelphia).

—— 1995. 'The papacy in the eighth and ninth centuries', in McKitterick (ed.) 1995: 563–86.

Österberg, E., & Lindström, D. (eds), 1986. *Crime and Social Control in Medieval and Early Modern Swedish Towns* (Uppsala).

Partner, P., 1972. *The Lands of Saint Peter* (London).

Patlagean, E., 1974. 'Les armes et la cité à Rome du VIIe au IXe siècle et le modèle européenne des trois fonctions sociales', *Mélanges de l'Ecole Française de Rome, Moyen Age, Temps Modernes* 86: 25–62.

—— 1977. *Pauvrété économique et pauvrété sociale à Byzance, 4e–7e siècles* (Paris).

Piétri, C., 1966. 'Le sénat, le peuple chrétien et les partis du cirque sous le pape Symmaque (498–514)', *Mélanges d'Archéologie et d'Histoire de l'Ecole Française de Rome* 78: 122–39.

Pini, A. I., 1986. *Città, Comuni e Corporazioni nel Medioevo Italiano* (Bologna).

Pizarro, J. M., 1995. *Writing Ravenna: The Liber Pontificalis of Andreas Agnellus* (Ann Arbor).

Raynaud, C., 1991. *La violence au moyen âge, XIIIe-XVe siècle d'après les livres d'histoire en françáise* (Paris).

Rich, J. (ed.), 1992. *The City in Late Antiquity* (London).

Rudé, G., 1964. *The Crowd in History* (New York).

Ruggiero, G., 1980. *Violence in Early Renaissance Venice* (New Brunswick).

Thrupp, S., 1963. 'The city as the idea of social order', in O. Handlin & J. Burchard (eds), *The Historian and the City* (Cambridge, Mass.), pp. 121–32.

Von Falkenhausen, V., 1986. 'Bari Bizantina. Profilo di un capoluogo di provincia (secoli IX-XI)', in G. Rossetti (ed.), *Spazio, società, potere nell' Italia dei comuni* (Naples), pp. 195–227.

Ward-Perkins, B., 1984. *From Classical Antiquity to the Middle ages: Urban Public Building in Northern and Central Italy, A.D. 300–850* (Oxford).

Waley, D., 1988. *The Italian City Republics* 3rd edition (London).

Wickham, C., 1981. *Early Medieval Italy* (London).

—— 1988. 'La città altomedievale: una nota sul dibattito in corso', *Archeologia Medievale* 15: 649–51.

Zimmermann, H., 1968. *Papstabsetzungen des Mittelalters* (Graz, Vienna & Cologne).

Zorzi, A. 1990. 'Contrôle sociale, ordre public et répression judiciaire à Florence à l'époque communale: élements et problèmes', *Annales* 45: 1169–88.

CHAPTER 4

Violence in the Carolingian world and the ritualization of ninth-century warfare

Janet L. Nelson

CHANGING ATTITUDES TO VIOLENCE AND WAR

In eighth-century narratives, the most obvious violence was perpetrated by Frankish armies against 'external peoples', Aquitanians, Saxons and, less systematically, Slavs and Avars. The sources suggest a strong ethnic element in these conflicts. *Fredegar*'s Continuators, for instance, portray Aquitanians as fickle betrayers of Frankish good faith, and so justify the destruction of Aquitanian leaders and vineyards (*Fredegar, Continuations*, 25, 41, 42, 46–47). This ethnic element sometimes looms larger in ninth-century texts: most infamously, perhaps, in Notker's description of Eishere, recalling how he 'spitted Bohemians and Wilzes and Avars on his spear as if they were little birds . . . and carried them about . . . squealing their incomprehensible lingo' (*Gesta Karoli* II.12). Closer investigation reduces such conflicts' ethnic element. Ethnicity was cross-cut by class when Saxon nobles allied with the Franks to suppress Saxon freemen (*ARF s.a.* 782). Nevertheless, early Carolingian writers could depict violence as essentially *outside* Frankish society itself.

In the original *Royal Frankish Annals*, the language of conflict is that of dispute. Waifar 'lies', 'fails to be mindful of his hostages and his oaths', seeks 'revenge' on Pippin (*ARF s.a.* 761). The revised (early ninth-century) version of these annals converts all this into a single protracted 'war', repeatedly resumed in the 760s; Pippin wants to 'put an end to it' and apparently does so after bringing about Waifar's death (*ARF s.a.* 762, 766, 767, 768). The shift from private to public language signals the reviser's use of classical models, but is also symptomatic of a new kind of justification for, and conception of, violence.

The influence of Augustine's views on just war (as of *augustinisme politique*) is especially evident in late eighth- and ninth-century 'mirrors' for lay leaders and kings. Alcuin justified Count Guy's military service, reassuring him that his calling did not exclude him from heaven; Paulinus did the same for Count Eric; and a series of writers from Agobard to Hincmar called on kings and emperors to engage in warfare to defend the church and the weak (for all these, see Anton 1968). Hincmar of Rheims' *De regis Persona et regio Ministerio*, a work shot through with Augustinian thought, justified prayers for warriors killed *in bello*, conducted at royal behest for the peace of the kingdom. Liturgy was also prominent in supplying and reinforcing the language of just war. The Christian *res publica* would be preserved by the efforts of rulers and those serving in their armies (Tellenbach 1934; McCormick 1986). The *laudes regiae* called on the aid of the saints, and of Christ as supreme victor, to bring victory for the army as well as the kings of the Franks (Kantorowicz 1946). Priests and bishops accompanied Charlemagne's troops, providing continued moral support. Monks throughout Charlemagne's empire chanted the more martial psalms as invocations of victory (McCormick 1986: 347–62; Nelson 1996a: xxiii). Liturgical performance constituted a practical supplement to Christian warfare, involving lay persons too; no more clearly than in the fastings and litanies that Charlemagne enjoined on 'everyone' (McCormick 1984). Such moral support was as important as the logistical support which Charlemagne organized so carefully.

Early Christian liturgy and the Fathers justified warfare against pagans and heretics who threatened the peace of the church. Had not Augustine urged compulsion against the Donatists (Brown 1964)? From his uncompromising *cogite intrare*, Carolingian propagandists took their cue. Pippin's first Aquitanian campaign in 760 was undertaken because Waifar 'refused to acknowledge the just claims [*iustitiae*] of Frankish churches in Aquitaine' (*ARF s.a.* 760). In Lombardy too, *iustitia* justified the Franks' invasion: this time the 'just claims' were those of the papacy (*ARF s.a.* 755). The decision to attack the Avars was made 'on account of the excessive and intolerable wickedness which they had committed against the Holy Church and the Christian people', and after Charlemagne's *missi* had sought and failed to get *iustitiae* (*ARF s.a.* 791). Pagans could be negotiated with, held responsible for their commitments, and justly punished if they reneged (see, e.g., *ARF s.a.* 791 (Avars), 798, 808 (Abodrites) and 811 (Danes)). Their obligations became all the weightier after conversion to Christianity. Truce-breaking became sin, back-sliding apostasy. Here, the Saxons were a special case. Their forced conversion was undertaken with particular speed and ferocity. From 779, pagan practices were punishable by death (*MGH Capit.* I, 26). Alcuin complained; he did not challenge the wars and conquests themselves, but did think that conversion must be voluntary – literally, a matter of personal will – and addressed his worries not only to Charlemagne but to his chamberlain Meginfred (*MGH Capit.* I, 18; *MGH Epp.* IV, 110–11). There is no evidence that Charlemagne, or Meginfred, heeded him. This regime rested on the recognition of lordship. Fidelity was essential, sustained by mutual obligation between lord and man. Both coercion and volition were involved. The exact balance of these ingredients varied, but Charlemagne had no doubts that power depended on force as well as on persuasion and consent. Divine power was lordship writ large. When Frankish armies implored Christ their lord for victory, they were not thinking metaphorically. The litanies preceding the 791 Avar campaign clearly show the Franks' confidence in the 'justice' of their lord's and their Lord's cause. Confidence breathes equally strongly through Ermold's accounts of Christian ritual associated with Louis the Pious' campaigns against Spanish Muslims and Bretons ('Christians in name only', ll. 322–33, 566–69, 1522–93; Smith 1992: 63–64). The ideology of just war was subtended by a clearly etched cosmology: within the earthly empire God-directed rulers maintained peace in and for the church; outside it, war was waged to defend the Christian people, and to extend the church's sway.

Justice meant giving each his due. Peace meant concord, a harmony of interests and ends. The maintenance of internal peace and justice was fundamental to the Carolingian regime's agenda: not new, but trumpeted now insistently and *con brio*. It remained an ideal, conflicting with the evidence of the Franks' own eyes. Read the capitularies, saints' lives and miracle stories, and records of dispute settlement; violence, actual or threatened, is frequent. Much of what we call violence was then perfectly licit: the husband's chastising of his wife (Regino, *s.a.* 883), the father's corporal punishment of his children (Nelson 1994a), the beating of madmen (Adrevald, *Miracula S. Benedicti*, 30). Legitimate, institutionalized violence was necessary for the state. Royal agents were authorized to flog or mutilate law-breakers among unfree (and sometimes also free) persons (*MGH Capit.* I, 28.v, x, xxiii; 33.xxxvi; 44.v; 130.ii). The death penalty was enjoined for those who broke oaths of fidelity to the king, or for Saxons persisting in pagan practices and acts of political insubordination. Sexual offences, especially incest, were punished with a new ruthlessness (*ibid.*: 13.i; 19.x; 20.v; 33.xxxiii) as the Carolingian state declared itself against not only crime but sin. Most significant of all in the present context, Carolingian rulers launched a determined assault on 'feud': a *faidosus* who persisted after Charlemagne's 'pacification' would be punished by a heavy fine and the loss of his hand (*MGH Capit.* I, 44.v; see also Introduction: 25–26).

Legal documents also testify to much illegitimate violence perpetrated by armies against the peasantry of their own kingdom encountered en route; by lords' agents against tenants and labourers; by assorted predators against widows and orphans and against local churches; by thieves and criminals generally (Nelson 1986a; 1986b; 1988; 1996b). Violent conflicts existed between the powerful: between regional magnates, sometimes ecclesiastical as well as lay, and between men of magnates' followings. One of the best-documented instances involved two of the most celebrated intellectuals of Charlemagne's circle, Alcuin and Theodulf, no less (Dutton (trans.) 1993: 116–19)! Later in the ninth century the word *werra* (> guerre) first appears, with the sense of private conflict (Niermeyer 1976: 1133–34), as distinct from *bellum* waged by public authority, that is by the king. When Charles the Bald in 877 arranged for the government of the kingdom by his son during his own absence in Italy, he ordered that royal *scarae* (rapid deployment forces) be ready for *bellum* to protect the realm from aggressors, but also that counts be ready to repress local *werrae*, and that if comital action failed, royal intervention be invoked (*MGH Capit.* II, 281.xix).

And yet, in the first century of Carolingian government, there were means of conflict resolution and of redress: courts of settlement and courts of appeal; pledges and sureties; mediators and arbitrators; and judges. While 'justice' often enough was 'the ordinary name of power', sometimes it meant what it said. Courts took account of rights. Kings and their agents tried conscientiously to protect the powerless and to punish criminals and aggressors. However inadequately, the regimes of Charlemagne and Louis the Pious strove not only to represent themselves as just, but to be just. There was a judicial system of sorts, central officers, *missi*, entrusted with the surveillance of local judges, and there was a right of appeal up to the ruler himself (Fouracre 1995). There was a measure of peace, not least in public places like courts, markets, and highways. Ecclesiastical sanctuary was upheld in theory. In the eighth century it was proverbially said of Edwin of Northumbria's reign that 'that there was such great peace in that time ... that if a woman with her new-born babe chose to wander throughout the land, she could without molestation' (*EH* II.16). The early Carolingians could not claim so much; but they could plausibly claim that theirs too was a kingdom of peace, and that they branded, mutilated, executed and made war to keep that peace.

How could rulers enforce it? The idea of public administration had not disappeared; indeed it revived as experienced earlier Carolingian *legislatores* took note of the provisions of the Theodosian Code. Counts, marquises, dukes were in principle agents of public authority. They worked largely by consensus, going with the grain and exploiting the weight of local opinion and the testimony of knowledgeable neighbours

(Nelson 1995; 1986b). The lowest level of public officer, the hundred-man, was entitled to call for informants on local criminals and to demand help in bringing malefactors to court (*MGH Capit.* I, 33.xiii, xxv; II, 260). Counts raised troops for the royal host. The capitularies sometimes imply that these consisted of all free men, or a selection thereof; and free men have often been glossed by modern historians as descendants of Tacitus' Germans. On the other hand, annals, saints' lives and other miscellaneous, mostly ninth-century, texts tend to show that those engaged in *werra* or *bellum* consisted of the followings of the powerful (Reuter 1985; Nelson 1996b; France 1985; cp. White 1986). In modern historiography, two ways of resolving this contradiction have commonly been adopted. One is Ganshof's diagnosis of 'Charlemagne's failure' – and *a fortiori* his successors'. Theodosian prescriptions simply could not be applied in this incipiently feudal society (Ganshof 1971; cp. now Reynolds 1994). Alternatively decline and fall is suggested after an initial period of success. Under Charlemagne and Louis the Pious the state held its own; after 840, it yielded to local lordship (Halphen 1977; Poly & Bournazel 1991: 64–106; cp. Nelson 1992: 19–40). In either reconstruction, a clear line is drawn between a period when a revived state attempted more or less effectively to 'monopolise the use of legitimate force' (I quote Max Weber's definition of the state, amended by Reynolds, forthcoming), and a succeeding period, often described as 'feudal', when force was privatized (Bisson 1994; but cp. White 1996).

The methodological problems raised by the source-materials of this period have not always been squarely addressed. Among the most intractable are the familiar gap between prescriptive and descriptive evidence, and the coexistence in the same texts of old law and contemporary practice. As an example, consider the contrast between Charlemagne's capitularies summoning all free men to the host, and Alcuin's letters recording the descent on St-Martin, Tours, of Theodulf's posse of *armati* (above: 93). We confront here an implicit contrast between *bellum* and *werra*, though the earliest source to mention *werra* is a couple of generations later (Hincmar, *Quierzy Letter* 15). But the methodological difficulties do not end there. Descriptive evidence of local social practice is extraordinarily thin for Charlemagne's reign, but positively and progressively thick from the 820s. This uneven distribution means that comparisons between Charlemagne's and subsequent reigns are insecure. Capitularies cannot substitute for descriptive material, though historians have frequently forced them to. By contrast, the scraps of genuinely descriptive evidence have been relatively unexploited. The Alcuin-Theodulf dispute has been played down as a little local difficulty over a nicety of canon law instead of highlighted as the tip of a large iceberg of inter-magnate violence involving the obligations of local lordship. Another piece of evidence, the complaints of the men of Risano in Istria against the oppressions of Duke John, a text dated 804, has been, as far as I can see, almost wholly ignored. Yet what it shows is a magnate requisitioning horses from lesser landowners and well in control of regional organization for war (Nelson 1996a: xxvi).

Reuter (1990) has undertaken major ground-clearing around some of these methodological problems. He observes that Charlemagne's earlier capitularies are concerned with long-range, aggressive campaigns against Saxons, Avars and others, that is, involving elite mounted forces, whereas the capitularies from c. 805 onwards deal with defence against external aggression, notably from Danes and Slavs. Only in the *lantweri*, the defence of the land, were all required to contribute or serve. The quaint vernacular term has seemed to indicate surviving primitive Germanic arrangements; it actually translates requirements affirmed in the Theodosian Code (Nelson 1989b). Fifth-century Germans and Romans possibly acknowledged the same military obligations. If so, it seems likely that the formulation in terms of public duty bears a Roman stamp. Yet eighth- and ninth-century armies were neither like Roman armies nor, even vestigially, peasant armies of stolid freemen answering the royal summons. The conquerors of the Saxons and Avars need to be reimagined as war-bands of noble youths in the followings of lords, competing with each other (individually and as groups) for glory and loot (Reuter 1985). Reuter (1990) offers an elegant solution to an apparent contradiction in the evidence: different capitularies relate to different types of warfare. At the same time Reuter squares the prescriptive/descriptive circle: the earlier capitularies (and also some of the later ones) fit after all with what is implied, sketchily, by annalistic and other evidence. Carolingian war-making was the business of noble specialists whose expensive equipment was paid for by the labours of dependent and more or less unarmed peasants.

Reuter's analysis has a further important implication: the Carolingian decline and fall did not take place – or not in the way so often presented. Warfare in the 870s, as in the 840s, or 820s, was, in one fundamental respect, essentially similar to that of the later eighth century. War-lords and war-bands were always the essence of Carolingian armies. True the balance of offensive and defensive warfare changed. In the ninth century the Carolingian realms came under frequent attack. What did this mean for participation in war? Reuter's model holds for the reigns of Louis the Pious and Charles the Bald, in that capitularies continue to indicate defensive military service required as a public duty. In the Edict of Pîtres (864), for instance, it is understood that the *pagenses* will serve with their counts in the host. Furthermore, forty days after being demobilized, 'let that command be reimposed which is called in the Germanic tongue *scaftlegi*, meaning the laying-down of arms' (*sit bannus resisus quod in lingua theodisca scaftlegi, id est armorum depositio, vocatur (MGH Capit.* II, 273.xxxiii(B))). Again *scaftlegi* looks ancient and Germanic, but translates a Roman phrase. The use of weapons is prohibited within the realm, against compatriots. Does this imply that the *pagenses* then handed their weapons in to some comital armoury, to be redistributed at the next call-up? That seems unlikely, though one of Charlemagne's capitularies mentions, à propos the contingents of men beneficed on church lands, the storage of weapons in churches (*ibid.*: 74.x; cp. Nelson 1986a, ch. 6). Are the *pagenses* here (whatever meaning the term may have had in earlier and other contexts) not in effect the counts' followings? The Edict of Pîtres was infused with late antique language and content, yet the world it addressed was one of lordly retinues. The same text thus has to be read in differing perspectives, mirroring both ideal and reality. Elsewhere in that edict, private fortifications (*castella*) are required to be royally (publicly) licensed (*MGH Capit.* II, 273.i(C)). The Carolingians tried to control and canalise violence towards public ends, collectively defined at assemblies where *latrones* (brigands; cp. Introduction: 14–15) were declared public enemies.

What they could not control was recruitment. The members of comital retinues were the count's men. All local *potentes*, counts or otherwise, could coerce. Their legitimate violence coexisted with and subtended that of the Carolingian rulers themselves. *Quis custodiet ipsos custodes?* The lords about whom we are best informed are the king and ecclesiastical *potentes*: the information is that armed men were not easily controlled – the king's *vassi*, the *caballarii* of palatine clergy, or the *homines* of bishops, were liable to use force on their own account (cp. García Moreno, above: 50–51). Yet the evidence comes largely from Hincmar of Rheims in querulous mood (*MGH Epp.* VIII, 125, 126); Hincmar could also (when it suited him) call those same men the *militia regni* (*Quierzy Letter*, 7).

Whoever they were – sons of great nobles, kinsmen of their lords, sons of local squires, *mediocres* on the make (Notker, *Gesta Karoli* I.3) – these were not classed as belonging to the *vulgus*. The Frankish sword was not a peasant's weapon, nor did peasants perform cavalry service (Le Jan 1991). *Arma et equi* denoted an elite (Nelson 1989a). When peasants banded together to resist aggressors, contemporary writers, in effect spokesmen for that elite, showed them little sympathy. They were, Regino of Prüm wrote of peasants attempting to fight off Vikings in 882, 'not so much unarmed as lacking in military discipline'. Peasants, that is, had some kind of weaponry but no experience of coordinated fighting. Hence they were 'slaughtered like cattle' (Regino, *s.a.* 882). Earlier, peasants were said to have acted *incaute*, and were 'slain by our more powerful ones', *potentiores*, nobles who saw the threat to their own social power outweighing any sense of Frankish solidarity against Scandinavian attackers (*AB s.a.* 859). Writers and legislators had no ideological problem with peasant revolt; *conjurationes* were unlawful and sinful, and violent resistance to lordly oppression was 'nobly' crushed (Nithard, IV.4). Such attitudes, incidentally, help to explain the otherwise surprisingly low-key and stereotyped accounts of Scandinavian 'plundering', 'ravaging' and 'laying-waste', whose language seldom becomes strongly and specifically emotive (*AB s.a.* 851).

Aristocratic rebels were altogether more serious, not least because they were so often aligned with rivalries within the royal family. Given that the aristocracy doubled as office-holders, rebellion was the greatest disturber of the peace. Both Charlemagne and Louis the Pious faced, and faced down, serious and widely supported revolts (Brunner 1979). Yet both kings and rebels acted in the name of peace, as restorers and preservers. Thus, although violence (and in 834 horrific violence; Nithard, I.5) was involved, it was locally or regionally contained. Furthermore, Carolingian ideology, shared by the aristocracy, was strengthened rather than shattered. Confrontations were smoothed over by discussions and defections. Even 'the most dangerous' rebellion against Charlemagne (785) was suppressed with only three men killed: 'some [rebels] were blinded, and all were exiled' (Einhard, *Vita Caroli* 20).

A pitched battle must have seemed very possible on 24 June 833, when Louis the Pious confronted his rebellious sons at Rotfeld in Alsace, 'so that if he had been unable to divert them from their shameless course of action by peace-making words, he could check them by force of arms, lest they do harm to the Christian people.' In fact, most of Louis' supporters slipped away, 'compelled by various forms of pressure applied by his sons' (Nithard, I.4; cp. *AB s.a.* 833; Astronomer, 48). Deportations ensued, but no deaths. Bluff cynicism soon renamed the place 'the Field of Lies' (*AB s.a.* 833, marginalia in MS 'O'). Yet this stand-off stemmed not only from treachery. Franks who relished warfare against 'outside peoples', and engaged in battle as a form of 'play' (*Ludwigslied*; Dutton (trans.) 1993: 483, 'romped'), surely found the prospect of slaying fellow Franks profoundly shocking. Better suffer accusations of cowardice than be guilty of fratricide. Further, these men had for their adult lives been the target-audience of an ideology of Christian empire. They were committed in principle to keep the peace. Louis' son Lothar was an adroit manipulator of opinion. He had Pope Gregory IV with him, and the papal case for peace was especially telling (Nithard, I.4; cp. Fried 1990). Agobard of Lyons justified climb-downs and compromises for the sake of 'keeping whole the one body of Christ' (*MGH Epp.* V, 16). What prevented a pitched battle was a combination of political circumstance and aristocratic hesitation. Churchmen naturally justified non-violence; defusing had always been part of their métier. But they also repaired and repowered the system after the political 'power-cuts' of such crises. Drogo of Metz, Hrabanus Maurus of Fulda and the contrite Abbot Hilduin of St-Denis re-established the credentials of Louis' restored regime in 834–835 (Nelson 1990). Like the fastings and prayers accompanying Louis' unveiling of his *Ordinatio Imperii* in 817, Louis' penance of Attigny in 822, and even the penance of Soissons in 833 imposed by his sons (however cynical a charade it appears in retrospect), Louis' reinvestiture at St-Denis in 834 and his recrowning at Metz in 835 were great ecclesiastical rituals performed 'in the presence of the people', devised to restore consensus and reaffirm the legitimacy of the Christian empire (*ARF s.a.* 817, 822; *AB s.a.* 833, 835; De Jong 1992).

Another episode comparable to the Field of Lies occurred in November 858. After Louis the German invaded his brother Charles' kingdom, the kings' armies faced each other for three days at Brienne (dép. Aube): 'finally on the third day, that is 12 November, when the lines of battle had already been drawn up on both sides, Charles realizing that his men were deserting him retreated . . .' (*AB s.a.* 858). Charles' temporary military weakness seems enough to explain the outcome; it is likely that there was a strong ritual element in the confrontation. Both Charles and Louis wished to secure a public manifestation of divine approval (*Quierzy Letter* 15). That Charles waited at Brienne for three days – a ritually significant period – could suggest that he would have fought had he seen a chance to win. It is possible that Louis was relieved that the outcome was secured without blood-letting. That outcome, however, was not the decisive judgement of a victor on the battlefield. Even the Field of Lies had been depicted as a judgement of God (Agobard, *Capit.* II, 197). That was possible – but not very convincing.

THE RITUALIZATION OF NINTH-CENTURY WARFARE

Bloodless victories had a painful alternative. The real crisis of the Carolingian empire came after Louis the Pious' death. What had not happened in 785, 792, 806, 817, 830 or 833, finally occurred in 841: mortal conflict between Franks erupted as Louis' sons Louis and Charles fought their elder brother Lothar. Not just one but two battles (*praelia*) occurred in early summer, 841. At the first (13 May), near the East Frankish-Bavarian frontier, King Louis the German slew Count Adalbert of Metz and 'an uncountable number of men'. The author of the *Annals of Fulda*, who previously mentioned Adalbert in quite neutral tones, now called him 'the instigator of disputes' (*AF s.a.* 841). Though Adalbert had been one of Louis the Pious' most loyal supporters, and after 840 maintained Lothar's cause in the Rhineland, his military challenge to a Carolingian king apparently sufficed to discredit him in this chronicler's eyes. Adalbert's fate prefigured that of many other aristocrats in 841. Armed conflict was no longer just a settling of scores in local magnate rivalry. 'Private' disputes were now 'public'. Contemporaries saw the difference.

The difference was blatant when Carolingian kings pitted themselves against one another in war that contemporaries labelled *bellum, proelium, certamen,* even *bellum civile* (Nelson 1996b). But how to cope with such conflict? The Battle of Fontenoy was as remarkable for the prolonged negotiations that failed to avert it as for the fact that it occurred at all. Fortunately, the days preceding the battle are exceptionally well documented. Nithard, an illegitimate member of the Carolingian family, a Frank, was a participant-observer, though by no means a neutral one (he supported Charles), and an able historian (Nelson 1986a; Leyser 1989: 19–26). Nithard began by establishing the credentials of Charles and Louis (partly by reporting Louis' victory of 13 May) and showing Lothar's unreliability (Nithard II.9). Lothar, encamped in the upper Meuse valley, failed to respond to envoys; he spread lies about Charles in order to kindle enthusiasm among his 'party' (*pars*); he pretended to rest his horses but in fact plotted an attack; he 'raged by deceit against his brothers and their men'. Louis and Charles did all they could to avoid this battle. They conferred with their bishops and leading laymen and agreed to send envoys to Lothar, reminding him of his debt to his father's memory, and to God, who required him 'to grant peace to his brothers and to God's whole church'. Louis and Charles offered 'all they possessed in their whole army, except for their weapons and horses'. If he refused, they would 'be able to hope for help from a divine gift'. Lothar now finally acknowledged that he wanted to settle matters by battle (*proelium*) and set off to rendezvous with his nephew, Pippin of Aquitaine. Only with this additional help was Lothar hopeful of victory.

Louis and Charles complained strongly at Lothar's determination to 'deny them peace without a battle'; but if battle there were – and it would be at his insistence – it must be conducted without fraud (Nithard II.10). A last effort would be made to avert battle: 'let us invoke God with prayers and fastings; then . . . let Lothar come to meet us under guarantee that there will be no ambush – alternatively let Lothar make the same offer and the same guarantee to us.' Lothar pretended to negotiate but while his brothers' envoys were bringing back his reply, Lothar quickly moved south to Fontenoy on 22 June. Charles and Louis, realizing what had happened, pursued and overtook their brother and pitched their camp just south of his.

Again Charles and Louis sent envoys to Lothar begging him to 'allow the church of God and the whole Christian people to have peace', and to 'grant them the *regna* which their father had granted them with his [Lothar's] consent'. They renewed their previous offer, adding substantial territorial concessions in a future partition of the *regnum*, and promising Lothar the choice of whichever of three 'equal shares' of Francia he wished. Still pretending to negotiate, Lothar on Thursday 23 June agreed to a truce until 7 a.m. on Saturday 25 June (a three-day period by some medieval reckoning), and waited. 24 June was St John the Baptist's day, which Charles and Louis wished to celebrate appropriately. The liturgy of that feast centred on cleansing and baptismal renewal (see Nelson 1992: 117). It was also the date on which, just eight years before, Louis and Charles had witnessed their father's failure and humiliation at the Field of Lies (above: 97). On this day in 841, Pippin of Aquitaine arrived to join his forces to Lothar's. Nithard says nothing about *their* celebrating St John's day. He reports Lothar's envoys' high-handed response to Charles and Louis, convincing them that 'all hope of justice and peace had gone'. They then informed Lothar that they would put their cause to the Judgement of God at 7 a.m. on the 25 June – and that this was Lothar's desire, not their own. Next dawn, Charles and Louis moved to a hill overlooking Lothar's camp. They waited, as their envoys had sworn, until 7 a.m. and then attacked . . .

Nithard was by no means the only contemporary to record that this was a 'great', and 'hard fought' battle (Nithard, II.10, . . . *proelium . . . magno certamine committunt*; III.1: *Proelio . . . strenue peracto . . . ingens cedes*). The author of the *Annals of Fulda* thought the slaughter such 'that no one can recall a greater loss among the Frankish people in the present age' (*AF s.a.* 841). Others also stressed exceptional carnage (Nelson 1996b). It is therefore surprising that we cannot identify a single casualty for certain. Not even Nithard names any slain comrades. Why this silence? Why the absence of epitaphs, such a common genre of the period? Perhaps a certain *damnatio memoriae* was cast over a conflict that brought no glory to the fallen. As Carolingian writers knew, *dulce et decorum est pro patria mori*. But to fight and die *pro parte*, for party rather than fatherland, was evidently thought neither sweet nor decorous.

The trauma of Fontenoy emerges from its aftermath, nowhere more clearly than in Nithard's account. He goes into detail here (Nithard III. 1). Even on the battlefield, while some, motivated by *ira*, urged a ruthless pursuit, Charles and Louis 'took pity on their brother and the people [that is, the combatants on his side] who had been crushed by the Judgement of God and by the blow they had suffered.' Rather than prolong the slaughter, Charles and Louis 'desired in the way they always had . . . that the defeated should repent their wickedness and greed, and . . . become of one mind with them in [the quest for] true justice.' The kings persuaded their followers to put everything in God's hands. Fighting and pillaging stopped. It was decided to spend Sunday on the battlefield. Mass was celebrated, the dead buried, 'friends and enemies, faithful and faithless, without distinction' (this was apparently unusual since other contemporary writers stressed it) and the wounded and dying of both sides cared for. Messengers offered pardon to those who had fled, provided they abandoned further resistance. Ecclesiastical guidance was now invoked. The bishops present (and, interestingly, they *were* present) held an impromptu council, which was at the same time a general assembly. They issued the following statement: Charles and Louis and their men had fought for justice and a Judgement of God had been declared. Therefore all present were to be regarded as God's ministers, whether advisers of God's will or active doers of it, and as such were 'immune', blameless. Any individual knowing himself to have been motivated by anger, hate or pride, was to confess that secretly, and was assigned penance accordingly. A three-day fast was then decreed 'for the remission of sins of their dead brothers' and 'so that God might continue to be a helper and protector of them all, as he had been up to then in their acts of justice.'

The crucial part of this passage, I think, contains two assertions: first that the battle had indeed constituted a Judgement of God; second, and consequently, that the victors (except for some ill-motivated individuals) bore no guilt for bloodshed. The significance of this becomes clear in the light of contemporary canonistic discussion of killing. Only a few years before Nithard wrote his *Histories*, Halitgar of Cambrai's *Penitential* distinguished between killing in warfare generally, a sin for which the due penance was a three-week fast, and killing in battle to defend oneself or one's close kin, not sinful and hence entailing only voluntary penance (Nelson 1989a). Even though Halitgar's remained a minority view among canonists, Nithard clearly shows that in 841 this view was adopted by bishops and warriors alike. The killings at Fontenoy, of Frank by Frank, brother by brother – for this was civil war – could have been expected to arouse exceptionally painful feelings of guilt and remorse. The victors might be persuaded that they had been tools of the devil (Nelson 1996b). Such doubts and anxieties had to be stilled. The old liturgy of victory was felt to be inappropriate here, both by those who had 'advised' and by those who had wreaked the carnage. A new liturgy was needed, and a newly explicit and unequivocal justification for what had been done. The bishops responded to the warriors' need; but bishops and warriors thought alike. The killing had had to be done in the cause of justice. The instrument of divine intervention, it had been justified because its context was a *bona fide* Judgement of God. Thus killers won 'immunity'. Their care for the dead, body and soul, and their voluntary fasting confirmed their piety. Some modern German scholarship has seen *urgermanisch* ritual in judgement by battle (Cram 1955: 20–47). It may be that churchmen were here adapting, subsuming and overlaying pre-Christian patterns of behaviour in conflict situations which, in any culture, are fraught with danger, social as well as personal (Flint 1991). Another reading is also possible: in the Judgement of God and attendant ritual, the ninth-century Christian Frankish elite attempted to come to terms with a new and specific threat to its integrity, self-perception, and even survival.

Just once again in the ninth century was a similar appeal made to a judgement of God, again with the object of legitimating otherwise intolerable internecine violence and conflict. In September 876, Charles the Bald, now emperor, attempted to exploit the situation following his brother Louis' death. Charles had long set his sights on territorial acquisitions in Francia's heartlands. Louis' death offered a uniquely favourable opportunity (Nelson 1992: 244–45). The only obstacle to Charles extending his eastern frontier to the Rhine was his nephew Louis the

Younger, newly king in East Francia, relatively inexperienced, and with resources in the Rhineland an unknown quantity. Charles surely aimed at a bloodless victory, hoping to overrule his nephew's objections, and override by sheer weight of numbers and imperial prestige Louis' claims to his father's lands west as well as east of the Rhine. Louis nevertheless determined to fight for what he, and most contemporaries apparently, saw as his just inheritance. There had been no pitched battle of Franks against Franks since Fontenoy, which Louis himself (born in the mid-830s) may not have remembered. Other contemporaries did remember, and surely helped inspire Louis' conduct in October 876 when he confronted his uncle just across the Rhine at Cologne.

First Louis exculpated himself by sending envoys to seek peace; his uncle spurned them. Thus far, the sources agree. Hincmar in the *Annals of St-Bertin* (*s.a.* 876) is alone in adding: 'when [Louis] and his counts then sought mercy from the Lord with fastings and litanies, the emperor [Charles]'s men jeered at them.' Hincmar, again, gives the unique, yet thoroughly credible, account of what happened next. Louis pre-empted Judgement by battle, organizing multiple taking of the three standard kinds of ordeal: hot iron, hot water and cold water. The results of all three were positive (*AB s.a.* 876). Though Hincmar gives no further details, other ninth-century evidence shows that these ordeals were administered by clergy. Hincmar himself was exceptionally vocal in advocating judicial ordeals in certain difficult cases, and they were already established in those contexts as a preferred instrument of the Carolingian state (Bartlett 1986; Moore 1987; Flint 1991; Bührer-Thierry 1992). Louis now extended the ordeal's application to the hardest case of all: a conflict between close kin, between senior and junior, between Franks and fellow Franks. Louis chose his ideological weapons wisely: before any blood was shed, he scored a moral victory, cemented the support of leading churchmen and doubtless inspired his men with a confidence that belied their inferior numbers. Immediately afterwards, he crossed the Rhine to offer battle at Andernach. The *Annals of Fulda* claim that Charles and his army were already demoralized:

> 'without doubt, God fought against Charles . . . for, as the prisoners who were led away reported, when Louis and those who were with him appeared, such fear filled all Charles' men that they thought themselves defeated before battle had begun, and . . . though they scored and gashed with their spurs the flanks of the horses on which they sat, these remained standing as if tied to posts' (*AF s.a.* 876).

Yet Charles had also attempted to keep morale high, having carefully timed the battle for the eve of the feast-day of St Denis, his own special protector and the West Franks' traditional patron. Had he won at Andernach on 8 October, he would have offered his victory to St Denis, and claimed the outcome a judgement of God.[1] Both contenders at Andernach, in other words, used registers of Christian ritual and symbolic power to boost their supporters' confidence and to forestall charges of failure to honour their world's most fundamental social obligations. By the ninth century it was impossible to claim justice without demonstrable ecclesiastical legitimation; conversely, whatever the outcome, contemporaries could justify it, and render it intelligible, by reference to religious meanings.

BY WAY OF CONCLUSIONS

No elite can live long with the perceived dissonance of values that conflict within the authorized political structure inevitably entails. Learned contemporaries perceived Fontenoy as civil war. The solidarities of family, group, realm, ethnicity were riven. Obligations were called into question. Legitimate authority was legitimately challenged. Yet unlike other civil wars where the unitary structure survives and reintegrates the dissident parts, the ninth-century inter-Frankish wars signalled permanent division. After 840, though the Frankish *regnum* continued to be seen as one, and aristocrats still moved to and fro within it, separate *regna* were in fact constituted (for the longer term, see Brühl 1990). Several generations were necessary for enduring new political structures to form and harden, yet the kings of the new successor states already demanded loyalty of their own aristocracies, and required that this be demonstrated in battle. The Frankish elite, descendants of the men who made the Carolingian empire, now had to participate in its splitting and reordering. They were co-designers, potential victims, as well as beneficiaries, of what was no natural process ('decline', 'dissolution') but a thoroughly man-made one. These aristocrats supported, and enabled, the creation of distinct successor states.

    Their own memories were purveyed in song and story as well as in writing. Hincmar could almost certainly call on oral tradition as well as history when in 878 he reminded Louis the Stammerer and his entourage of the battle of Vinchy in 717, 'the last time Franks fought Franks until Fontenoy' (Hincmar, *Instructio ad Ludovicum Balbum*, col. 986). These were painful memories. The two battles framed an age of Frankish unity and successes in war against external enemies. Some of Hincmar's audience would remember that golden era, as Hincmar himself did. Other, younger men knew only the post-Fontenoy world, and they had learned to live in it. The future France and Germany had taken

---

1. It can be argued (Nelson 19974b) that in the aftermath of Andernach, Hincmar wrote up his account to criticize what he saw as Charles' unjust action against his nephew. Readers, including Charles himself, would not miss the significance of a date so loaded with meaning for a devotee (as Charles was) of the cult of St Denis.

shape during the half-century after Fontenoy, and Andernach had confirmed this. Internal frontiers within Francia, as well as external ones,
had solidified. The two battles had been crucial. To live with the consequences of political division it was necessary to believe that the ends
justified the means. Here churchmen played an indispensable role. They
taught not only that God might choose to work through war (he was
after all a God of Battles),[2] but that he could speak through civil war.
Hence to fight in such a war was defensible, and necessary. Fratricidal
strife could be understood as an irrefragable manifestation of God's will.

Furthermore, its result, in theory at least and in the victors' hopes,
would have the finality of a battle's outcome: the winners' cause would
be manifestly justified, as, therefore, would be both sides' acquiescence
in the further consequences. What to men was uncertain (as are the out-
comes of battles) acquired the certainty of divine judgement. Men torn
between apparently irreconcilable demands of family and royal lordship,
and of rival royal lords, could find dilemmas resolved. Men anguished
by guilt at the killing of compatriots and kinsmen could know themselves 'immune' as agents of divine intervention. To be told all this by
churchmen acknowledged as God's spokesmen on earth was surely important in motivating and reassuring those who fought. No less important, the church constructed rituals before and after battle through which
warriors were enabled to feel themselves engaged in a cosmic event.
Fasting and prayer, battle-field assemblies, ordeals, these were not
merely external performances passively observed. On the contrary, these
rituals actively involved warriors. At Fontenoy and at Andernach, they
were organized to make sense of, and legitimize, war, not against pagan
outsiders, but of Christian Franks against Christian Franks. These were
battles earmarked, consecrated, as instruments in a divine plan of campaign. The Franks could see themselves, still, as a chosen people.

Two things gave all this a longer-term importance. The ritualization
of ninth-century inter-Frankish warfare eased the formation and acceptance of new political structures, the *regna* that by 900 were becoming
France and Germany. Elites had switched loyalties, and self-definitions
of membership, from one single Christian empire to a plurality of
Christian realms. Finally, those same elites, who well before the close of
ninth century were being identified as *bellatores*, *belligerantes*, and a
militia regni, could find legitimation for their own specific social
behaviour, for their military activities off as well as on the battlefield.
Their violence had been ecclesiastically validated, consecrated in the
service of God. The ninth century was already an age of chivalry. The
world of the three orders, of the crusades, of *Gesta Dei per Francos*, was
being born.

---

2. This theme emerges strongly in the *Ludwigslied*, composed a few years after
Andernach to celebrate a Frankish victory against Vikings (Fouracre 1985).

BIBLIOGRAPHY

Primary sources

Adrevald, *Miracula S. Benedicti*: PL 124 cols 909–48.

Agnellus, *Liber Pontificalis Ecclesiae Ravennatis*: O. Holder-Egger (ed.), *MGH Scriptores Rerum Langobardorum et Italicarum* (Hanover, 1878).

Agobard of Lyon, *Episcoporum de Poenitentia, quam Hludowicus imperator professus est relatio Compendiensis*: A. Boretius & V. Krause (eds), *Capitularia Regum Francorum* II (*M.G.H. Legum* Sect. II vol. 2) (Hanover, 1897), pp. 51–56.

Agobard of Lyon, *Epistolae*: E. Dümmler (ed.), *MGH Epp.* V (Berlin, 1899), pp. 150–59.

Alcuin, *Epistolae*: E. Dümmler (ed.), *MGH Epp.* IV *Epistolae Aevi Karolini II* (Berlin, 1895), pp. 1–481. Selection in P. E. Dutton (trans.), *Carolingian Civilization* (Ontario, 1993), pp. 106–19.

Annals of Fulda: G. H. Pertz & F. Kurze (eds), *MGH SRG* 7 (Hanover, 1891); T. Reuter (trans.), *The Annals of Fulda (Ninth-Century Histories* vol. 2) (Manchester, 1992).

Annals of St-Bertin: G. Waitz (ed.), *MGH SRG* 5 (Hanover, 1883); J. L. Nelson (trans.), *The Annals of St-Bertin (Ninth-Century Histories* vol. 1) (Manchester, 1991).

Astronomer, *Life of the Emperor Louis*: E. Tremp (ed.), *MGH SRG* 64 (Hanover, 1995), pp. 279–555; A. Cabaniss (trans.), *Son of Charlemagne: A Contemporary Life of Louis the Pious* (Syracuse, NY, 1961).

Bede, *Ecclesiastical History*: B. Colgrave & R. A. B. Mynors (eds & trans.) *Bede's Ecclesiastical History of the English People* (Oxford 1969).

Capitularies: A. Boretius (ed.), *Capitularia Regum Francorum* I (*M.G.H. Legum* Sect. II vol. 1) (Hanover, 1883); A. Boretius & V. Krause (eds), *Capitularia Regum Francorum* II (*M.G.H. Legum* Sect. II vol. 2) (Hanover, 1897).

Epistolae variorum Carolo Magno regnante scriptae: E. Dümmler (ed.), *MGH Epp.* IV *Epistolae Aevi Karolini II* (Berlin, 1895).

Einhard, *Vita Caroli*: G. Waitz (ed.), *MGH, SRG* 25 (Hanover, 1880); L. Thorpe (trans.), *Einhard and Notker the Stammerer. Two Lives of Charlemagne* (Harmondsworth, 1969).

Ermold, *In Honorem Hlodowici Pii*: E. Faral (ed. & trans.), *Ermold le Noir. Poème sur Louis le Pieux* (Paris, 1964).

Fredegar's Chronicle and its *Continuations*: B. Krusch (ed.), *MGH SRM* II (Hanover, 1888), pp. 1–193; J. M. Wallace-Hadrill (trans.), *The Fourth Book of the Chronicle of Fredegar with Its Continuations* (London, 1960).

Hincmar of Rheims, *De regis Persona et regio Ministerio*: PL 125, cols 833–56.

Hincmar of Rheims, *Epistolae*: E. Perels (ed.), *MGH Epp.* VIII *Hincmari Archiepiscopi Remensis Epistolae* (Berlin, 1939).

Hincmar of Rheims, 'Quierzy Letter': W. Hartmann (ed.), *MGH Concilia* IV *Concilia Aevi Karolini, 843–59* (Hanover, 1984), pp. 403–27.

Ludwigslied: P. E. Dutton (trans.), *Carolingian Civilization* (Ontario, 1993), pp. 482–83.

Nithard, *Histories (Libri Historiarum IV)*: E. Müller (ed.), *MGH SRG* 44 (Hanover, 1907); B. Scholz (trans.), *Carolingian Chronicles* (Ann Arbor, 1972), pp. 129–74.

Notker, *Gesta Karoli*: H. F. Haefele (ed.), *MGH SRG* n. s. 12 (Berlin, 1959); L. Thorpe (trans.), *Two Lives of Charlemagne: Einhard and Notker the Stammerer* (Harmondsworth, 1969).

Regino of Prüm, *Chronicon*: F. Kurze (ed.), *MGH SRG* 50 (Hanover, 1890).

Royal Frankish Annals: F. Kurze (ed.), *MGH SRG* 6 (Hanover, 1895); P. D. King (trans.), *Charlemagne. Translated Sources* (Lambrigg, 1987), pp. 74–107; B. Scholz (trans.), *Carolingian Chronicles* (Ann Arbor, 1972), pp. 37–125.

Secondary bibliography

Airlie, S., 1993. 'After empire – recent work on the emergence of post-Carolingian kingdoms', *Early Medieval Europe* 2.2: 154–62.

Anton, H. H., 1968. *Fürstenspiegel und Herrscherethos in der Karolingerzeit* (Bonn).

Bartlett, R., 1986. *Trial by Fire and Water. The Medieval Judicial Ordeal* (Oxford).

Bisson, T., 1994. 'The "feudal revolution"', *Past and Present* 142: 6–42.

Brown, P. R. L., 1964. 'St. Augustine's attitude to religious coercion', *Journal of Roman Studies* 54: 107–16, reprinted in Brown 1972.

—— 1972. *Religion and Society in the Age of Saint Augustine* (London).

Brühl, C. R., 1990. *Deutschland-Frankreich. Die Geburt zweier Völker* (Cologne & Vienna).

Brunner, K., 1979. *Oppositionelle Gruppen im Karolingerreich* (Vienna).

Bührer-Thierry, G., 1992. 'La reine adultère', *Cahiers de Civilisation Médiévale* 35: 299–312.

Cram, K. G., 1955. *Iudicium Belli: Zum Rechtscharakter des Krieges im deutschen Mittelalter* (Munster & Cologne).

Flint, V. I. J., 1991. *The Rise of Magic in Early Medieval Europe* (Oxford).

Fouracre, P. J., 1985. 'The context of the OHG *Ludwigslied*', *Medium Aevum* 54: 87–103.

—— 1995. 'Carolingian justice: the rhetoric of reform and contexts of abuse', *La Giustizia nell'Alto Medioevo, Secoli V-VIII (Settimane di Studi 42)*, pp. 771–803.

France, J., 1985. 'The military history of the Carolingian period', *Revue Belge d'Histoire Militaire* 26: 81–99.

Fried, J., 1990. 'Ludwig der Fromme, das Papsttum und die fränkische Kirche', in Godman & Collins (eds) 1990: 231–73.

Ganshof, F. L., 1971. *The Carolingians and the Frankish Monarchy* (London).

Godman, P., & Collins, R. J. H. (eds), 1990. *Charlemagne's Heir. New Perspectives on the Reign of Louis the Pious* (Oxford).

Halphen, L., 1977. *Charlemagne and the Carolingian Empire* (G. de Nie, trans.) (Amsterdam & London).

Kantorowicz, E., 1946. *Laudes Regiae. A Study in Liturgical Acclamations and Medieval Ruler Worship* (Berkeley).

Le Jan, R., 1991. 'Satellites et bandes armées dans le monde franc (VIIe-IXe siècles)', in *Le Combattant au Moyen Age* (Nantes), pp. 97–107.

Leyser, K., 1984. 'Early medieval canon law and the beginning of knighthood', in L. Fenske, W. Rösener & T. Zotz (eds), *Institutionen, Kultur und Gesellschaft. Festschrift für Josef Fleckenstein zu seinem 65. Geburtstag* (Sigmaringen), pp. 549–66, reprinted in K. Leyser, *Communications and Power in Medieval Europe. The Carolingian and Ottonian Centuries* (T. Reuter, ed.) (London, 1994), pp. 51–71.

McCormick, M., 1984. 'The liturgy of war in the early Middle Ages: crises, litanies and the Carolingian monarchy', *Viator* 15: 1–23.

—— 1986. *Eternal Victory. Triumphal Rulership in Late Antiquity, Byzantium and the Early Medieval West* (Cambridge).

Moore, R. A., 1987. *The Formation of a Persecuting Society. Power and Deviance in Western Europe, 950–1250* (Oxford).

Nelson, J. L., 1986a. *Politics and Ritual in Early Medieval Europe* (London).

—— 1986b. 'Dispute settlement in Carolingian West Francia', in W. Davies & P. Fouracre (eds), *The Settlement of Disputes in Early Medieval Europe* (Cambridge), pp. 45–64, reprinted in Nelson 1986a.

—— 1988. 'Kingship and empire', in J. H. Burns (ed.), *The Cambridge History of Medieval Political Thought* (Cambridge), pp. 211–51.

—— 1989a. 'Ninth-century knighthood: the evidence of Nithard', in C. Harper-Bill, C. J. Holdsworth, & J. L. Nelson (eds), *Studies in Medieval History Presented to R. Allen Brown* (Woodbridge), pp. 255–66, reprinted in Nelson 1996a.

—— 1989b. 'Translating images of authority: the Christian Roman emperors in the Carolingian world', in M. M. Mackenzie & C. Roueché (eds), *Images of Authority. Papers Presented to Joyce Reynolds* (Cambridge), pp. 194–205, reprinted in Nelson 1996a.

—— 1990. 'The last years of Louis the Pious', in Godman & Collins (eds) 1990: 147–60.

—— 1992. *Charles the Bald* (London).

—— 1994a. 'Parents, children and the church in the earlier Middle Ages', *Studies in Church History* 31: 81–114.

—— 1994b. 'History-writing at the courts of Louis the Pious and Charles the Bald', in A. Scharer & G. Scheibelreiter (eds), *Historiographie im frühen Mittelalter* (Vienna), pp. 435–42.

—— 1995. 'Kingship and royal government', in R. McKitterick (ed.), *The New Cambridge Medieval History* vol. 2 (Cambridge), pp. 383–438.

—— 1996a. *The Frankish World, 750–900* (London).

—— 1996b. 'The quest for peace in a time of war: the Carolingian Brüderkrieg, 840–843', in J. Fried (ed.), *Träger und Instrumentarien des Friedens im Hohen und Späten Mittelalter* (Vorträge und Forschungen 43) (Sigmaringen), pp. 87–114.

Niermeyer, J. F., 1976. *Mediae Latinitatis Lexicon Minus* (Leiden).

Poly, J. P., & Bournazel, E., 1991. *La Mutation Féodale, Xe-XIIe Siècle* 2nd French edition (Paris).

Reuter, T., 1985. 'Plunder and tribute in the Carolingian empire', *Transactions of the Royal Historical Society* 5th series, 35: 75–94.

—— 1990. 'The end of Carolingian military expansion', in Godman & Collins (eds) 1990: 391–405.

Reynolds, S., 1994. *Fiefs and Vassals. The Medieval Evidence Reinterpreted* (Oxford).

—— forthcoming. 'The state in the Middle Ages', in M. Bentley (ed.), *The Routledge Companion to Historiography* (London).

Tellenbach, G., 1934. 'Römischer und christlicher Reichsgedanke in der Liturgie des frühen Mittelalters', *Sitzungsberichte der Heidelberger Akademie der Wissenschaften* (phil. hist. Klasse 25).

White, S. D., 1986. 'Feuding and peace-making in the Touraine around the year 1000', *Traditio* 42: 195–263.

CHAPTER 5

Regicide in early medieval Ireland[1]

N. B. Aitchison

SACRAL KINGSHIP AND RITUAL DEATH

Early medieval Irish kingship's well-known sacral dimension[2] is exemplified by inauguration rituals (Dillon 1973), *specula principum* ('mirrors of princes'; Smith 1927), and the circumscription of kings by *geisi* or *ugarta* ('taboos', 'proscriptions').[3] However, the ritual killing of kings, demonstrated by Frazer (1890) to underlie many sacral kingships, has received less attention.

Drawing on Frazer's study of the ritual killing of the *Rex Nemorensis*, Macalister (1919: 326) proposed that the kings of Tara were killed ritually; of '110 kings enumerated in *Flaithiusa hÉrenn* . . . eighty are said to have been killed by their successors'. According to Dalton (1970: 1), 'the kings of Tara were killed on a particular day of the year, in a ritual manner, for religious reasons, and at the end of a fixed term of [seven] years or of some multiple of this term. All the principal elements of a ritual killing are thus present.' However, Macalister (1919: 327) admitted that 'Improbabilities . . . are too frequent in the lists of kings . . . to accept it literally.' Indeed, Macalister's only evidence belongs to 'the

---

1. I wish to express my thanks to Patrick Wormald, whose ISN lectures in the University of Glasgow during 1981–82 first stimulated my interest in early Irish kingship. In addition, I am very grateful to Ross Samson for encouraging me to develop this theme and to Guy Halsall for his editorial comments. Any opinions expressed or errors made are my responsibility alone.

2. Binchy 1970: 8–12; Byrne 1973: 117–27; Mac Niocaill 1972: 44–47; Mac Cana 1979; Wormald 1986; McCone 1990: 107–37.

3. Dillon 1947: 252; 1951; Greene 1979; O'Leary 1988.

pseudo-history of pre-Christian Ireland which was elaborated during the ninth and tenth centuries, [in which] most of the mythical "kings of Ireland" are slain by their successors' (Binchy 1970: 10).

Dalton's (1970) analysis of the killing of the kings of Tara relied upon annalistic entries recording the celebration of the *Feis Temro* ('Feast of Tara'), the inauguration ceremony of the kings of Tara (Carney 1955: 334–39; Binchy 1958: 134–37), between c. 450 and 560. Although accepted as historical sources (most recently Byrne 1973: 80, 83), contemporaneous annals were not kept until c. 550 at the earliest (Byrne 1967: 180; Smyth 1972); that some celebrations are entered two or three times, under different years, within the same annals suggests confusion. Dalton attributed the regular celebration of the *Feis* to the need to install a new king after his predecessor's ritual murder. However, the fixed length of reigns is characteristic of the synchronizing (or 'synthetic') historians (Carney 1955: 337). Moreover, the *Feis Temro*, and the kingship of Tara itself, may be later, ideological constructs (Aitchison 1994a: 37–38).

For the ritual nature of the Tara king-killings, Dalton also depended on mythological sources of the late first millennium AD. The 'three-fold death', comprising transfixion, burning and drowning, features in the death-tales of Conaire Már mac Eterscélae, Muirchertach mac Erca, and Diarmait mac Cerbaill; having broken his *geisi*, a king seeks shelter at a mysterious hostel (*bruiden*), but during the night is attacked and wounded, and the hostel fired. Trying to escape, the king throws himself into a vat of ale or wine and drowns.[4] Variations on this theme constitute the dénouement of some of the most vivid Old and Middle Irish mythology, such as *Aided Muirchertach mac Erca*. Muirchertach's death is also recorded in a mythologically inspired interpolation in the annals (*CS s.a.* 531; see also *AFM s.a.* 527; *AU s.a.* 533), and a poem by Fland Mainistrech (d. 1056) (*LL* 15800–01) relates how 'in Cleitech [Muirchertach was killed] by a spearpoint – clear deed – wine drowned him, fire burnt him.'

The culmination of the three-fold death may be of symbolic significance. The twelfth-century Anglo-Norman commentator, Giraldus Cambrensis (*TH* III.102), described a probably earlier or archaic inauguration ritual as including the inauguree's bathing in a vat of broth; the motif of the 'drink of sovereignty' features prominently in the mythology of early Irish kingship.[5] Bhreatnach (1982: 259) interpreted Muirchertach's drowning as the killing of an unjust king, 'overwhelmed by the symbol

---

4. Jackson 1940; Rees & Rees 1961: 335–40; Nic Dhonnchadha 1964: ix-xi; Ó Cuív 1965; 1974; Byrne 1973: 97–102; Ó Concheanainn 1974; Guyonvarc'h 1983; Radner 1983; Sayers 1992.

5. O'Rahilly 1946: 14–16; Mac Cana 1956: 77–78, 84–86; Byrne 1973: 51, 75, 100; Bhreatnach 1982: 243, 256–57; see also Bhreatnach 1953; Herbert 1992.

of his own sovereignty'. Drowning in ale or wine may represent a ritual 'unkinging', inverting the inaugural immersion and 'drink of sovereignty'. This phenomenon is recognized by anthropologists: 'deposition from high office . . . often mirror[s] in reverse the rites and procedures by which the tenure is inaugurated' (Fortes 1962: 6).

The three-fold death, involving a king's supernatural killing by elemental forces – iron, fire and water – was the consequence of transgressing supernatural injunctions. It appears as a mythological motif (Byrne 1973: 97; Ó Cuív 1974) and some of its victims are mythical rather than historical (Byrne 1973: 59, 102). A similar death also appears in late seventh-century hagiography. Adomnán described St Columba's prophecy that Áed Dub mac Suibne, over-king of *Ulaid*:

> 'pierced with a spear (*lancea iugul*[*a*]*tus*), will fall from wood into water, and die by drowning. He has deserved such an end much sooner, who has slaughtered the king of all Ireland.

> 'And Áed Dub, priest only in name, returned to his former evil deeds, and, pierced with a spear by treachery, fell from the prow of a ship into the water of a lake, and perished' (*Vita Sancti Columbae* 37a-37b).

Aed had previously murdered Diarmait mac Cerbaill, whose death-tale, *Aided Diarmaid*, describes his three-fold death.

In addition to the mythological theme of the ritual killing of kings who had broken their *geisi*, *Lebor Gabála Érenn* suggests another motive. Although a twelfth-century source, it contains mythological traditions which allegedly 'go back at least as far as the seventh century' (Doherty 1985: 47; Byrne 1973: 62 for significance), and the three-fold death does appear to contain strands of considerable antiquity. The Berne scholiasts' commentary on Lucan (I.445) describes the sacrifice of victims to the Celtic god Teutates by drowning in a vat.

The fundamental debate between 'nativists' and 'anti-nativists' is of relevance here. The 'nativists' trace the origins of early Irish literature to an orally transmitted 'tradition' derived from a pagan Celtic and Indo-European past (e.g. Dillon 1947), whereas the now ascendant 'anti-nativists' regard these texts as having a Christian social and historical context (McCone 1990: 1–28). While nativists emphasize the conservative and pagan elements within early Irish kingship (e.g. Binchy 1970; Mac Cana 1979), others place it firmly within a Christian and wider European context (Wormald 1986: 160–62; McCone 1990: 9). To anti-nativists, the three-fold death is 'an explicitly Christian narrative device' (Radner 1983: 187) within tales which insist that 'there can be no ruler's truth without Christian faith in God and proper respect for the Church' (McCone 1990: 145). For our purposes, it is significant that the three-fold death attests the *concept* of ritual regicide in early medieval Ireland.

Previous studies of ritual regicide in early medieval Ireland draw almost exclusively on mythology, rather than historical evidence. Binchy (1970: 10) could 'find no direct evidence in Irish sources of the ritual slaying of the king by his successor', while Wormald (1986: 161) noted that 'It is not easy to find unimpeachable historical evidence of ritual sacrifice.' Byrne (1973: 103) claimed that there 'is no explicit reference' to the sacrifice of a king 'for peace and a good year', in contrast to Scandinavian sources (Snorri Sturluson, *Ynglingasaga* 16, 42–43). Mac Niocaill (1972: 45) was non-commital: 'Whether in fact any king was ever deposed – and deposition usually meant, in the historical period at least, his death – because of the occurrence of plague or famine, poor corn crops or other such misfortunes, is far from clear.'

THE RECORDING OF REGICIDE IN THE ANNALS

A primary concern of early medieval Irish annals was the recording of battles, *mirabilia*, and the deaths of kings and senior clerics. According to Binchy (1970: 26), 'examination of the annals shows that the life of an Irish king was highly uncertain . . . the chances of his perishing in battle or by assassination were much more than even.' These, then, may contain evidence of early medieval Irish regicide.

The annals employ widely varying terms to record violent deaths and chronological trends in terminology are discernible. There may be a parallel with the diverse formulae used to record ecclesiastical obits, reflecting the idioms of different monastic centres (de Paor 1971: 107–08). Wormald (1986: 161, referring to *AU s.a.* 650 and 658) highlights one term: '*iugulatio* . . . might seem to have ritual associations, but it was applied to a Northumbrian king whom we know simply to have been murdered and to a Frankish king who (probably) died in his bed.' However, in addition to the disputed identification of the Frankish king (Wormald 1986: 178, n. 49; Picard 1991: 41–42), these are not representative *iugulatio* entries. The kings concerned were not Irish, and consequently the circumstances of their deaths may not have been known. Moreover, the relevant part of the entry *s.a.* 658 is '*iugulatio* of Orc Doith mac Sechnusaich, and of Conchenn mac Laidcnén, and of Flodobuir, king of the Franks.' 'Flodobuir's' name appears simply to have been appended to the list (cp. its absence from a parallel entry, *CS s.a.* 655). Here, *iugulatio* may have had no special significance.

The *Annals of Ulster* contain 218 *iugulatio* entries (usually in the abbreviated form, *iugul*). Most concern individuals, usually kings or members of royal kin-groups, but some record the *iugulationes* of two or three royals, often brothers (*AU s.a.* 595, 633, 650, 662, 692, 709, 718, 776, 809). As the *Annals of Ulster* are derived from records which, until c. 740, were compiled on Iona (Bannerman 1968; Smyth 1972: 33–41), some entries relate to *iugulationes* of Scottish or Pictish kings. Three entries record the *iugulationes* of larger groups: *generis Cathboth* (*AU s.a.* 700; a Scottish entry), *Cenél Cairpre* (*AU s.a.* 741), and the ecclesiastical *familia* of Suibne in Armagh (*AU s.a.* 718; see also *CS s.a.* 833 on the *iugulatio* of the *familia* of Clonmacnoise). *Iugulatio* entries occur between *s.a.* 483 and 982, but concentrate between the late sixth and late ninth centuries, peaking around 710. This may reflect changes in the language and idiom of recording rather than in the events themselves. Old Irish entries appear in the *Annals of Ulster* from c. 810 (Hughes 1972: 129; Dumville 1982) and increasingly from the mid-tenth century, while, in Latin entries, *occisio* begins to supplant *iugulatio* from the ninth century.

Iugulatio means 'the cutting of the throat (of)', but is usually trans-lated as 'killing' or 'slaying'. The terseness of *iugulatio* entries makes it difficult to assess their significance. Before 800, of 149 entries in the *Annals of Ulster*, eighty-six give only the victim's name, forty-one record the victim's kingship and only fifteen identify the killer, although further information is sometimes available from parallel entries in other annals (the other entries concern larger groups or unnamed victims). A typical entry is '*Iugulatio Conaill m. Feradaigh*' (*s.a.* 708). Later *iugulatio* entries are more detailed and possibly atypical. Of thirty-four ninth-century entries, ten concern senior clerics (*s.a.* 804, 813, 815, 816, 832, 838, 848, 862, 881, 889), three Vikings (*s.a.* 843, 848, 895), and one the *iugulatio* of a Viking by a Welsh king (*s.a.* 855). These entries may reflect the close links which existed between some royal dynasties and churches – the prior of Armagh, whose *iugulatio* is recorded *s.a.* 862, was also king of *Ind Airthir* – and the impact of the Vikings.

Iugulatio may therefore have had a pejorative sense, throat-cutting denoting murder and therefore illegitimate killing. This may be re-flected in the saints' lives, where McCone (1986: 5) noted that it was 'usually applied to the activities of murderous brigands'. This would also account for the use of *iugulatio* in entries recording killings of ecclesi-astics or in front of an oratory, in breach of sanctuary, and, in secular contexts, the murder of brothers, allies and subjects. This perhaps ex-plains those ninth-century entries recording the *iugulationes* of senior clerics and Vikings at a time when *occisio* was supplanting *iugulatio* in the *Annals of Ulster*. While the *iugulationes* of clerics would constitute illegiti-mate killings, Vikings were presumably undeserving of treatment within the bounds of accepted Irish convention, just as they failed to observe established Irish codes of conduct in warfare (cp. Binchy 1970: 17). Throat-cutting was all they deserved.

However, some entries hint at a deeper significance. The deaths of Tuathal Máelgarb, king of Tara (*AU s.a.* 543, 548), and Colmán Már mac Diarmata (*AU s.a.* 554, 557, 562), are recorded as *iugulationes*, as is that of Áed Dub mac Suibne (*AU s.a.* 587), whose death was recounted by Adomnán (above). Although these may be later, mythological interpola-tions, and do not mention the three-fold death, the use of *iugulatio* to record the killings of the kings of Tara may suggest ritual associations. Indeed, one element of the three-fold death appears to be described as *iugulatio* (*AU s.a.* 599, 718; see also *CS s.a.* 600):

> *Iugulatio* of Suibne mac Colmán Már . . . by Áed Sláine in Brí Dam in the Suaine, i.e. in a stream.
>
> *Iugulationes* in Loch Uaithne of the two lords, i.e. two sons of Máel Fothartaig, with their kinsman, namely Cremthann Corrach.

It is unclear whether these killings were simply drownings or, as in the three-fold death, a combination of transfixion and drowning: killing in water. *Iugulatio* may have occurred in conjunction with other forms of killing (*AI s.a.* 642): 'The burning and *iugulatio* of Máel Dúin in Inis Caín Dega' (but cp. *AU s.a.* 640 which record the burning and *iugulatio* in separate entries, and *AT*, which record the burning and drowning of two different men of this name).

Other *iugulationes* appear to have been committed in similar settings to these drownings and may be analogous. An interpolation in an entry recording the *iugulatio* of a king of Uí Failge states that it occurred 'on the brink of Loch Semdid' (*AU s.a.* 603; see also *AFM s.a.* 600; *CS s.a.* 604), while *AU s.a.* 633 (see also *AFM s.a.* 630; *CS s.a.* 634) has '*iugulatio* of the two sons of Áed Sláine by Conall mac Suibne at Loch Treitni opposite Fremainn'. These aquatic or waterside killings represent only a small proportion of *iugulationes*, but they amount to four of the nine entries recording the place of death, the others being within ecclesiastical settlements (*AU s.a.* 718, 788, 832, 850) and a *ráith* (fort; *AU s.a.* 805). This may suggest the unusual nature or circumstances of some *iugulationes*.

Terseness and linguistic ambiguity hinder the interpretation of recorded drownings: *dimersus est* is used of both accidental (e.g. *AU s.a.* 736) and deliberate (e.g. *AU s.a.* 850) drownings. The *Annals of Ulster* record no drownings of kings which are unequivocally accidental (a quatrain *s.a.* 621 is a later interpolation), while others are of uncertain status (*AU s.a.* 621, 845, 1021, 1083; see also *AFM s.a.* 742, 869). In contrast, the accidental drowning of clerics is recorded (*AFM s.a.* 744; *AU s.a.* 690, 736, 748), although deliberate drownings are also noted (*AFM s.a.* 834; *CS s.a.* 823).

The *Annals of Ulster* record five drownings between 845 and 940, two of them by the same high king of Ireland (*s.a.* 844, 850; see also *AFM s.a.* 843, 849; *CS s.a.* 845, 851):

> Turgéis was taken prisoner by Máel Sechnaill and afterwards drowned in Loch Uair.
>
> Cináed mac Conaing, king of Ciannachta, was drowned cruelly in a lake (*dimersus est in lacu crudeli*) by Máel Sechnaill and Tigernach, despite the guarantees of the nobles of Ireland, and the successor of Patrick in particular.

Another drowning is also recorded as having been perpetrated '*in lacu crudeli*' (*AU s.a.* 911; *CS s.a.* 911). One drowning features another element of the mythological three-fold death (*s.a.* 939; *CS s.a.* 939): 'Niall mac Fergail was wounded and drowned (*do ghuin ocus badud*), that is, [by] Muirchertach mac Niall.' The fifth drowning was by a Viking, Amlaíb, 'king of the foreigners' (*s.a.* 863; see also *AFM s.a.* 862; *CS s.a.* 864; *LL* 5950). Turgéis was also a Viking leader, while Cináed mac Conaing was drowned by Máel Sechnaill because he 'had allied himself with the Norse of Dublin' (Byrne 1973: 263). Although Byrne (1973: 263) claimed that drowning was 'a form of execution probably borrowed from the Norse', deliberate drownings occurred long before the Vikings reached Ireland (e.g. *AU s.a.* 599, 603, 633).

Two Scottish entries record the drowning of Picts, Talorg mac Congusso and king Talorgan mac Drostain (*AU s.a.* 733, 738; *AC s.a.* 731).[6] The drowning of kings, or others of royal blood, is recorded elsewhere in Britain. The drowning of Dungarth, *rex Cerniu* (Cornwall), is recorded in the *Annales Cambriae* (*s.a.* 875), although whether this was deliberate or accidental is unclear. Of clearer relevance is a Northumbrian annal, preserved in Simeon of Durham's *Historia Regum* (*s.a.* 791), which records how King Æthelræd of Northumbria forcibly took Oelf and Oelfwine, sons of his predecessor but one, Ælfwold, from York and had them 'miserably killed' in *Wonwaldremere* (possibly Windermere).

These entries suggest similar practices in early medieval Britain and Ireland, and highlight the victims' circumstances. Ælfwold's sons were taken captive. Talorg is described as a prisoner; five years before his drowning Talorgan mac Drostain was 'apprehended and manacled near Arcem Ollaigh' (*AU s.a.* 733). Talorgan's capture in Dál Riata may be unrelated to his later drowning by Oengus, king of the Picts. However, these events mirror Talorg's fate, and the entry recording Talorgan's capture immediately follows that of Talorg's drowning. Amongst the Picts and the Northumbrians, at least, drowning appears to have been a means of executing royal prisoners.

This may also have been the case in Ireland. A marginal quatrain recording the drowning of Cináed mac Conaing, king of Ciannachta, states that he was 'taken, bound, to a pit' (*AU s.a.* 850), while a quatrain following a parallel entry (*AFM s.a.* 849) contains the line 'Great grief that Cináed mac Conaing is in a sack approaching the pool'. Turgéis, although a Viking, was also a prisoner (*AU s.a.* 844). The drowning of royal prisoners was still practised in the twelfth century (*AU s.a.* 1121). Some victims of *iugulationes* also appear to have been prisoners. Scottish entries in the *Annals of Ulster* record the capture of Conamail mac Cano,

---

6. Of possible relevance in this context, the Glamis manse Pictish symbol stone depicts two pairs of human legs protruding from a cauldron. See Allen & Anderson 1903: 221-23.

s.a. 672 and his *iugulatio s.a.* 704, although it is unclear if he spent the intervening period in captivity.

THE INTERPRETATION OF REGICIDE

The annals' terseness hinders analysis of the socio-political contexts of, and motives behind, these regicides. This is exacerbated by the range of types and circumstances of death to which *iugulatio* is applied. Most early medieval Irish kings, it seems, died violently, usually in battle or as a result of intra-dynastic dispute. Succession was based on 'the claims of the most powerful royal [member of a royal *derbfine* (kin-group)] with the widest support' (Ó Corráin 1980: 156). For those of royal blood, succession provided the principal context for frequent private violence. This appears to be reflected in the use of the formula '*a fratribus iugulatus est*' (or similar) in the *Annals of Ulster* (*s.a.* 798, 802, 838, 849, 853, 866, 912, 936). However, intra-dynastic disputes could sometimes occur on a scale that eroded the distinction between private and public violence. Some of the resultant killings were recorded as *iugulationes* (e.g. *AU s.a.* 727): 'The battle of *Ailenn* between two brothers, the sons of Murchad mac Brain; and Dúnchad the elder having been killed (*iugulatus*), Fáelán, the younger, reigns.' Such disputes presumably underlie the annalists' concern to record the killing not only of kings but also of other members of the royal *derbfine*, *rígdomna* (literally 'kingly material'), by kinsmen [7] or their own people. [8]

Whilst the motive behind the killing of most kings and members of royal kin-groups was apparently political, the means employed suggest that these killings were more than simple executions of royal prisoners or the elimination of rival contenders to the kingship. Drowning exhibits a high degree of premeditation because of the necessity of an adequate source of water (e.g. *AFM s.a.* 907; see also *AC s.a.* 904; *AU s.a.* 911; *CS s.a.* 911):

> 'The violation of Armagh by Cernachán mac Duilgén, i.e. a captive was taken from the church and drowned (*a bhadhadh*) in Loch Cirr [Loughnashade; Warner 1988], to the west of Armagh. Cernachán was drowned (*do bhadhadh*) by Niall mac Áeda, king of the North, in the same loch, in revenge of the violation of St Patrick.'

Of particular interest in this context is that the river Calann, in which Niall mac Áeda, high-king of Ireland, 'died by drowning' (*mersione*

---

7. *AU s.a.* 979; *CS s.a.* 920. On *rígdomna* see Greene 1968: 83–84; Mac Niocaill 1968; Charles-Edwards 1971; Ó Corráin 1971.

8. *AU s.a.* 886, 922, 1007, 1017 (twice), 1019 (twice), 1074, 1097; *CS s.a.* 980.

mortuus est),[9] has to be crossed if travelling from Armagh to Lough-nashade. That the drownings were not committed in the Calann indicates that Loch Cirr was deliberately selected. In this instance at least, the presence of water alone was not significant. The choice of Loch Cirr thus suggests that, even if the primary motive of these drownings was political and/or revenge, there may have been more enigmatic undertones; the context was clearly important.

Anderson (1980: 299) labelled the Pictish drownings (*AU s.a.* 733, 738) as 'ritual' but offered no support for this, and they are 'seen by some to represent a survival of pagan ritual sacrifice' (Laing & Laing 1993: 108). Early Irish kings' sacral qualities existed within narrowly defined limits of consanguinity (Aitchison 1994b: 65–67) and 'it was the royal blood that was sacred rather than a particular individual in whose veins it flowed' (Binchy 1970: 38, see also 20). Such beliefs are likely to have accompanied anxieties concerning blood pollution. Particularly in succession disputes, bloodshed may have been perceived to dissipate those sacral qualities with which the royal blood was imbued. This may explain why not only kings but also other members of the royal *derbfine* were drowned. In addition to the challenge it posed to a kin-based social structure, this may also be why *fingal* ('kin-slaying') was regarded with such abhorrence in the early Irish laws (Kelly 1988: 127–28); a king guilty of kin-slaying could, theoretically, lose his honour price (Kelly 1988: 18) and hence his kingship.

An Old Irish Penitential (III.1b) supports the association of forms of ritual killing with fears of blood pollution. This links categories of martyrdom, two of them bloodless, with the three-fold death: 'for its [avarice's] sake men suffer red martyrdom and blue martyrdom and white martyrdom, even slaying and burning and drowning.' The penitential attempts to explain the types of martyrdom and the three-fold death 'as forms of killing which do not literally involve "shedding blood"' (Stancliffe 1982: 22, n. 5).

Within the context of public violence, specific formulae used to record regicides in the *Annals of Ulster* are particularly interesting: *iugulatus est a sociis suis* (or similar; *s.a.* 737, 823, 831, 852, 868, 883, 884, 885, 886), and *occisus est a sociis suis* (or similar; *s.a.* 895, 896, 897, 901). A typical entry (*s.a.* 885) records that 'Fiachna mac Ainfíth, king of Ulaid, *a sociis suis iugulatus est*'. Mac Airt and Mac Niocaill translated *sociis* as 'associates' or 'adherents', and the singular, *socio*, as 'companion'. Parallel entries, however, give a different perspective. The *Annals of the Four Masters* (*s.a.* 886) record that: Fiachna mac Ainfíth, king of *Ulaid*, was killed by the *Ulaid* themselves (*do mharbhadh la hUltaibh budhdhéin*)', while *Chronicum Scotorum* (*s.a.* 886) has 'Fiachna

---

9. *AU s.a.* 845; see also *AFM s.a.* 846; *AI s.a.* 846; *CS s.a.* 846; *LL* 15926–29.

mac Ainfíth, king of *Ulaid,* [was slain] by his own (*a suis*) [people]'. Five other entries in the *Annals of Ulster* are paralleled in this way.[10] Again, there are similar (Scoto-) Pictish practices (*AU s.a.* 877): 'Aed mac Cináed, king of the Picts, was killed by his own people (*a sociis suis occisus est*).'

Later entries employ *a suis* with *iugulatus* (*AU s.a.* 924, 961, 979, 992; *CS s.a.* 962), *interfectus* (*AU s.a.* 993), and the Irish *marbad* (*AU s.a.* 1007, 1023, 1065, 1095, 1096), but increasingly from *s.a.* 958 (*AU*), with *occisus*. *Chronicum Scotorum* also uses *a suis* without a verb (*s.a.* 886, 897, 923, 953, 962). The Irish equivalent, *do marbadh dia dhoinibh fein* ('was killed by his own people') is also used (*AU s.a.* 1043, 1104), as is *do marbadh a suis* (*CS s.a.* 1093). Other entries record the killing of kings *a genere suo* (*AU s.a.* 604, 1015) or *a gente sua* (*AU s.a.* 869, 979). While these entries may record the killing of kings by their own people, the annals also use *generis* as the Latin equivalent of *cenél* ('kindred'). It is uncertain how wide a social group was included in the *cenél* (Byrne 1973: 36) and unclear, therefore, whether these entries record instances of private violence of uncertain motive(s). These distinctions, however, are clearer in the *Annals of the Four Masters,* which record the killing of kings and *tighearna* ('lords', used by the *AFM* of tributary kings) by their own *derbfine* (*s.a.* 601, 962), *cenél*,[11] and *muinntir* (people).[12]

The *muinntir* entries describe the killing of kings by their own subjects, as do entries such as 'Congalach mac Gairbíth, *tigernach* of *Conaille Muirthemne,* was slain by the Conaille themselves'.[13] Another entry clearly distinguishes between royal kin-group and subjects, indicating the involvement of both in a regicide (*AU s.a.* 864): 'Tadc mac Diarmaid, king of Uí Cheinnselaig, was treacherously killed by his own kinsmen and his people (*a fratribus suis & a plebe sua*).' Here we not only see public violence directed against kings, but the formulaic recording of these regicides suggests that this practice belonged to a recognized pattern of behaviour.

A possible context for a king's killing by his own subjects may be provided by his sacral role in ensuring fertility within his *túath* (petty kingdom), achieved through his own physical well-being and observance of a code of conduct, including *geisi*. This guaranteed the maintenance of those sacral properties, such as *fír flathemon* ('the prince's truth' or

---

10. *AU s.a.* 823 and *AFM s.a.* 822; *AU s.a.* 884, *AFM s.a.* 882 and *CS s.a.* 885; *AU s.a.* 895 and *AFM s.a.* 891; *AU s.a.* 896 and *CS s.a.* 897; *AU s.a.* 897 and *AFM s.a.* 897.

11. *s.a.* 833, 897 (twice), 941, 950, 965, 985, 999, 1006, 1057, 1059, 1096.

12. *s.a.* 582, 798, 822, 898, 991, 992, 999, 1000, 1003, 1034, 1039, 1040, 1050, 1051, 1100; see also *AU s.a.* 942; *CS s.a.* 1002.

13. *AFM s.a.* 908 (see *AU s.a.* 912 for a parallel entry), *AFM s.a.* 882, 960, 1005, 1016 (twice), 1018 (twice), 1034, 1065, 1077, 1083, 1102; *AU s.a.* 1003, 1017, 1102 for similar entries.

'the justice of the ruler'),[14] perceived as fundamental to the *túath*'s prosperity. According to *Audacht Morainn* (17–21), a *speculum principis* of c. 700:

> 'It is through *fír flathemon* that abundance of great tree-fruit of the great wood are tasted.
>
> It is through *fír flathemon* that milk-yields of great cattle are maintained [?].
>
> It is through *fír flathemon* that there is [?] abundance of every high, tall corn.
>
> It is through *fír flathemon* that abundance of fish swim in streams.
>
> It is through *fír flathemon* that fair children are well begotten.'

Conversely, the actions of an unjust king revealed his *gáu flathemon* ('the falsehood of the prince'), bringing defeat and disaster on his *túath*, and the blighting of land and livestock. These themes are expressed in several *specula principum*, such as *The Instructions of Cormac* (no later than c. 850) and the seventh-century *On the Twelve Abuses of the World*, in which the unjust king, the ninth abuse, brings defeat and disorder upon his kingdom and storms that destroy crops, fruit and fishing. *The Battle of Mag Mucrama*, preserved in a ninth-century version but containing elements which may date to around 700, is typical of mythological tales recording an unjust king's fate:

> 'After that [the king's false judgement] he [Lugaid mac Con] was a year in the kingship of Tara and no grass came through the earth, nor leaf on tree, nor grain in corn. So the men of Ireland expelled him from his kingship for he was an unlawful ruler (*an-flaith*)' (*Cath Maige Mucrama* 66)

The annals contain few entries recording the expulsion of kings (*AU s.a.* 696, 699, 713; *CS s.a.* 710) and it is apparent that these did not involve regicide, ritual or otherwise (*pace* Mac Niocaill 1972: 45). That Old/Middle Irish has a word for 'unkinging', *athrígad*, suggests that expulsion from kingship did occur in early medieval Ireland, although it is used only rarely, in late contexts (*AT s.a.* 1064; *AU s.a.* 1064).

Hughes (1972: 56) suggested that 'It would be interesting to work out from the annals just how often a run of bad luck had fatal consequences for a king'. However, the laconic nature of these entries and the annalists' disinclination to record, or at least explicitly link, both cause and effect means that the annals are of little help here. Nevertheless, one juxtaposition of entries suggests that kings were killed for a perceived failure to live up to their sacral responsibilities (*AU s.a.* 992):

---

14. On which see Dillon 1947: 250–51; Binchy 1970: 10; Wagner 1970: 8–9; Byrne 1973: 24–25, 115, 187–89; Aitchison 1994b: 59–67.

'Cléirchéne mac Máel Dúin, King of Uí Echach, was killed by his own people (*a suis iugulatus est*).
'A great mortality of people, cattle and bees throughout Ireland this year.'

The entries' ordering may be irrelevant because they are not always listed chronologically under a specific year (Hughes 1972: 109-10; Dumville 1985: 84).

Other possibly significant associations of annalistic entries occur. The first entry *s.a.* 699 (*AU*) is 'The cattle mortality broke out in Ireland on the Kalends of February in Mag Trega in Tethba'. The fifth entry under the same year concerns the expulsion of Aurthuile ua Crunmáel, while the sixth entry is 'Famine and pestilence prevailed in Ireland for three years, so that man ate man.' Furthermore, two entries below the entry recording the expulsion of king Fogartach ua Cernaich of Brega (*AU s.a.* 713) occurs 'Great drought', although a parallel entry (*AFM s.a.* 713) says that Fogartach was expelled by Fergal mac Máel Dúin, king of Aileach. External involvement in some expulsions may still indicate the exploitation of internal weaknesses by hostile kingdoms.

However, the annals also contain many records of natural disasters that are not juxtaposed with the killing or expulsion of kings. It should be noted that, in early medieval Europe, natural disasters were often regarded as omens, including portents of a king's death (e.g. Gregory of Tours, *LH* IV.9, IV.51, V.18, VII.11), and ecclesiastical writers on the continent may have seen a divine link between them. A similar association may have resulted in such events being juxtaposed in some Irish annals. Natural disasters may, moreover, be expected to have heightened stress within an early medieval Irish kingdom, which, in turn, could have exacerbated intra-dynastic tensions. These could have resulted in a king's killing. Thus any link between, for example, famines and acts of regicide, need not have been direct.

Another motive for regicide appears to have been retribution for the violation of sanctuary, even though the plunder and destruction of churches was commonplace in early medieval Ireland (Lucas 1967). Cernachán mac Duilgén was drowned for drowning a cleric from Armagh (*AC s.a.* 904; *AFM s.a.* 907; *AU s.a.* 911; *CS s.a.* 911), while another king, Branacán ua Máeluidir was drowned for plundering a shrine (*AFM s.a.* 1021; *AU s.a.* 1021). Another king, Cináed mac Conaing, was drowned for unspecified acts against the church (*AFM s.a.* 849; *CS s.a.* 851).

Drowning, therefore, appears not only to have been a means of killing royal prisoners, but also a punishment for kings who had violated sanctuary. However, although the mode of killing employed in some of these regicides was possibly 'ritual', the close links between some dynasties and churches suggests that the motives which lay behind them may have been political. The identity of the regicides is therefore important. One entry, linking Congalach mac Gairbíth's slaying by his own people to his killing of an abbot (*AFM s.a.* 908; *AU s.a.* 912), indicates that some kings did meet their deaths as a result of their lack of due respect for the church (cp. McCone 1990: 145).

CONCLUSION

While mythology attests the *concept* of ritual regicide in early medieval Ireland, the historical evidence does not support the practice of regicide on purely ritual grounds. Most regicides appear to have occurred within unambiguously private or public contexts, as an integral part of intra-dynastic succession struggles or in the course of warfare between kingdoms. However, the annals do record several regicides which possess enigmatic elements, distinguishing them from the contexts in which kings were usually killed. These features include the drowning of kings, the killing of kings by their own people, and the juxtaposition of a small number of annalistic entries recording regicides and natural calamities. The interpretation of any of these as ritual regicides rests upon whether the ritual element is identified as the circumstances and mode of death and/or the motive(s) behind it. Motivation poses particular problems because of the sources' terseness and the notions of sacrality inherent within early medieval Irish concepts of kingship. For example, the elimination of rivals for the succession constitutes undeniably political motivation but, given the perceived sacral qualities of the royal blood, it is possible that opponents were killed in a manner dictated by ritual requirements. This may also have been the case with the killing of royal prisoners. Indeed, throughout early medieval Europe public executions, such as that of Brunechildis in Francia in 613 (*Fredegar* IV.42), often involved a strong element of ritual, in part as justification.

In particular, the drowning of kings and other royals provides an interesting link between the private, public and ritual elements of early medieval Irish regicide. Drowning, it seems, was practised in both private and public domains. It is recorded as a means of killing captives of royal blood who presumably included potential rivals to the kingship, and Irish and Viking kings captured in battle. A sacral dimension, reflecting concerns about blood pollution, has been suggested for drownings, often as an element of the three-fold death. However, the sources' brevity does not permit the identification of common elements in, and motives behind, royal drownings in either private or public contexts.

Although the killing of kings by their own people may have had a ritual dimension, the annals record neither the motive(s) behind these regicides nor the mode(s) of death employed. While an unjust or oppressive king's deposition constitutes a political act, the sacral dimension of Irish kingship may have invested it with further significance because a king's conduct was perceived to determine his possession of the metaphysical properties essential to the *túath*'s well-being. A king's killing by his own people, therefore, *may*, in some cases, have represented an act of propitiation in order to avert or end the misfortunes perceived to result from his misdeeds. This, however, cannot be confirmed from the historical evidence available, although it appears to be supported by *tecosca ríogh* and mythological sources.

Indeed, this interpretation contradicts the view that 'the tribal kingdom . . . and the sacral tribal king with his taboos, had become things of the past long before the year 800' (Ó Corráin 1972: 31; cp. Mac Niocaill 1972: 47). In contrast, the entries recording the killing of kings by their own people are dated mainly *after* AD 800. The significance of this is unclear. It may stem from the circumstances of recording, or reflect a rising level of violence within society. The latter is an indicator of social and political upheaval, perhaps a result of increasing political centralization and/or the impact of Viking raids and settlement. Alternatively, these entries may attest the recrudescence of archaic social practices, possibly including ritualized regicide, during times of political stress. As McCone (1990: 136) notes in the case of *geisi*, 'even unreal or ostensibly outmoded features may provide a means of articulating very real contemporary concerns', and this may have applied to other aspects of early medieval Irish kingship. In this manner, historical reality may have emulated mythology.

Politics and ritual were inextricably linked in early medieval Ireland and one must be wary of over-emphasizing one at the expense of the other. In recent studies the emphasis has swung towards the political character and powers of kingship. However, mythology attests the enduring concept of sacral kingship, within which ritual regicide appears to have been perceived as an integral element, throughout the early medieval period. The annals record a number of regicides, both public and private, that appear to have had a political motive, the elimination of rival contenders for the kingship or of political enemies and captives. What seems likely, however, is that at least some of these may have had a ritual dimension and that this is most readily apparent in those entries recording the drowning of royal captives and members of royal kingroups and the killing of kings by their own people.

BIBLIOGRAPHY

Primary Sources

Adomnán, *Vita S. Columbae*: A. O. Anderson & M. O. Anderson (eds & trans.), *Adomnán's Life of Columba* 2nd edition (Oxford, 1991).

Aided Diarmaid: S. H. O'Grady (ed. & trans.), *Silva Gadelica (I-XXXI): A Collection of Tales in Irish with Extracts illustrating Persons and Places* (London 1892), pp. 76–88.

Aided Muirchertaig meic Erca: W. Stokes (ed. & trans.), 'The death of Muirchertach Mac Erca', *Revue Celtique* 23 (1902), pp. 395–437; L. Nic Dhonnchadha (ed.), *Aided Muirchertaig meic Erca*, Medieval and Modern Irish Series 19 (Dublin, 1964).

Annales Cambriae: E. Phillimore (ed. & trans.), 'The *Annales Cambriae* and Old-Welsh genealogies from Harleian MS 3859', *Y Cymmrodor* 9 (1888), pp. 141–83.

Annals of Clonmacnoise: D. Murphy (ed.), *The Annals of Clonmacnoise: Being Annals of Ireland from the earliest Period to AD1408. Translated into English AD 1627 by Conell Mageoghan.* (Dublin, 1896).

Annals of the Four Masters: J. O'Donovan (ed. & trans.), *Annala Ríoghachta Éireann: Annals of the Kingdom of Ireland by the Four Masters, from the Earliest Period to the Year 1616* 2nd edition 7 vols (Dublin, 1856).

Annals of Inisfallen: S. Mac Airt (ed. & trans.), *The Annals of Inisfallen (MS Rawlinson B503)* (Dublin, 1951).

Annals of Tigernach: W. Stokes (ed. & trans.), 'The Annals of Tigernach', *Revue Celtique* 16 (1895), pp. 374–419; no. 17 (1896), pp. 6–33, 119–263, 337–420; no. 18 (1897), pp. 9–59, 150–97, 267–303.

Annals of Ulster: S. Mac Airt & G. Mac Niocaill (eds & trans.), *The Annals of Ulster (to AD 1131). Part 1: text and Translation* (Dublin, 1983). See also W. M. Hennessy (ed. & trans.), *Annala Uladh. Annals of Ulster, otherwise Annala Senait: a Chronicle of Irish Affairs from AD 431 to AD 1540.* vol. 1, *AD 431–1056* (Dublin, 1887).

Audacht Morainn: F. Kelly (ed. & trans.), *Audacht Morainn* (Dublin, 1976).

Berne Scholiasts, *Comentary on Lucan*: I. Zwicker (ed.), *Fontes Historiae Religionis Celticae (Fontes Historiae Religionis ex Auctoribus Graecis et Romanis,* fasc. V.1) (Berlin, 1934).

Book of Leinster: R.-I. Best, O. Bergin, M. A. O'Brien. & A. O'Sullivan (eds), *The Book of Leinster. Formerly Lebar na Núachongbála,* 6 vols (Dublin, 1954–83).

Cath Maige Mucrama: W. Stokes (ed. & trans.), 'The Battle of Mag Mucrime', *Revue Celtique* 13 (1892), pp. 426–74; S. H. O'Grady (ed. & trans.), *Silva Gadelica (I-XXXI): a Collection of Tales in Irish with Extracts Illustrating Persons and Places* (London, 1892), pp. 347–59; M. O. Daly (ed. & trans.), *Cath Maige Mucrama: The Battle of Mag Mucrama* (Irish Texts Society 50) (London, 1975).

Chronicum Scotorum: W. M. Hennessy (ed. & trans.), *Chronicum Scotorum: a Chronicle of Irish affairs from the Earliest Times to AD 1135: With a Supplement Containing the Events from 1141 to 1150* (London, 1866).

Fredegar's Chronicle and its *Continuations*: B. Krusch (ed.), *MGH SRM* II (Hanover, 1888), pp. 1–193; J. M. Wallace-Hadrill (trans.), *The Fourth Book of the Chronicle of Fredegar with its Continuations* (London, 1960).

Giraldus Cambrensis, *Topographia Hiberniae*: J. J. O'Meara (trans.), *Giraldus Cambrensis (Gerald of Wales): The History and Topography of Ireland (Topographia Hiberniae)* rev. edition (Portlaoise, 1982).

Gregory of Tours, *Histories*: B. Krusch and W. Levison (eds), *MGH SRM* I, part 1 (Hanover, 1951); L. Thorpe (trans.), *Gregory of Tours. History of the Franks* (Harmondsworth, 1974).

Lebor Gabála Érenn: R. A. S. Macalister (ed. & trans.), *Lebor Gabála Érenn: The Book of the Taking of Ireland* 5 vols (Irish Texts Society 34, 35, 39, 41, 44) (London, 1938–56).

Old Irish Penitential (MS Royal Irish Academy 3 B 23): E. J. Gwynn (ed. & trans.), 'An Irish penitential', *Ériu* 7 (1914), pp. 121–95.

Pseudo-Cyprianus, *De Duodecim Abusivis Saeculi*: S. Hellmann (ed.), *Pseudo-Cyprianus, De Duodecim Abusivis Saeculi* (Texte und Untersuchungen zur Geschichte der altchristlichen Literatur 3.4) (Leipzig, 1910).

Simeon of Durham, *Historia Regum*: T. Arnold (ed.), *Symeonis Monachi. Opera Omnia* vol. 2 (Rolls Series) (London, 1885); J. Stephenson (trans.), *Simeon of Durham. A History of the Kings of England* reprinted (Lampeter, 1987).

Snorri Sturluson, *Ynglingasaga:* E. Wessén (ed.), *Snorri Sturluson: Ynglingasaga* (Nordisk Filologie 6) (Norstedts/Stockholm, 1952).

Tecosca Cormaic: K. Meyer (ed. & trans.), *The Instructions of King Cormac Mac Airt* (Todd Lecture Series 15) (Dublin, 1909).

Secondary Bibliography

Aitchison, N. B., 1994a. *Armagh and the Royal Centres in Early Medieval Ireland: Monuments, Cosmology and the Past* (Woodbridge).

—— 1994b. 'Kingship, society, and sacrality: rank, power, and ideology in early medieval Ireland', *Traditio* 49: 45–75.

Allen, J. R., & Anderson, J., 1903. *The Early Christian Monuments of Scotland* (Edinburgh).

Anderson, M. O., 1980. *Kings and Kingship in Early Scotland* 2nd edition (Edinburgh).

Bannerman, J., 1968. 'Notes on the Scottish entries in the early Irish annals', *Scottish Gaelic Studies* 11: 149–70, reprinted in J. Bannerman, *Studies in the History of Dalriada* (Edinburgh, 1974), pp. 9–26.

Bhreatnach, M., 1982. 'The sovereignty goddess as goddess of death?', *Zeitschrift für celtische Philologie* 39: 243–60.

Binchy, D. A., 1958. 'The Fair of Tailtiu and the Feast of Tara', *Ériu* 18: 113–38.

—— 1970. *Celtic and Anglo-Saxon Kingship* (O'Donnell Lectures for 1967–68) (Oxford).

Breatnach, R. A., 1953. 'The lady and the king: a theme of Irish literature', *Studies: An Irish Quarterly Review of Letters, Philosophy and Science* 42: 321–36.

Byrne, F. J., 1967. 'Seventh-century documents', *Irish Ecclesiastical Record* 108: 164–82.

—— 1973. *Irish Kings and High Kings* (London).

Carney, J., 1955. *Studies in Irish Literature and History* (Dublin).

Charles-Edwards, T. M., 1971. 'The heir-apparent in Irish and Welsh law', *Celtica* 9: 180–90.

Dalton, G. F., 1970. 'The ritual killing of the Irish kings', *Folklore* 81: 1–22.

de Paor, L., 1971. 'The aggrandisement of Armagh', in T. D. Williams (ed.), *Historical Studies 8: Papers Read before the Irish Conference of Historians, 27–31 May, 1969* (Dublin), pp. 95–110.

Dillon, M., 1947. 'The archaism of Irish tradition', *Proceedings of the British Academy* 33: 245–64.

—— 1951. 'The taboos of the kings of Ireland', *Proceedings of the Royal Irish Academy* 54C: 1–36.

—— 1973. 'The consecration of Irish kings', *Celtica* 10: 1–8.

Doherty, C., 1985. 'The monastic town in early medieval Ireland', in H. Clarke & A. Simms (eds), *Comparative History of Urban origins in Non-Roman Europe: Ireland, Wales, Denmark, Germany, Poland and Russia from the Ninth to the Thir-*

teenth Century (British Archaeological Reports, International Series 255) (Oxford), pp. 45–75.

Dumville, D., 1982. 'Latin and Irish in the *Annals of Ulster*. AD 431–1050', in Whitelock *et al.* (eds) 1982: 320–41.

—— 1985. 'On editing and translating medieval Irish chronicles: the *Annals of Ulster*', *Cambridge Medieval Celtic Studies* 10: 67–86.

Ford, P. K. (ed.), 1983. *Celtic Folklore and Christianity: Studies in Memory of William W. Heist* (Los Angeles).

Fortes, M., 1962. 'Ritual and office in tribal society', in M. Gluckman (ed.), *Essays on the Ritual of Social Relations* (Manchester), pp. 53–88.

Frazer, J. G., 1890. *The Golden Bough: a Study in Magic and Religion* (London).

Greene, D., 1968. 'Some linguistic evidence relating to the British church', in M. W. Barley & R. P. C. Hanson (eds), *Christianity in Britain, 300–700: Papers Presented to the Conference on Christianity in Roman and Sub-Roman Britain* (Leicester), pp. 75–86.

—— 1979. 'Tabu in early Irish narrative', in H. Bekker-Nielsen, P. Foote, A. Haarder, & P. M. Sorensen (eds), *Medieval Narrative: A Symposium* (Odense), pp. 9–19.

Guyonvarc'h, C.-J., 1983. 'La Mort de Muirchertach, fils d'Erc, texte irlandais du très Haut Moyen Age: la femme, le saint et le roi', *Annales* 38: 985–1015.

Herbert, M. 1992. 'Goddess and king: the sacred marriage in early Ireland', in L. D. Fredenburg (ed.), *Cosmos 7, Women and Sovereignty* (Edinburgh), pp. 264–75.

Hughes, K., 1972. *Early Christian Ireland. An Introduction to the Sources* (London).

Jackson, K., 1940. 'The motive of the threefold death in the story of Suibhne Geilt', in J. Ryan (ed.), *Féil-sgríbhinn Eóinn Mhic Néill: Essays and Studies Presented to Professor Eoin Mac Neill* (Dublin), pp. 535–50.

Kelly, F., 1988. *A Guide to Early Irish Law* (Early Irish Law Series 3) (Dublin).

Laing, L., & Laing, J., 1993. *The Picts and the Scots* (Stroud).

Lucas, A. T., 1967. 'The plundering and burning of churches in Ireland, 7th to 16th century', E. Rynne (ed.), *North Munster Studies. Essays in Comemoration of Monsignor Michael Moloney* (Limerick), pp. 172–229.

Macalister, R. A. S., 1919. 'Temair Breg: a study of the remains and traditions of Tara', *Proceedings of the Royal Irish Academy* 34C: 231–399.

Mac Cana, P., 1956. 'Aspects of the theme of king and goddess in Irish literature', *Études Celtiques* 7: 76–114, 356–413.

—— 1979. '*Regnum* and *sacerdotium*: notes on Irish tradition', *Proceedings of the British Academy* 65: 443–79.

McCone, K. R., 1986. 'Werewolves, cyclopes, *díberga*, and *fíanna*: juvenile delinquency in early Ireland', *Cambridge Medieval Celtic Studies* 12: 1–22.

—— 1990. *Pagan Past and Christian Present in Early Irish Literature* (Maynooth Monographs 3) (Maynooth).

Mac Niocaill, G., 1968. 'The "heir designate" in early medieval Ireland', *Irish Jurist* 3: 326–29.

—— 1972. *Ireland before the Vikings* (Dublin).

Ó Concheanain, T., 1974. 'The act of wounding in the death of Muirchertach mac Erca', *Éigse* 15: 141–44.

Ó Corráin, D., 1971. 'Irish regnal succession: a reappraisal', *Studia Hibernica* 11: 7–39.

—— 1972. *Ireland before the Normans* (Dublin).

—— 1980. Review of Byrne 1973, *Celtica* 13: 150–68.

Ó Cuív, B., 1965. Review of Nic Dhonnchadha (ed.) 1964, *Éigse* 11: 146–50.

—— 1974. 'The motif of the threefold death', *Éigse* 15: 145–50.

O'Leary, P., 1988. 'Honour-bound: the social context of early Irish heroic *geis*', *Celtica* 20: 85–107.

O'Rahilly, T. F., 1946. 'On the origin of the names *Érainn* and *Ériu*', *Ériu* 14: 7–28.

Picard, J.-M., 1991. 'Church and politics in the seventh century: the Irish exile of King Dagobert II', in *id.* (ed.), *Ireland and Northern France. AD 600–850* (Blackrock), pp. 27–52.

Radner, J. J., 1983. 'The significance of the threefold death in Celtic tradition', in Ford (ed.) 1983: 180–200.

Rees, A., & Rees, B., 1961. *Celtic Heritage: Ancient Tradition in Ireland and Wales* (London).

Sayers, W., 1992. '*Guin agus crochad agus gólad*: the earliest Irish threefold death', in C. Byrne, M. Harry, & P. Ó Siadhaill (eds), *Proceedings of the Second North American Congress of Celtic Studies, Halifax 1989* (Halifax, N.S.), pp. 65–82.

Smith, R. M., 1927. 'The *speculum principis* in early Irish literature', *Speculum* 2: 411–45.

Smyth, A. P., 1972. 'The earliest Irish annals: their first contemporary entries, and the earliest centres of recording', *Proceedings of the Royal Irish Academy* 72C: 1–48.

Stancliffe, C., 1982. 'Red, white and blue martyrdom', in Whitelock *et al.* (eds) 1982: 21–46.

Wagner, H., 1970. 'Studies in the origins of early Celtic civilisation I: Old Irish *FÍR* "truth, oath"', *Zeitschrift für celtische Philologie* 31: 1–45.

Warner, R., 1988. 'Loch Cirr/Cúl Chíre', *Emania* 4: 36.

Whitelock, D., McKitterick, R., & Dumville, D. (eds), 1982. *Ireland in Early Mediaeval Europe. Studies in Memory of Kathleen Hughes* (Cambridge).

Wormald, P., 1986. 'Celtic and Anglo-Saxon kingship: some further thoughts', in P. E. Szarmach (ed.), *Sources of Anglo-Saxon Culture* (Studies in Medieval Culture 20) (Kalamazoo), pp. 151–83.

CHAPTER 6

Violence in eleventh-century Normandy: feud, warfare and politics

Matthew Bennett

'Feud: A state of bitter and lasting mutual hostility; especially such a state existing between two families, tribes or individuals, marked by murderous assaults in revenge for some dreadful insult or wrong' (*Shorter O. E. D.* 1986: 744).

Much violence in the early medieval period is ascribed to feuding. Periods of 'feudal anarchy' are represented as producing a plethora of feuds. Few historians use the phrase 'feudal anarchy' nowadays, but they do talk about periods of anarchy and continue to use the term 'The Anarchy' to describe the reign of King Stephen of England (1135–1154; e.g. King: 1994: 1–5). The 'anarchy' of Duke William of Normandy's early reign, when he was still a minor and until he secured his position (1035–1053), forms the starting point for this essay. What it will suggest is that violent political activity, extending even to warfare, has been mis-read as feud, and that violence was an accepted part of the lifestyle of the military classes in a way that modern historians seem reluctant to

---

1. What follows has been delivered in various forms, most fully to the Early Medieval Seminar at the Institute of Historical Research. I am grateful to two of the seminar's convenors, Professors Janet Nelson and John Gillingham, for their helpful criticisms of, and disagreements with, my argument. Professor Robert Bartlett has been kind enough to allow me to use unpublished material from one of his lectures. Dr Jean Dunbabin also provided helpful criticism. Above all I owe an enormous debt of gratitude to Dr Kathleen Thompson who has helped me to avoid errors of fact and interpretation, and enabled me to finish this project. I must also thank my editor for his patience.

grasp.[2] Furthermore, in the absence of a proactive superior authority capable of resolving or at least assuaging a dispute then recourse to violence was common. But these were not feuds nor was the result anarchy, rather a self-regulating system operating in much the same way as the wars of princes, but on a smaller scale. I shall also be arguing that attempts to regulate violence, through the Peace and Truce of God and ducal ordinance, recognized this essential truth.[3]

DEFINING 'FEUD'

First, what is meant by feud? A standard dictionary definition such as heads this paper places the emphasis upon the taking of life in response to a perceived injury. But recent historical studies of the subject make more nuanced distinctions. Paul Hyams distinguished between 'strong' and 'weak' feud in medieval England.

> 'By "strong" [he means] the ritual of blood vengeance in forms prescribed by custom, and even, on occasion, recognized by formal law . . . By following proper procedures, avengers wished to proclaim higher motives than lay behind conventional crimes . . . Where wrong to an individual was perceived also as an injury to the honour of some group to which he belonged, thus shaming himself and them into action . . . But the "weak" sense turns on the emotions motivating actions that hostile observers and public law may term criminal' (Hyams 1991: 6).

Icelandic sagas and law have provided a rich field for study of feud. From this evidence, William Miller's definition is: 'Localised hostility between groups which have a collective responsibility to act on matters concerning honour and which involves turn-taking and score-keeping during which responses are appropriate to the status of a victim and for which there are mutually acceptable means of reconciliation [which may be only temporary]' (Miller 1990: 180–81). Both Hyams and Miller place

---

2. In contrast, Barthélemy (1993) is convinced that historians misread secular society through the distorting mirror of clerical chronicles and charters. See esp. pp. 298–300, 858, 1006–07. I owe thanks to Dr Jean Dunbabin for drawing my attention to this work, whose arguments seem to support my own. See also Barthélemy 1992, esp. his analysis of 'public order' contrasted with 'private warfare', wrongly in his opinion pp. 772–74. These references came to hand after this text was completed.

3. Bisson (1994: 14) reluctantly admits as much when he says: 'Violence became institutionalised within as well as outside the regalian legal order.' Although here he is making an assumption about 'regalian legal order' and goes on to talk about the 'tension between old public order and the new vassalic régime' (1994: 24). Finally (1994: 410) he is critical of Barthélemy for 'flying in the face of the evidence', which is a matter of opinion.

an emphasis upon honour in what anthropologists call 'shame' cultures.

Yet Peter Sawyer concluded that: 'The bloodfeud flourished best, not in the real world, but in the fictions of poets, storytellers and lawyers.' He doubts, for example, 'that there was much kin solidarity; some of the most disruptive conflicts were within families, not between them.' Rather, 'throughout medieval Europe . . . revenge and compensation were accepted as legitimate. In threatening one and obtaining the other, kinsmen were normally expected to help, but the support of lords often proved more effective . . . What is interesting is not so much feud itself but the great and growing means for settling disputes and preventing violence from being too disruptive' (Sawyer 1987: 36, 27, 35).

Stephen White (1986) has investigated the resolution of feud in the Touraine c. 1100. He gives various definitions of feud, ranging from 'relations of mutual hostility among intimate groups in which a resort to violence is anticipated on both sides' or 'the state of lasting mutual hostility which exists between groups where one part has suffered injury from the other (usually by homicide) and retaliation by means of recip-rocal killing is sought' to J. M. Wallace-Hadrill's 'working definition' of supposed early medieval Frankish blood-feuds: 'We may call (feud) first, the threat of hostility between kins; then, the state of hostility between them; and finally; the satisfaction of their differences and a settlement on terms acceptable to them both.' White is critical of the term 'private wars' since 'during our period, revenge often considered 'private' by modern scholars was something other than a disorderly and dis-reputable alternative to 'public' prosecution by *a state that barely existed*' (White 1986: 199).[4] White provides seven case studies from Noyers charters to exemplify monastic mediation. They are highly formulaic, but several interesting features emerge. Killing did not necessarily pro-voke a feud, although it might later be represented as having done so (sometimes one party was not able to respond even if it wished to do so). Killings were more likely to provoke what White terms a feud (though see Introduction: 24, for reservations) when there was already conflict between the killer's and the victim's kin. White cites the con-cluding scene in the late-twelfth-century *chanson de geste, Raoul de Cambrai*, where the clergy stage an impressive ceremony to bring the warring parties together. Perhaps such dramatic occasions actually worked (White 1986: 208–09, 262–63).

Finally, Robert Bartlett has drawn attention to the term 'mortal enmity'. It is preferable to vague concepts such as feud since it has a

---

4. The italics are mine. White hits upon an important point here, recognizing the existence of dispute resolution by military action at a level below that of the rulers of eleventh-century French 'principalities'; but his last phrase is rather overstated. (See his n. 21 for further investigation of the terms 'state' and 'anarchy'.)

clear and legally definable status, expressing a situation of declared hostility in which the parties will attempt to harm one another. Most of his evidence is twelfth-century or later, but two examples are close enough to eleventh-century Normandy to be worthy of comparison.[5]

'FEUDS' DURING DUKE WILLIAM'S MINORITY

When Duke Robert I died in far-off Nicea in western Asia Minor, whilst returning from pilgrimage to Jerusalem (1035), William, his illegitimate heir, was only seven years old. His authority as ruler of the duchy could not be said to have been secure until, at the earliest, 1047, when with the assistance of the King of France he defeated a rebellion in open battle at Val-ès-Dunes; or, more realistically, after he had broken the power of his cousin, Guy of Burgundy in 1051, his uncle, William of Arques, in 1053 and another uncle, Archbishop Malger, in 1054.

After the death of Robert, archbishop of Rouen, the young duke's great-uncle in 1037, William was left without a powerful protector; rather his potential protectors did not survive for long. Count Alan III of Brittany died in October 1040, allegedly of poison. His successor, Count Gilbert of Brionne was murdered a few months later at the instigation of Archbishop Robert's son. Another supporter, Turchetil de Neufmarché, was killed about the same time. William's steward, Osbern, was even assassinated in the ducal bedchamber whilst at his family holdings of Vaudreuil. According to Orderic Vitalis, his mother's brother had to sleep in the same room and on occasion spirited the boy away in the middle of the night for fear of attack (OV VII.82).[6] To David Douglas this was an expression of feudal anarchy: 'Longstanding feuds among the secular aristocracy were re-opened, and each crime was made the occasion for further bloodshed.' Douglas goes on to talk about 'private war' and 'unspeakable crimes', identifying castles as a characteristic feature of this disorder. These were 'family strongholds' from which to 'conduct hostilities against each other, and defend themselves against the onslaught of their enemies' (Douglas, 1964: 40–41). Admittedly, he was writing thirty years ago. Yet William's most recent biographer, David Bates, is in general agreement that

> 'clearly the young William was quite unable to control events even within his own household, let alone stop the feuds which were taking place throughout the rest of Normandy. . . . These were times of quite dramatic violence; in a crime which shocked even

---

5. I am extremely grateful to Professor Bartlett for allowing me to read and draw material from his unpublished article: '"Mortal Enmities": the legal aspect of hostility in the Middle Ages'. See below: 136–37.

6. Admittedly, Searle sees this story as a literary flourish in William's supposed death-bed speech (Searle 1988: 248–49, 324, n. 22).

contemporaries, the southern Norman lord William Giroie attended a wedding feast given by one of his lords, William de Bellême [William Talvas], and left cruelly disfigured, without ears, eyes and genitals' (Bates 1989: 26–27).

Douglas draws his purple passage from William of Jumièges, whose *Gesta Normannorum Ducum* was completed about 1070. However, he may have written the following passage in the 1050s; good contemporary evidence:

> 'During his [William's] m:.ority many of the Normans, renouncing their fealty to him, raised earthworks in many places and constructed for themselves the strongest fortifications. When they felt themselves sufficiently secure, a number of them immediately rebelled, stirred up sedition, and inflicted cruel destruction upon the whole country. In such a storm of disorder, indeed, while Mars rampaged, whole troops of warriors lost their lives in vain, as when Hugh de Montfort and Walkelin [de Ferrières] fought and both were killed' (*GND* VII: 115–16). [7]

What is absent from this passage is any indication that the men described were pursuing a feud; they were engaged in warfare. Rather they are seen as rebels against the duke, the representative of peace and good order.

Eleanor Searle prefers to see such conflict as part of the 're-arrangements' of property which took place whenever ducal authority was weak. This is how she reads 'The "Anarchy" of the 1030s' (a chapter heading) in her book *Predatory Kinship and the Creation of Norman Power 840–1066*. In fact, such 're-arrangements', or attempted 're-arrangements' could take place when there was a mature and active duke like Robert I in power (Searle 1988: 179–89).[8] Searle cites the example of Count Gilbert of Brionne who attempted to take advantage of his neighbours, the Giroie family (probably in the early 1030s). Despite having seven sons, Giroie left only two of fighting age when he died. Orderic Vitalis was very well informed about the Giroie family since they were the founders of his abbey of St Evroult. This is his account of what transpired:

> 'When Giroie died most of his sons were minors, only Arnold and William having assumed knighthood (*milites erant*). So Gilbert count of Brionne, who was chafing to enlarge his estates, judged

---

7. It is worth noting that the *GND* is a composite work including interpolations by the twelfth-century chroniclers Orderic Vitalis and Robert of Torigny, a point stressed by Van Houts, its most recent editor.

8. Robert's position may have been weakened by his defiance of his elder brother Richard III in 1026, followed by Richard's convenient death soon after. There was suspicion of poisoning (Searle 1988: 150).

himself strong enough to attack the boys with armed force, and
attempted to take Montreuil from them. They, however, were able
to make a stand against him in open battle with a strong company
of kinsmen and dependants; and after driving them back with
heavy loses they soon wrested the town of Le Sap from him. Duke
Robert succeeded in reconciling them, and, taking pity on the
orphans who had shown such splendid courage he persuaded
count Gilbert to let them keep Le Sap as a pledge of peace' (OV
II: 24).

As Orderic's language makes plain, this is a fairly straightforward
piece of territorial aggrandizement by Gilbert, who was seeking to
exploit the youth of his neighbours. The Giroie brothers then employed
the traditional mechanisms of their society to defeat him. Kin and
dependants rallied round and even took property away from Gilbert.
They were so successful in their warfare that the duke's negotiated
peace permitted them to keep Le Sap. Unfortunately, Gilbert now had a
grievance. He had not only failed to win lands from the Giroie family
but had lost some of his into the bargain.

Orderic continues: 'Finally, some years later the count turned against
the seven sons of Giroie and tried to recover Le Sap; and he met death
through their courage and daring, though he was closely guarded by his
own men' (OV II: 24).

By around 1040, count Gilbert had become the guardian of the
young Duke William the Bastard, which meant that the was in a position
to reverse Duke Robert's decision to award Le Sap to the Giroie family.
Not surprisingly he decided to take it back. To get at the details of what
follows we have to turn from Orderic's *Ecclesiastical History* to his interpolations in the work of William of Jumièges, where he describes how
Gilbert was killed at the instigation of Ralph de Gacé the son of Archbishop Robert (the former ducal guardian). But the tool Ralph used was
Robert fitzGiroie, the fourth son of the Giroie family. This begins to
look less like feud and more like politics. What could be more natural
than an alliance between Ralph, the duke's cousin and son of the former
regent, who clearly wished to gain control of the young duke, and the
Giroie family whose earlier gains, made with ducal blessing, were threatened now that Gilbert controlled the young duke and exercised on his
behalf ducal authority?

Unfortunately, another Giroie brother, Fulk, was riding in the entourage of the duke's guardian at the time when Robert was involved in
the assassination of the count. The plot between the aspiring ducal
guardian Ralph and the Giroie family, who feared Gilbert's acquisition
of ducal authority, had the unfortunate effect of killing a fitzGiroie as
well as Gilbert, but with a quiverful of sons this was not a great price to
pay. Orderic gives no hint of how he felt about the death of Fulk fitz-

Giroie, brought about by his brother; not in the *Ecclesiastical History*, anyway. In his interpolations into William of Jumièges, and in the context of listing the murders described by David Douglas, he cites the death of Count Gilbert as a crime (*GND* VII: 94), but he does not say exactly what sort of crime, and there is no sense of the Giroie being entitled to his life as a part of a feud. This is because it was not part of a feud at all.[9] It was not a private murder which might require some act of revenge, but a clear political assassination.

Let us now return to the gory incident I described earlier – the horrible mutilation of William fitzGiroie at the hands of William Talvas (the son of William of Bellême). This might appear a clear case for the exaction of retribution under any notion of feud. In the previous generation the families had co-operated. Giroie and William of Bellême had united to defeat an attack by Herbert Wakedog, count of Maine. In fact, this had been the occasion of the introduction of Giroie into the duchy through his marriage to a daughter of Heugon who held estates close to Giroie's on the march with Maine. Indeed, according to Orderic's interpolations into William of Jumièges, William Talvas owed his lands to the support of William fitzGiroie (*GND* VII: 108). So his attack upon his vassal was unexpected as it was savage. Or was it?

William fitzGiroie was also a vassal of Geoffrey of Mayenne (a dependant of the count of Maine). In around 1044, William found himself defending the castle of Montaigu for Geoffrey and against William Talvas. So to William Talvas, William fitzGiroie was a contumacious vassal, even though he had been doing loyal service to another lord.[10] When William Talvas captured Geoffrey, William fitzGiroie arranged his freedom by agreeing to the destruction of the castle, which seemed to have secured a victory for William Talvas. But what may have rankled is that Geoffrey then built another castle at St-Céneri-sur-Sarthe. William fitzGiroie may also have held this too, as his brother Robert did later (Thompson 1985: 219; Searle 1988: 181–82). Naturally, Orderic censures the attack on William fitzGiroie and asserts that William Talvas' son, Arnulf, rebelled against him and deprived his father of his fiefs (*GND* VII: 112).

The truth is difficult to fathom, but Dr Kathleen Thompson has recently devised a plausible scenario. The expulsion probably took place in 1048. Arnulf was dead by 1049, and his father may have recovered his land in 1052. His daughter, Mabel, married Roger de Montgommery,

---

9. It may be that it was the deceitful nature of the attack on Gilbert *nil mali suspicans*, which made the killing criminal. Chibnall points out that Orderic does not make the same charge in his *Ecclesiastical History* and that the changes made in this interpolation are clearly visible in the Rouen ms. (OV vol. 2, pp. 94–95 n. 3).

10. Chibnall draws attention to William Giroie's 'ambiguous position', and accepts that c. 1044 is a quite possible date for the event (OV III: 26–27).

the duke's cousin who was to become one of his chief supports, his wealth bolstered by the Bellême inheritance. William Talvas survived to 1060 (Thompson 1985: 222). His actions against William fitzGiroie were those of a lord seeking to set an example to other recalcitrant castellans. No feud seems to have resulted, the Giroie lost out and the Mont-gommery benefited.

We return to the issue of how Duke William survived his minority. For Douglas (1964) it was a result of the intervention of his overlord, Henry, King of France. This *deus ex machina* interpretation may reflect the attitude of an older generation of scholars to 'central authority'. In contrast, Eleanor Searle stresses the importance of kin solidarity. It does seem that William was protected by his relatives (who also sought to dominate him). First, he had to rely upon his fraternal kin, but this was dangerous as both his cousin Guy and his uncle William had good claims to his position (Searle 1988: 176–77, 219–21). This is probably why Duke Robert had chosen different guardians before his departure on pilgrimage; seeking to establish checks and balances within the power structures of Normandy.

So William turned to his mother's family. They were not as low-born as was formerly (and romantically) supposed. Herleva's father, Fulbert, was not a tanner, but a prominent Rouen merchant and Duke Robert's chamberlain (Van Houts 1986; *GND* VII: 96). After Robert's death she soon married Herluin de Conteville, a prominent lord of central Normandy, and quickly produced two half-brothers who became polit-ical figures in the 1050s. Odo was made bishop of Bayeux in 1049, and his younger brother acquired the county of Mortain in 1055/56. They were to become invaluable allies. But until such time, William also had the support of his cousins: Roger de Montgommery II and William fitz-Osbern, upon whose loyalty and competence he came to rely. Allen Brown and Eleanor Searle alike write affectingly of the close bonds forged between these young men in their career in arms. She (like me) plays down the threats to the young duke (Brown 1969: 38; Searle 1988: 197, 205). For, in Peter Sawyer's words 'Kinship was most important in matters of inheritance, and the revenge of kinsmen was more likely when family interests, especially in property, were threatened' (Sawyer 1987: 35).

William fitzOsbern provides an example of feud *not* being pursued by a close blood-relative. Both Douglas and Searle note that William did not take revenge upon his father's killer. Rather, he 'allowed' his steward to do it (Douglas 1964: 42; Searle 1988: 196).[11] Was this because he was not motivated by the concept of feud? (It could be, of course, that by

---

11. Orderic's interpolations into the *GND* describe this as a night-raid upon the murderer's hall in which he and his 'accomplices' were sleeping and quickly despatched, 'as they deserved' (*GND* VII: 94) cf. n. 6.

not committing the act himself he sought to avoid getting involved in potential feud.) Yet this is pretty much what happened as Duke William asserted himself. He fought to control his duchy and eliminate rival claimants. But he was not vindictive towards them. They were exiled not imprisoned or killed (see Introduction: 11 for reasons, and cp. Nelson, above: 97).

Recently, Professor John Gillingham has commented on the dangers of eleventh-century Norman political life. He argues that the descriptions of violent deaths of notables in two periods, first in the years before William established himself as duke and later during the rule of his son Robert Curthose (1087–1106), indicate a significant shift of behaviour. While before, such men were murdered, by the end of the century they died gloriously in battle, mourned by their chivalrous opponents, because: 'Between the two twenty-year periods of political anarchy aristocratic opinion in Normandy had turned against the blood feud' (Gillingham 1994: 36). Even with this proviso, the expectation of aristocrats to settle their property disputes by military action remains.[12]

A nobleman's life was dangerous. Of the seven Giroie sons, four died violent deaths simply learning their trade: one was killed by a wrestling fall, another by a lance in weapon practice, another died when returning from a raid on nearby church lands and Fulk, in Count Gilbert's body-guard (Searle 1988: 181). William was another victim of violent politics, as we have seen; whilst Robert died defending St-Céneri against Duke William in 1060, allegedly of poison (OV II: 78–80, 79 n. 3).[13] Orderic speaks quite matter-of-factly about men dying in the course of 'military life' in Book III, when speaking of the Giroie brothers. He says that they were; *'strenui et dapsiles, in militia callidi et agiles, hostibus terribiles, sociisque blandi et affabiles'* ('valiant and courtly; in war nimble and cunning, to their enemies a scourge, to their friends gracious and gentle'; OV II: 24–25). It is worth commenting that in this little rhymed passage Orderic is here presenting an epitome of chivalry in form close to that found in vernacular material. Orderic was writing a tract for the first quarter of the twelfth century, of course, but his view springs from the reality of noble competition in political life (OV II: xv).

There were some who chose to escape this life. Orderic cites Robert de Grandmesnil, who became a monk at St-Evroult in 1050 (and later abbot) after serving as Duke William's squire for five years and being knighted. But, 'He often called to mind the perils of earthly warfare

---

12. I am extremely grateful to Prof. Gillingham for allowing me to see his work at proof stage. He argues that blood feud *was* practised in Normandy in the first half of the eleventh century, and that the development of chivalry transformed attitudes to violence (Gillingham 1994).

13. The fifth son, Ralph also enjoyed a military career although being educated for the spiritual life, hence his name 'Ill-Tonsured' (OV III, 28).

endured by his father and many like who had met the death they intended for others whilst bravely attacking their enemies. For on one occasion [about 1040] his father Robert fought with Roger de Tosny against Roger de Beaumont, and in that conflict, Roger [de Tosny] together with his sons Elbert and Elinant was slain, and Robert received a mortal wound in his bowels. . . . Deeply moved by this tragedy, Robert set his mind on fighting better warfare' (OV II: 40–41). Not everyone viewed earthly warfare in this way though. In his old age Roger de Beaumont boasted that his destruction of the Tosny was a useful and loyal service to the duke (Searle, 1988: 186; OV IV: 206). Warfare was endemic and it was not particularly frowned on by rulers – as long as it was directed to their own ends.

The dispute between the Beaumont and Tosny families has long been seen as a classic example of 'feud'. Roger de Tosny's father had been a loyal supporter of Richard II and held the important castle of Tillières-sur-Avre as a result. Roger still held the castle, and 'Besides Tosny and nearby settlements, he held Conches and its huge forest, south-west of Evreux and in all probability lands further west, stretching to the Risle' (Searle 1988: 185–86). This made him one of the most powerful men in the Evrecin. He had as an ally Robert de Grandmesnil, holding lands in the Lieuvin and French marches near Argentan, and who was married to Giroie's daughter Hawise. Eleanor Searle points out de Tosny's possible weakness by not allying with other Norman families. She suggests that he was isolated. She then goes on to see the resulting events and bloodshed as feud (Searle 1988: 185–86).[14] But the connection is not so certain. Certainly there was competition and conflict between Humphrey de Vieilles, supported by his son, Roger de Beaumont, and Roger de Tosny. It resulted in the encounter in which de Tosny was killed. According to David Bates (1982: 101), 'In retaliation, Roger de Clères, a Tosny follower, slaughtered Robert, another of Humphrey's sons.' This is emotive language predicated upon the existence of feud. Again it is explicable within the context of a struggle for power and possessions in the region. Eventually the victory went to those who were better established and could possibly call upon ducal support. Searle recognizes as much when she identifies Tosny as 'other', by which she means someone who could not claim to be part of Gunnor's kin. De Tosny is alleged to have been scornful of William's illegitimacy. This comes from Orderic; but he is a poor guide, having both the benefit of hindsight and a clear bias against the losers (Searle 1988: 185–86). For what happened, essentially, was that 'incomers' – the Giroie and Tosny –

14. Searle does go on to say that the killings of Gilbert de Brionne, Robert de Grandmesnil and Roger de Tosny 'had a more purposive look, as if a coalition were ridding the area of rivals and expanding at the expense of their enemies' (Searle 1988: 185–86).

were eventually overcome by a group within the duchy. When Tosny and Grandmesnil banded together, it was to form an alliance with, momentarily at least, a common aim. If the stakes were higher in the sense of the loss of life, this was because the competitors could not exercise the same claims as ducal relatives to clemency in defeat.

So, in these case studies from the years of the Norman 'anarchy', the apparent feuds disintegrate upon closer scrutiny. We are dealing with a society where the kin-group played a vital part in the acquisition of assets and retention of wealth. Rivalry between families was endemic, and at the slightest opportunity kin-groups sought to advance their own fortunes at the expense of their neighbours. They had, moreover, readily at their disposal the violent means to do so. In such a situation some families profited and some did not, and those who suffered setbacks might have more than one reason for hostility against another group. The Girioe family clearly had a series of grudges against the Bellême family and their feelings found their way into Orderic who can scarcely find a good word to say about the descendants of William Talvas. But the grievances of the Giroie were not personal quarrels which could be resolved in series of tit-for-tat revenge killings. They were products of the society described, in which violence might easily break out between kin-groups, and they remained essentially grievances.

CONCLUSIONS: ENMITY, 'PRIVATE WAR' AND THE LIMITATION OF VIOLENCE

So far I have stressed that what can be seen happening in Normandy are expressions of politics and warfare, not feud. Crucial to the issue of feud seems to be the significance of mortal enmity – open hostility – identified by Robert Bartlett, declared by formal defiance (*diffidatio* in Latin; *desfi* in Old French).[15] This appears most dramatically in the twelfth-century popular literature of the *chansons de geste*. In the *Chanson de Roland* (ll. 2000–02), Ganelon declares his enmity by defying Roland; and when a wounded and confused Roland strikes Oliver at Roncesvals his companion is bewildered that he has not been defied (Whitehead 1978: 65). Bartlett draws on the well-known story of *The Murder of Charles the Good, count of Flanders*, in 1127. Burchard of the Erlembald clan was the murderer (Galbert XII.12). His act sprang from an enmity developed not against the count but against Thancmar, a neighbour, who had appealed for Charles' intercession. Burchard is condemned by Galbert of Bruges for his covert actions against his enemy, in concert with his kin. 'He pretended in public that he grieved to see his nephews

---

15. Gillingham (1994: 48–49) sees the *diffidatio* as novel in the England of 1138; but does admit that the word was used in Aquitaine a century earlier. These statements are not mutually exclusive, of course.

engaged in so much strife and killing although he himself had incited them to all these crimes' (Galbert X.9). [16]

Bartlett's second example is in a Norman context, although admittedly from Italy, and describes a dispute between Robert Guiscard and his younger brother Roger, in 1062. Roger declared his opposition by fortifying a castle and summoning his vassals. According to Geoffrey Malaterra's chronicle (II.21.xxxvi), Roger refrained from attacking his brother for forty days. I know of no evidence for such regulated violence in the Normandy of the young Duke William. It may that similar conditions prevailed, but that contemporaries do not refer to them in the same way. Certainly there are later – royal – pronouncements by King William and his sons which may have had some precedents (see below). More palpably, there was the peace legislation employing the Peace and Truce of God.

The Peace of God had been introduced into northern France at the Treaty of Compiègne in 1023 and was sponsored by Richard II of Normandy as part of his peace-making between King Robert and Odo of Blois. David Bates sees its first appearance as part of a firm 'political programme' when William instigated a Peace and Truce just before or after his victory at Val-ès-Dunes in 1047 (Bates 1982: 176; cf. Brett 1994: 131–32). It was then reinforced by church councils, specifically at Lisieux in 1064 and Lillebonne in 1080. This supposedly meant that warfare conducted by anyone except ducal forces was restricted to engagements permitted only from Monday to Wednesday and also set out unacceptable targets: church personnel and property, merchants, peasants, widows and orphans. The use of Peace Councils is often portrayed as an admission of governmental weakness in the face of 'private' warfare. I suggest that it should be seen as supplementing ducal authority and enabling means of resolution of conflicts. Certainly it has been linked to William's wider policy of ensuring stability. David Bates points to the duke in 1075 forbidding private vengeance in cases of murder, unless the victim had been either a father or son (Bates 1989: 154; Gillingham 1994: 36). [17] But he also stresses William's political skill and energy rather than any legal guidelines as the reason for his successes. So, before he reached mature authority, William the Bastard tolerated – had to tolerate – 'illegal' castle-building despite the Norman chroniclers' assertion that the duke destroyed such castles after 1047. He preferred to put in charge of them loyal men, or men newly loyal after a period of

---

16. Bartlett points out that Burchard's crime is not his violence against his neighbour, but his disregard of established rules. The chronicler Walter of Thérouanne draws attention to Burchard's devastation of his enemy's lands as contrary to the restraints of *guerra* (war).

17. His source is two annals, or rather variants of one, and not any 'legislation' assigning the declaration to Fécamp, Easter 1075 (Bates 1982: 164 and n. 69).

exile and expropriation of their estates, such as Nigel of St-Sauveur (Bates 1982: 167).

As regards the issue of 'private' warfare, I am not sure that this term is actually helpful. The twelfth-century evidence about *guerra* deals with the nature of the conflict, with rulers seeking to control burning and the destruction of slow-growing crops: vines and orchards. Orderic comments on Henry I's severe punishment of Ivo de Grandmesnil for 'waging war (*guerra*) in England and burning the crops of his neighbours, which is an unheard-of crime in that country and can be atoned only by a very heavy penalty' (OV VI: 18). Yet it is interesting that Orderic refers to the kingdom of England as 'that country' but passes no comment on the situation in the duchy of Normandy. This may be significant.[18]

Towards the end of the century, prohibitions on violence appear in the *Consuetudines et Justicie*, supposedly of William I, reaffirmed by William II and Duke Robert at Caen, in 1091 (Haskins 1928: 277–84). The document is said to 'demonstrate a very strong continuity from Carolingian notions of authority' (Bates 1982: 163) and is worthy of a brief review. The first clause (1) forbids any man taking charge of his enemy (*inimicus*) at court, or travelling to or from it, which David Bates reads as an injunction against blood-feud. It could be seen as more of a precaution against political opportunism, though, reminiscent of the miserable fate of the atheling Alfred whilst in the hands of Earl Godwin in Danish-ruled England, in 1036 (*ASC* C(D) 1036, Whitelock 1961: 103–04). Similar restrictions were enjoined for service in the host (2). If an affray occurred: 'the instigator made amends according to the measure of the misdemeanour' (3). The penalties mentioned in the first two clauses are unspecified sums of money.

The *Customs* go on to forbid the construction of fortifications, destruction of mills, ambushes, challenges leading to ambushes, mutilation (unless a criminal was discovered *in flagrante delicto*), house-breaking, burning and rape, together with the harassment of merchants or pilgrims against whom the aggressor had a grudge. Bates (1982: 163) comments: 'Violence as such was not condemned; but many forms of it were.' Like Orderic's condemnation of the murders during William's minority, it is unexpected assaults, without open declaration of enmity which are most forbidden. The provisional nature of the *Customs* is epitomized by the penultimate passage, which states that only the most essential points had been written down (allowing for the recovery or invention of other rights later).

There follows a fourteenth clause, perhaps more in hope than ex-

---

18. This may be read as part of the propaganda attack on Robert Curthose identified by Gillingham, contrasting his inability to restrain disorder with his sterner brother King Henry (Gillingham 1994: 35).

pectation: 'No one was allowed to capture a man in war, or ransom him, nor take money from a war or a fight, nor take away arms nor a horse' (Haskins 1928: 284). What is being forbidden here is pursuit of the knightly pastime of war for profit, not feud. It may even refer to tournament, that watered-down version of true military activity. How much was enforceable in 1091, let alone forty of fifty years earlier, is open to doubt.

Karl Leyser (1991: 108) has ventured to turn Clausewitz's famous phrase on its head and suggest that medieval politics were the continuation of warfare. In this context, there is nothing really unusual about the conflicts described above. Historians, with the usual problem of hindsight, have tended to see eleventh-century events through the eyes of twelfth-century evidence. Even without the difficulties of the minority there was not as much distinction to be made between the count/duke of Normandy and his comital vassals in the 1030s – or even the 1090s – as there was by the time Henry I had established his rule. When members of the ruling comital family were engaged in competition to exercise that authority then warfare was inevitable. The problems that Robert Curthose faced in the 1090s serve to illustrate that proposal (Gillingham 1994: 34). Without a truly fearsome representative of central authority then warfare was endemic amongst those families capable of exercising a military potential. If the disputes between the great barons in Stephen's reign are seen in the same light then there is no need to create contrasting images of them as warlords or peace-seekers. Pragmatic politics required them to be both. War was one type of dispute resolution to be tried along with many others, and it was one which the military classes found congenial. But to represent it *all* as 'feuding', is really to miss the point.

Bibliography

Primary Sources

Anglo-Saxon Chronicle: D. Whitelock, D. Douglas & S. Tucker (trans.), *The Anglo-Saxon Chronicle: A Revised Translation* (London, 1961).

Galbert of Bruges: J. B. Ross (trans.), *The Murder of Charles the Good, Count of Flanders by Galbert of Bruges* (New York, 1957).

Geoffrey Malaterra's Chronicle: E. Pontieri (ed.), *De rebus gestis Rogerii Calabriae et Sicilae comitis et Roberti Gusicardi ducis fratis eius* (Bologna, n. d.).

Orderic Vitalis: M. Chibnall (ed. & trans.), *The Ecclesiastical History of Orderic Vitalis* (6 vols) (Oxford, 1968–80).

William of Jumièges: E. Van Houts (ed.), *The Gesta Normannorum Ducum of William of Jumièges, Orderic Vitalis and Robert of Torigni* (2 vols) (Oxford, 1992, 1995).

Secondary Bibliography

Barthélemy, D., 1992. 'La mutation féodale a-t-elle eu lieu?', *Annales* 47: 767–77.

—— 1993. *La Société dans la comté de Vendôme, de l'an mil au XIVe siècle* (Paris).

Bates, D., 1982. *Normandy before 1066* (London).

—— 1989. *William the Conqueror* (London).

Bisson, T., 1994. 'The feudal revolution', *Past and Present* 142: 6–42.

Brett, M., 1992. 'Warfare and its restraints in England 1066–1154', in *'Militia Christi' e Crociata nei secola XI-XIII, Miscellanea del Centro di studi medioevali* 13: 129–44 (Milan).

Brown, R. A., 1969. *The Normans and the Norman Conquest* (London).

—— 1984. *The Norman Conquest* (Longman Documents in Medieval History 5) (London).

Douglas, D. C., 1964. *William the Conqueror* (London).

Gillingham, J. B., 1994. '1066 and the introduction of chivalry into England', in G. Garnett and J. Hudson (eds), *Law and Government in Medieval England and Normandy; Essays in Honour of Sir James Holt* (Cambridge), pp. 31–55.

Haskins, C. H., 1960. *Norman Institutions* (New York).

Hyams, P. R., 1992. 'Feud in medieval England', *The Haskins Society Journal* 3: 1–21.

Kay, S., 1994. *Raoul de Cambrai* (Oxford).

King, E., 1994. *The Anarchy of King Stephen's Reign* (Oxford).

Leyser, K., 1993. 'Early medieval warfare', in J. Cooper (ed.), *The Battle of Maldon: Fiction and Fact* (London), pp. 87–108.

Millar, W. I., 1990. *Bloodtaking and Peacemaking: Feud, Law and Society in Saga Iceland* (Chicago).

Sawyer, P., 1987. 'The bloodfeud in fact and fiction', *Tradition og Historieskrivining* (Acta Jutlandica 63.2) (Humanistik serie 61) (Aarhus), pp. 27–38.

Searle, E., 1988. *Predatory Kinship and the Creation of Norman Power 840–1066* (Los Angeles).

Thompson, K., 1985. 'Family and influence to the south of Normandy in the eleventh century: the lordship of Bellême', *Journal of Medieval History* 11: 215–25.

Van Houts, E., 1986. 'The origins of Herleva, mother of William the Conqueror', *English Historical Review* 101: 399–404.

White, S. D., 1986. 'Feuding and peace-making in the Touraine around the year 1100', *Traditio* 42: 195–263.

Whitehead, F., 1942. *La Chanson de Roland* (Oxford).

CHAPTER 7

Violence and late Viking Age Scandinavian social order

Guy A. E. Morris

The famous association of Vikings with violence stems almost entirely from non-Scandinavian records, concerning Viking activities outside Scandinavia. This paper examines the use of violence to assert social and political order within Scandinavia itself. Any account or interpretation of violence essentially depends upon the ethical and moral attitudes of those involved. In the tenth and eleventh centuries Christianity only spread gradually in Scandinavia, sporadically encouraged by great lords (Sawyer 1987). Thus the Vikings differed from the rest of western Europe, and to analyze their use of violence within Scandinavia, it is best to use their own perspective.

THE PROBLEMS OF 'SKALDIC' VERSE

This is made difficult by a general lack of written source material for Viking Scandinavia itself. Even the available non-Scandinavian texts are severely limited in scope, and the sources from within Scandinavia were mostly written down after the end of the Viking age, surviving in manuscripts of the mid-thirteenth century at the earliest. The nature and problems of this later source material have been much considered elsewhere.[1] This writer's research has concentrated on the 'skaldic' verses contained within the earliest sagas, and the *Snorra Edda* (an early thirteenth-century treatise on this poetry by one of the saga authors, Snorri

---

1. Andersson 1985 and Clover 1985 give a general survey.

Sturluson), which were used as a form of contemporary evidence (Frank 1985: 162; Andersson 1985: 222; Whaley 1991: 75–77). It is difficult to corroborate such assumed authenticity; the period of at least two centuries between composition and the earliest surviving manuscripts obscures the verses' transmission. However, analysis is possible when based on variations between manuscripts, as preserved in their diplomatic edition (Jónsson (ed.) 1967).[2] Occasionally the texts show distinctly different readings of verses between and amongst their earliest manuscripts. The rigidly defined verse structure (Frank 1978: ch. 1) limits variation as long as the verse was understood by those using it. Strong indications suggest that the verse texts evolved separately from the saga texts until the early fourteenth century, with more than one tradition, and location of preservation.[3]

Further analysis of the verses is complicated by difficulties in establishing authenticity, and by the literary analysis which has been applied to them (Frank 1985: 166–69; Poole 1987: 266; 1991: 3–7). Various attempts have been made to utilise the poetry, but even those that recognise that some re-assessment is needed have failed to take it far enough back to basic editing principles to produce a historically acceptable, and useful, source.[4] We must further limit the verses for analysis to those in the certain early thirteenth-century texts: the 'literary' corpus is potentially distorted by its inclusion of romantic, mythical, and idiosyncratic verses, many from sagas of minimal authenticity (Frank 1985: 172–73).

The 'historical' selection covers over three quarters of the surviving verses that are probably dated to the Viking Age, about 900 in all, and a greater percentage of *dróttkvætt*, 'court-speech', poetry of particularly strict metre and rhythm. It has proved necessary to take each verse from its diplomatic text, with all variations from the historical sagas' earlier texts,[5] and the *Snorra Edda*, and re-evaluate its reconstruction, edition and translation. The resolution of manuscript conflicts, unusual or incomprehensible syntax or vocabulary, and particularly the solution of interpretational difficulties, all involve much subjective judgement, based on personal, or established, theories of literary criticism (Frank

---

2. Though Jónsson's accuracy may be criticised (Frank 1985: 162–64), there is little alternative except the manuscripts themselves, in Reykjavik.

3. Possibly including Norway, as well as Iceland.

4. Sawyer (1993: 36–37), quoting Frank (1985: 174); however it is invalid simply to dismiss skaldic poetry because it is supposedly only eulogistic: apart from the fact that it frequently is not (Frank 1985: 181–83, and this article), this has not been, and should not be, an excuse to avoid analysis of any potential source material.

5. Manuscripts K, F, 39, 47 (*Heimskringla*), 2, 4, 61, 68, 75a (*Oláfr saga helgi*), B, A, (*Fagrskinna*), Mk (*Morkinskinna*), R, W, T, U, 748 (*Snorra Edda*), variations listed for each verse in Jónsson 1967.

1985: 166–69; Poole 1987: 166). The validity of any is extremely variable, from a historical perspective, which requires, for example, the establishment of manuscript seniority and analysis of variations. Unclear, conflicting, ambiguous, or even incomprehensible readings must be acknowledged rather than resolved or obscured for the sake of translation. Textual emendations, or other readings based on hypothetical forms, syntax or vocabulary must be limited to those clearly proven from the poetry itself. The removal of all but the most acceptable forms of resolution produces a historically acceptable rendition, which is not often pretty.[6]

This provides a basis for analysis of Viking attitudes to violence. The surviving verses mostly concern the Norwegian kings from Harald *Gráfeldr* (c. 960) onwards, but coverage is patchy until the reigns of Magnus the Good and Haraldr Sigurðarson (c. 1034–1066). Their wars against the Danish kings and activities within Norway are extensively covered. In Norway, Haraldr seems to have had problems with individuals called *þegnar*, as reported by the poet Þjóðolfr Arnórson (ÞjóðA 3.18; 3.19; 3.20; 3.21; 3.24; 3.25).

KINGS, LORDS AND RETINUES: VIOLENCE AGAINST SUBJECTS AT HOME AND ABROAD

These verses indicate action both against individual leaders (ÞjóðA 3.25), and a broader class of lords (in position to act tyrannously). Harald's action was ferocious, and though justified by treason, Þjóðolfr was not convinced of its righteousness. Arnórr Þórðarson's version however is favourable:

> 'Acting like his kin, the *Yngvi* burnt Uplanders' houses; people paid for the lord's anger, who is famous amongst men; a strong generation did not want to attend to profit-adorner, before they were steered into danger; gallows benefited from the lord's fury' (Arn 6.7; see also Arn 6.8).

There is repetition: both poets mention Harald's attacks on the

---

6. The translations given include frequently used general translations ('lord', 'ruler', 'retainer', 'retinue'), as used by the main editors of skaldic verse (Jónson 1973, Kock 1923–44, Aðalbjarnson 1941–51) for some terms more specifically analyzed in unpublished research, so as to give a 'correct' translation without forcing unknown conclusions on the reader. Almost all skaldic verses have two distinct halves – for many only one half survives, and the pairing of some halves is uncertain. Translations are not given of both halves unless they are clearly associated and relevant (in many verses both halves contain much the same subject matter), nor of sections where editorial or manuscript difficulties prevent the establishment of a reading (though some variant readings are included, indicated by brackets, or '/'). The abbreviations used to denote the verses (see Abbreviations, above: viii–ix) are those established by the main editors.

Danish islands, use the word *öld* ('generation'), and refer to Uppland, Heiðmark and Raumarike, the burning of property, and severe physical punishment. The victims are *land-karlar* ('slaves to the country'), *þegnar*, *búendr*, *her-togi* (*her-*'leader') and *rekkar*. They have local power, and Harald's attack is based on the destruction of property, and the punishment of certain individuals. Exceptionally in these verses, there is little mention of a clash of arms, just destruction. Harsh punishments are recorded elsewhere, usually for robbery and piracy, but the 'crime' here is more that of treason, non-cooperation with Harald.

There are many references to lords defending land, as in Ott 1.6, 'battle-brave defends the land; few kings may so', Hfr 3.11, 'who defends broad lands', or as a source of 'order', such as Gldr 2, 'death-knower to din-outcast thieves', Sigv 11.13, 'thief's reverser', and Arn 2.12 and 2.17, where 'thieves' oppressor' is used. Hanging was a typical treatment for 'undesirables', and in Hál 7, 'gallows drooped on the headland with that inlets' dealer'. Sigv 12.4 also refers to this as a punishment for raiding.

This protection of property was a duty derived from mastery over land (Sigv 12.5; 12.6). Violence was used to protect those within a lord's territory, which might conversely be defined as the area he was capable of protecting. When Harald directed just this sort of violence against those within his territory, it was on the pretext that they had abused and rejected his lordship: his violence within his territory was 'legitimized' by their treason, which made them a threat to his territory, and they were dealt with as such.

Sigv 12.6 also shows that the status of *víkingr* was not desirable, primarily because of the 'crime' of *rán*; it is notable that in the early verses of *Bersöglisvísur*, when Sigvatr referred to the good features of Magnus's predecessors, praised Oláfr Tryggvesson for defending 'hard lords' inheritances' (Sigv 11.3), 'I believe that the people, and Earls, chose rightly in that they gave the peace of Oláfr to mens' inheritances' (Sigv 11.5), and that 'Hákon, who fell at Fitjar, promised much good and (resolved *þegnars*' war's *rán*)/(firmly punished war's *rán*) when men liked him' (Sigv 11.4). *Rán* also described Knut's activities against England (Sigv 10.9): he did not have to commit much *rán* before he gained a territory of his own. [7]

This can be further examined in *Bersöglisvísur*, presented to Magnus the Good, Harald's predecessor, on the grievances against certain of Magnus's activities of a group which appears similar to Harald's later 'victims'.

> 'Who eggs you to hew at *þegnars*' farms, martial one? It is presumptuous for a lord to make gain inside the land; no one has so before advised a young ruler: I think *rán* is loathesome to your *rekkar* – *herr* is angry' (Sigv 11.11).

---

7. Note also Ott 2.16, Ott 2.17, Ott 2.18, Edað 5, and Hál 7.

'It is said, where such can be spoken, that my lord seizes *þegnars'* *óðal* property; *búendr* are angry at officials – a decent man, who has to hand over his own father's leaving to a king's reeve, as the result of the outcome of a struggle, may therefore consider it *rán*' (Sigv 11.14; see also Sigv 11.8).

The 'victims' are again *buendr, búmenn, rekkar, þegnar,* and *herr.* In later times *búendr* and *þegnar* could not, as here, be the same. The words vary sufficiently to indicate that *búendr* did not yet have its later meaning, and a hybrid exists in the form *bú-þegn. Bú-* compounds indicating a 'farm'-holder (*bú* is used for farm or small settlement) occur sixteen times in the poetry, for the first nine in the form *búendr,* then as *bú/-menn/-and/menn/manna,* which sudden variability in usage suggests variation in meaning or interpretation. With one exception the early verses fall into a pattern, wherein *búendr* are villagers, and the (militarily inadequate) victims of warfare. In *Bersöglisvísur* (Sigv 11.13) the first compound, *bú-menn,* men from *bú-* (farmsteads), appears and there is a change in status as well as terminology in this period: Sigv 12.20, on St Óláfr's defeat at Stiklarstaðir, in the late 1020s, describes them further:

'People brought about the lord's death: rock's tree's terrors had not before then known *búandr*-men's strength, nor *hersir's,* when wound-fire's trees felled such a ruler, as Óláfr was thought to be, in battle – many worthy men lay in gore' (Sigv 12.20).

Some *búendr* were now militarily competent, and so needed differentiation. This memorial poem on St Óláfr could not have been composed until early in Magnus's reign, not long before *Bersöglisvísur,* in which *bú* and *búendr* were the poem's main concern. It is notable that *herr,* 'army'[8] is applied to both sides in *Bersöglisvísur's* dispute, some distinction being achieved by the compound with *land.* The *þegns* are *land-karls* according to Þjóðolfr, so the term *land* is probably used to denote a general status. The *þegns* can thus be *herr,* and distinct from the *land-herr,* though one is also a *her-togi,* 'army-leader'.

A further twist is inherent in the term *rekkar.* In Hfr 3.2, on his ship, the Long Serpent, Óláfr Tryggvesson 'did not bid his *rekkar* to think of flight; *þjóð sessa* live by this speech of strength': *rekkar* equal *þjóð sessa,* 'people of benches', amongst *drengir,* retainers. The term probably indicates a quality, rather than a particular status, but Sigvatr's lament, 'I went past the lord's retinue's *rekkars'* game; my spirit was not improved; . . .: I recalled myself how my well-reputed lord had also often formerly played with us at his men's *óðal* tofts' (Sigv 13.24), indicates a further link between the retinue's function, and its retainers' inherited property.

---

8. In all verses it has a firmly military situation, and frequently seems to be a collective for military individuals.

Such references are also found on Norwegian runic inscriptions, at Sele (NR236),[9] *eign* and *oðal* are property, as in *Bersöglisvísur*. More interesting is the inscription at Oddernes church[10]: 'Eyvindr made this church, the godson of St Oláfr, on his *oðal*'. Though the raiser cannot be identified with certainty, and the stone probably post-dates the establishment, this emphasises the importance of *oðal*, and St Oláfr's use of alliances with major nobles, here featuring Christianity. The status of *óðal* cannot be defined in legal terms from the verses, but it clearly has significance, in association with *þegns*: 'Men's lord, you took into your ownership *þegns' oðal*, all Norway; . . .' (Arn 2.8; see also ÞjóðA 3.9; Ott 2.19).

Rule of an area is thus defined as a relationship whereby a lord controls men of the *þegn* status, who possess *oðal*, defined in *Bersöglisvísur* as heritable property, and was the subject of dispute: Magnus took it, by *rán*, 'illegal seizure'. When the *þegns*, the property's owners did not 'attend on' Harald, he attacked their property. Magnus tried to ignore the *þegns*, in favour of closer counsellors, but Harald utilized their dependence on property to coerce them. Harald first shared Norway with Magnus, and then ruled alone. Magnus apparently backed down after *Bersöglisvísur*, but Harald was in a very much stronger position, able to destroy the *þegns'* land.

Bersöglisvísur probably preceded Magnus's invasions of Denmark, where Harald's violence in Norway is paralleled in his and Magnus' attacks on Denmark:

> 'the ruler did such there that retainers' *lið* was drained for the *Jarl*, when we took plunder: *herr* takes ships to strip' (ÞjóðA 1.12; see also ÞjóðA 1.20; 1.22)
> 'Ring-shirt's colourer reddened flashing standards at Fyn; people's lord sought land; *herr* paid for *rán* from him;...' (Arn 3.18).

The latter verse implies that Danish forces had committed *rán* against Norway. The concentration on settlement destruction and the defeat of Sveinn's forces is continuous:

> '*bør* keel over with flames' greyness about householders near Fyn; roofs and thatch endure distress; Northmen burnt hall' (ÞjóðA 4.2).[11]
> 'We have born to eagle ice-cold iron upon the leader's *lið*; . . .; red fire played sudden as madness ruled about wide villages, . . .' (ÞjóðA 4.5).

---

9. Every reference to a runic inscription, except the next, is given by an abbreviation for their publication (see Abbreviations, above: viii–ix); the Swedish volumes in particular are recorded in several different fashions in different libraries.
10. *Oslo Universitetets Oldsakamlings Årbok* 1991/2: 175f.
11. ÞjóðA 1.19 refers to an earl's 'lords' seat' being destroyed.

'Bright fire burnt *seggirs*' [as with *rekkr*, implying some credit-
able status] boothes all over Denmark; the ruler destroyed
dwellings as he moved in great *herr*; . . . we were allotted victory
when Sveinn's men ran wounded before us' (ÞjóðA 4.6).

The *fylgjurar*, 'followers' of ÞjóðA 1.20, were Magnus's target. When
they were dead, the earl had to flee, deprived of retainers whose *bú* had
been destroyed. A similar pattern emerges under Harald:

'The lord reddened gleaming edges in Fyn, when Fyn-dwellers' *lið*
then became thin; . . .' (Arn 6.1).
'Jutes' swift-spoken *vinr*'s choice ship must float deserted,
because of the ruler's flight from dead retinue' (Arn 6.4).

The extent of fighting seems greater, with references to greater lords'
support (until it became betrayal) for Sveinn, and destruction beyond
just Fyn:

'Sveinn does not have to reward liberally for fight six Danish *Jarls*
who were where attack grew in battle; battle-bright Finn Arnason,
gallant hearted who did not want to escape, was captured in the
force's midst' (ÞjóðA 3.17).
'Harald, you made a plundering sortie over all Zealand; . . . ;
konungr went with many to Fyn, where he did not find helm little
work; . . .' (Valg 7; see also Valg 8; Valg 9 [12]).

There was more than one raid, by both kings. The verses show
consistency, particularly in the Norwegian rulers' 'policy' of attacking
Sveinn's supporters. Magnus achieved ultimate victory from his timely
destruction of a large invading Wendish army: he gained territory in
Denmark from performing the duty to defend in which Sveinn failed.
The results of Harald's policy are more interesting:

'Ruler's *vinir* offered *seggirs*' lord great reconciliation: those who
had lesser *lið* soothed hard-minded battles, and quick and resolute
búendr delayed their attack when they received the news: men's
kin's breath was not corpse-like' (Þfagr 9).
'Valiant *búendr* tell much report of either's conduct, when *seggir*
met each other, there was much men's grief; *þegnar* who contest
all the time put in a prolonged opposition to concord; great mind
swells in the lords' (Halli 4).
'Lords' great anger becomes all-danger, if terms should be
agreed; men, who can mediate, fence with speeches in halls; it

---

12. This verse suggests the severity of the violence, as it is one of the very few
references in the historical sagas' skaldic verses to women suffering: in most
cases they are represented as valued individuals, or bereft of their beloved, or in
mythological circumstances.

may be help to say to the rulers all such which *herr* agree, if lords
should understand/separate worse, they would want it so because
of greed' (Halli 5).

'I have heard it that Harald and Sveinn gladly set hostages
between each other against baseness; that is good business; so
they held to/with oaths and all full peace, that either reduce expeditions: settlement was then completed with witnesses' (Halli 6).

'Danes' ruler would not have submitted – we must spread truly
about most blest's wise kin – if men there held forth from south-
wards with *herr*-force; it would do well for raven-food, swords
were carried to expedition' (Steinn 1.7).

The speeches in halls in Halli 5 seem to represent *herr*'s opinions,
while Þfagr 9 proposes four parties: the ruler, his *vinir*, *seggirs*' lord (the
other ruler), and *búendr* who are detached from, and only hear of the
proceedings. Halli 4 also makes *búendr* detached, though commentators,
while the *seggir* who met each other must be Harald and Sveinn, with a
party opposed to the peace, *þegnar*, and lords with swelling pride. The
last are usually taken as Harald and Sveinn, though Halli 6 makes them
gladly accept a settlement. Whatever the case, the verses indicate a consistent opposition party (*þegnar*, and lords called *jöfrar* and *hölðar*).

This is difficult to untangle, but there are further consistencies with
the verses on ravaging. The peace treaty involves the reduction of *ferð*,
'expeditions', the victims of Steinn 1.7 and Valg 9, and of Magnus (in
Þjóða 1.13 and Þjóða 1.21). Those with lesser *lið* propose peace, and
Sveinn's *lið* is the target, on land and sea, of Arn 6.1 and Þjóða 4.5,
(also Steinn 1.4 and Þjóða 1.12). In Þjóða 3.17 *Jarlar* are present in
Sveinn's force. Where the poems Þjóða 1 and Arn 2 consistently call
Sveinn a *Jarl*,[13] it implies a rank below, (and subject to) Magnus. Sveinn
clearly has supporters of this calibre, who may be the *lands-menn* victims
of Valg 8, part of Sveinn's *ferð*. The occurrence of *lands-menn* in Sigv
13.19 suggests powerful lords supporting St Oláfr with their *herr*: the
plaintiffs in Halli 5, and victims of Magnus in Arn 3.18. The destruction
is aimed at the *lands-menn*'s dwellings, repeated in Þjóða 1.19, 20, 4.2, 5,
6, and Valg 8. Further forms of reduction are noted in Þjóða 4.1, Valg 7
and Valg 9. The results of all this are notable in that Sveinn's own power
seems reduced. In each major battle Sveinn's personal defences were
easily breached, and his ship cleared of his retinue. Thereafter those
lacking *lið* press for peace negotiations: Sveinn's followers lost as many
as 30 ships in 4.3. Steinn 1.2 is at pains to emphasise Harald's numerical
inferiority, so it was apparently not Sveinn's lack of ships that led to his
downfall. However Þjóða 3.11 proposes the division of Sveinn's support
that is mirrored in the verses on the peace negotiations: 'it is learnt that

---

13. Þjóða 1: 8, 12, 13, 18, 19, 20, 22; Arn 2: 15.

sveit [one of many terms for a retinue or a section of a retinue] has divided itself by deed and good lord against Sveinn; that retainers' strife is long in the memory', this allegedly precedes the final battle, and is supported by Steinn 1.7 in its emphasis of retinue terminology.

Some Danish runes can be added to the predominantly Norwegian skaldic evidence (though Þórleikr fagri's verses were for Sveinn).[14] On the Glavendrup stone (Mr209, Fyn),[15] the deceased, Alle, was *gode* of Solver, *þegn* of *uia-lið*, with a pagan formula. This, two other commemorative stones, and a ship-setting are all for the same deceased. The *þegn* was a *gode*, a rank given to chiefs in Iceland, allegedly with religious status, certainly important. *Gode* also appears on Helnaes (MR190, Fyn) where the raiser is *gode* of Nes' inhabitants, a position associated with a district or people. The Gunderup *þegn* was lord to the rune-carver, using the term *dróttinn* which is almost always used in skaldic poetry to indicate the specific lord-retainer relationship. The Södra Villie (MR277, Skåne) deceased was most prominent of *þegnar*, so a position with variable status. *Lið* also appears on Karlevi (MR411, Öland), which includes a *drottkvætt* stanza probably composed by a Norwegian or Icelander, raised on the island by a follower (*fylghu*, as in Sveinn's *fylgjurar*, ÞjóðA 1.20, targets for Magnus) in the deceased's *lið*. The dead lord 'ruled' land in Denmark, and the verse calls him a ship's captain (in a kenning), so was on a naval expedition away from home. This *lið* concurrs with the skaldic meaning, as do the ship-setting and *lið* title at Glavendrup. On Västra Strö 2 (MR335, Skåne), the deceased was joint owner of a ship with the erector, who also raised Västra Strö 1 (MR334) for Asser, his brother, who died *í víkingr*.[16] There are also compounds of *land-*, as on Skivum (MR133, North Jutland; 'the foremost and best *land*-man in Denmark'), and on Lund 1 (MR314, Skåne; 'good *land*-men', suggesting an achieved status). This concurs with the skaldic material and indicates a powerful class of lords.

Examples of lords and their retinues forming parts of greater forces

---

14. Actual overlap, other than in terminology, between skaldic and runic evidence is rare, though the Karlevi stone has a *dróttkvæt* verse, and in Norway Stangeland (NR239) was raised by Þórbjorn Skald for a son who died in Denmark, so the skald had sufficient status to raise a runestone. Galteland commemorates one who died *í lið* when Knútr *sótti*, 'sought' England, a very typical skaldic phrase.

15. The main problem with Glavendrup is the meaning of *uia-*, which has been taken to have religious significance, and its association with *lið*. Contrary to the skaldic meaning of *lið*, a direct retinue association has been assumed, which makes *uia*'s position as a qualifier difficult, and inexplicable.

16. There is otherwise little use of *víkingr* in Danish runes: Tirsted (MR216, Lolland), where the deceased was part of a group (possibly *lið* – the carving is blundered), all of whom were *víkingr*. In Gårdstånga 2 (MR330, Skåne) some commemmorate their *félagi*, 'fellow', also *drengr*, who were *í víkingr*.

are limited, primarily because the verses rarely consider subordinate nobles. The most notable congregation is represented in Sigv 1.4, when 'all peace amidst lords' *lið* was sundered in fearful Suðrvík, known by the Danes'. ÞKolb 3.6 mentions Erling as hostile to the *Jarlar*; Sigvatr's verses on his position suggest military support (Sigv 7.9; 7.1).

This is potentially expanded by Sigv 12.21, where St Oláfr's rule of the upper land includes 'each *herr*'s *land*-ruler has further recognized him to the country's northern ends'. St Oláfr's first downfall, as a result of Knut's bribery, includes further *sveits*, 'retinues', *lands-menn*, and another *ferð*, 'expedition' (Sigv 13.19).

Both Danish and Norwegian ruler's armies consisted of multiple retinues, supplied by supportive lords. These were primarily powerful individuals such as Erling, and Sveinn's six earls. In Vell 23, 'seven *land*-rulers rushed to sea-kings' meeting with Hákon', so earlier great lords were dependent on the support of powerful 'subjects'. This could be extended as far as *Jarl* Hákon of Norway's support for Harald Bluetooth of Denmark against Saxon invasion (in the 1060s Vell 26, 27). It seems unusual that Magnus and Haraldr paid so much attention to individuals without great power, but as Magnus found with the *Bersöglisvísur* episode, this level of society had become potentially decisive. In Sigv 12.20, quoted above, St Oláfr's defeat and destruction was by this same group of lesser landholders, *þegn* and *hersir*, and though Erling was considered a *hersir*, his power was the creation of Oláfr Tryggveson, and extraordinary. The structure of society changed whereby the greatest lords did not use, or could not rely on, a number of powerful subjects to supply all the support they might require. Magnus initially used legal and administrative authority to take advantage of the lesser landholders, implying that he could do so because there was no powerful subject to prevent such activity. However, there were still great lords within Norway, including Kalf Arneson, who 'let young lord have inheritance in that you determined his return; truly, Sveinn had to sit alone in Denmark' (BjH 6). Thus the social structure must have been considerably flexible. Though Harald captured at least one figurehead, his violence was clearly directed at all those who did not support him as required, in contrast to the earlier methods of encouraging support by dealing with single powerful individuals (as in the creation, and subsequent destruction, of Erling). Harald apparently had to deal directly with the *þegns* and *búendr* to secure their support, and supply the forces he required for fighting in Denmark.

LIÐ, LEDUNG AND LEIÐANGR

One small problem arises: many believe or assume that by the middle of the eleventh century (if not long before) national levies were the dominant military mechanism.[17] The question of the relative existence of retinue-based forces and levied forces in Denmark has been well considered (Lund 1986; 1993), as defined by the words *lið* and *ledung*, but the skaldic verses add some notable points (though there is not space to explore them fully).[18] The use of the word *lið* continues throughout the period, without diminishing in frequency but changing somewhat in usage. Before Magnus the Good, all but four out of twenty-eight occurrences of the word are unequivocally naval in context. After c. 1034 six are thoroughly naval, while ten are simply overseas operations on land. The degree to which the meaning is specifically naval, rather than originally a ship-borne force, declines. However, *lið* remains essentially naval, whether or not it is a fleet (in Þloft 2.2 *lið* clearly equals *flota*, 'fleet'), or just operating overseas. Clearly it cannot refer to retinues in general. It could refer to retinues only on maritime operations, but frequently refers to general groups, not a lord's own forces, as in: ÞKolb 3.12 ('English *lið*;') and Sigv 4 ('. . . all men's *lið*;')[19] All these are post-1000, and could indicate a change from retinues to levies. However, ÞjóðA 1.2 has a *lið* of *húskarlar* (definitely retainers). The term is also used for Harald Sigurðarson's Varangian army (Böl 4; Valg 1). In Arn 6.15 and ÞjóðA 2.1 the presence of *liðsmenn* indicates a firm conceptual base. There is no indication of dependence on retinue content, nor of the development of levied forces. It can be a retinue, of randomly recruited, rewarded, and skilled men, but it can also be their congregation in general. In later verses it can refer to almost any kind of expeditionary force (particularly a *ferð*), and specifically includes Magnus's Swedish mercenary army.

The verses spell *ledung* as *leiðangr*, and editors have frequently assumed[20] that when they come across the word *leið* in some form in a verse, it is a contraction. This is definitely not the case; on none of its appearances can *leið* indicate a levy, and although many of its wide range of meanings were utilized (including 'tomb'), most are associated with 'a way' on the sea. The word *leiðangr* appears only four times: once for a Danish sea-borne force attacking Norway (ÞKolb 3.4), once part of a *lið* (ÞjóðA 3.12), then used for one of Harald's fleets assembled to attack Denmark (ÞjóðA 4.22), where though the term *almenningr* is used, later a term for a levy in a specific legal framework, its early meaning is 'common pastures', with a base of 'common', 'public': in the verse it is

17. Particularly amongst Swedish archaeologists, though, as noted by one exception, (Jakobsson 1992: 92–94), this is an extrapolation from later medieval practices, with no real proof of any such institution before 1200.

18. Lund (1993) has covered all but the skaldic material; this analysis complements his criticisms.

19. Also Ott 2.6, Ott 3.2, Þórf lv 2, Arn 3.17, Arn 6.1, Pfagr 2.

20. Such as for Tindr 1.4 (Jónsson (ed.) 1967: 145, Aðalbjarnson 1941: 286).

used for the fleet, *herskip*, and could be used in the sense of 'the entirety'. Finally in Böl 8:

> 'You prepared *leiðangr* next year out of fair land, you raised an increased adorned stud of sea-horses; sea embraced ships: worthy trunks lay on dark waves – Danes were there badly checked: *herr* saw ships piled up before land.'

This concerns building ships for a fleet; *af*, *a loco*, 'out of', denoting motion, suggests its launching. On every occasion *leiðangr* is a naval expedition – a natural derivation from *leið*, a 'path' associated with the sea: *leiðangr* would be an outing on that path. This accords with its equalling of *lið* which precludes a levy. The later levy associations could be based on ship-crewing requirements, *leiðangr* originally indicating ships on a naval expedition.

There is further information for *lið* on Swedish runestones: on Sponga (SS164, Södermanland) and at Gripsholm (SS179, Södermanland) where Harald, Ingvar's brother, went *drengiliga* after gold to the east. This adjective strongly epitomises military, retinue aspects of *drengr*: bravery in the face of battle, and lust after gold. On Turinge (SS338, Södermanland) the brothers of Torsten, best of *landmanna*, out in *lið heldu* their *húskarlar* well. To 'hold' *húskarlar* is the terminology for retainer used in Sigv 3.19, a treaty between St Oláfr and earl Rögnvaldr, where it is equated with *drengr*. Several *liðs forungi* ('leader') are named. The most famous is Ingvarr, who led a disastrous expedition into Russia, commemorated in numerous runestones, mostly in Södermanland.

The composition of Ingvar's *lið* includes those stated as ship owners or *styrismaðr* (Steninge (SU439, Uppland), Varpsund (SU654, Uppland), Svinnegarn (SU778, Uppland), Ajä (SU136, Uppland)). There are others known, including Uppsala (SU922, Uppland) and particularly on Esta (SS171, Södermanland), suggesting the composite forces of the skaldic verses, and Tuna (SM42, Småland) commemorates a *skibari* of *Haraldr konungr*, Harald Harefoot or Harald Sigurðarson. If the former it would conform to a number of stones which explicitly record that the deceased was associated with England. Yttergarde's (SU344, Uppland) deceased 'took geld three times in England: first Tosti payed, then Thorkell, then Knut'. At Grinda (SS166, Södermanland) the deceased took his share of geld, and sacked *borg* in Saxland. The last comment echoes Kungs hållet (SS106, Södermanland), whose deceased went west, broke *borgar* (forts), and killed *borgmen* because he was skilled in all such. In terms of inscriptions many Swedes went abroad, mostly on military expeditions, very reminiscent of Magnus's recruitment in Sweden recorded in skaldic verses (Jónsson (ed.) 1967: 248–49).

Another skaldic incident (Sigv 1.4, above) was when there was fighting between *jöfrars*' *liðs*, probably in Jutland where Husby-Lynhundra's (SU539, Uppland) deceased died when he should have gone to England.

Similarly Vändle Sörgarden (SV5, Västmanland) died in Jutland on the way to England, probably in a *lið*. There are few references to *víkingr*, though Bjudby (SS54, Södermanland) commemorates a group where all were *víkingr*. Bro (SU617, Uppland) commemorates a son of Hákon *Jarl* (probably an unknown Swede) who was *vörðr* against *víkingr*, combining all the skaldic poetry indications of the lord's duty to defend an area, epitomized in the use of *vörðr*.

CONCLUSIONS

Thus Sveinn's Danish and Magnus' and Harald's Norwegian forces apparently consisted of lesser lords bringing their own forces together. This is also suggested by the *Encomium Emmae*'s (I.3) description of Knút's forces (Lund 1993: 120). Harald's violent treatment, particularly of alleged ring-leaders, reflected his need for support, the loss of which (to bribery) earlier cost St Oláfr his rule. The destruction of property was used to subdue both Harald's opponents and Sveinn's supporters. Thus, as the wars between Denmark and Norway lasted almost all of Harald's reign, his violence within Norway would have 'encouraged' any who tired of warfare and Sveinn's attacks: Harald on the rampage was worse. This allowed him to be more brutal and successful in exerting authority over *þegns*. This was an answer to a relatively new problem: the 'traditional' methods of exerting political authority had involved dealings with particularly powerful individuals, but by the mid-eleventh century this approach was clearly not adequate, and Harald's 'solution' was to employ violence to intimidate his supporters into loyalty.

The growth of lesser lords, and their participation in composite military expeditions, involved retinues. Retinue service included a basis of trust and loyalty but depended primarily upon reward for service. Though there are indications of maintenance and the provision of armour (Sigv 13.5), the reward was principally bullion. There is a general emphasis of the linkage of gold and retinue, such as Vell 33 ('lord distributes earth's gold: lord gladdens an army of retainers'), Sigv 11.1, Þfagr 12 ('lord cast crucible-cargo from slain's splendid harbours towards *þegnar*; young leader gave out glowing arm's embers'), and Þfagr 13 ('Gold-thrower gains for himself a faithful retinue with a lord's deeds'). Retinue payments also entail the inducement of treachery, as Sigvatr emphasized in his verses on St Oláfr's first expulsion from Norway by Knút (Sigv 5.4). In Sigv 13.16, 'the lord's foes go there with loose money-bags; people often bid heavy metal for a lord's unsold head: sells his loyal lord for gold' (see also Sigv 13.18). This 'professional quality' is also indicated in the compounds *heið-þegnar* (Sigv 2.6), *heið-mann* (Sigv 3.17), and *heiðmildr* (Bersi 1.3, Arn 6.3), where *heið* clearly indicates fee. The importance of this reward, and the consequence of inadequate remuneration, was repeatedly stressed: a lord who failed to

give sufficient payment lacked retainers, or had a retinue susceptible to
bribery, and lost the battle.

Runic inscriptions demonstrate careers in retinue membership, from
the level of *drengr* and *félagi* up through ship-ownership to the ability to
organise a *lið*. Those capable of the latter two activities were also of
considerable standing within their localities, although they hardly ever
had titles such as *Jarl*, but were *þegn*s or *landsmen*. These are also the
new lords of the skaldic poetry: their status in society was based on their
careers as retainers, or retinue-leaders. Only a small part of this was
based on *víkingr* activities, the rarity of which within Scandinavia, and
the fact that it was positively disapproved of, confirms the prevalence of
legitimate retinue service, as opposed to piracy. It was even a source of
power to be a defender against *víkingr*, though for Knút, St Oláfr and
others *víkingr* activity was the basis of their own future power. Thus the
successful pursuit of warfare brought a stronger retinue and more
power. A force gathering many lesser lords' retinues brought as much
collective strength as one of a few great lords, but without constituents
powerful enough to threaten the gatherer.

Stiklarstaðir and Harald Sigurðarson's problems in Raumarike indicate the consequences of this policy: the first rank now had to deal
with those previously subordinate to the second rank, and whom they
had been encouraging against the second rank. Where there were new
great lords, *landsmenn* such as Erling, there was no great change in
policy, but the rest of the 'lower ranks', *þegnar*, *búendr* and *hersir*, had
benefited from the decline in the second rank, and prospered especially
from the rewards of retinue-membership. Thus the great lords had to
deal with the aspirations not just of a rising class in society, but of a class
on whom they depended for their own retinues, and power. This is the
cause of *Bersöglisvísur*, where Magnus' (or powerful advisors', as Sigvatr
alleged) apparent weakness in the face of this contrasts with Harald
Sigurðarson's dealings with Raumarike. But Magnus early in his reign
was in a much weaker position, without a great career, and treasure
from Byzantium, and the problems seem much greater; Magnus's own
retinue, represented by Sigvatr, was discontented, and was needed to
quell some form of revolt in Sogn.

The great lords of the late Viking age were clearly capable of great
undertakings; their source of power was their retinues, filled on the
basis of reward. Power grew from increasing ability to fund large
retinues. However, in the wake of this growth of power Scandinavian
society was restructured. As a few great lords became more powerful,
they weakened those immediately beneath. The break-down in social
hierarchy combined with the opportunity provided by the retinue to increase wealth and power by enterprise. The need for constant remuneration translated into constant warfare. There were many political opportunities for warfare between the greatest lords, and from the mid-tenth

to mid-eleventh centuries there was little peace within Scandinavia or between it and its Anglo-Saxon neighbours. Ultimately this could not continue. No one lord could continually conquer. There was no concept of nationhood involved in the struggles between Harald and Sveinn, rather a struggle for personal superiority. Though the respective 'nations' started their formation in this period, the rulers' influence was indirect. In Denmark and Norway the great lords fought themselves to a standstill, and in the process helped to define their territorial influence and the geographical scope of later nations.

There are many further ramifications to these circumstances, and verses, particularly incorporating the growth and development of 'royal' power in Norway. However, within such wider concerns, violence in Scandinavia at the end of the Viking age had an important part. The roots of power lay in heritable property and its owners' support, so an opponent could be weakened by attacking his supporters. Yet the opponent could reply with further violence, either against the aggressor's support, or by intimidating his own. This potential spiral of violence, not unlike some situations of more modern times, was curtailed firstly by the lower landowners on each side pressing for peace, and then by Stamford Bridge's 'removal' of one of the main protagonists.

BIBLIOGRAPHY

Primary Sources

Encomium Emmae Reginae: A. Campbell (ed. & trans.), Camden 3rd ser. LXXII (London, 1949).

Jónsson, F., 1967. *Den norsk-islandske skjaldedigtning* vol. IA (tekst efter håndskrifterne) (Copenhagen, reprint, original Copenhagen, 1912).

Moltke, E., 1985. *Runes and their Origin: Denmark and Elsewhere* (Copenhagen).

Norges Innskrifter med de Yngre Runer, 1951, Annet Binde, V. Buskerud fylke, VI. Vestfold fylke, VII. Telemark fylke, M. Olsen (ed.), with additional material from S. Bugge, O. Rygh, I. Undset, utgitt for Kjeldeskriftfondet, Norsk Historisk Kjeldeskrift-Institutt (Oslo).

Norges Innskrifter med de Yngre Runer, 1954, Tredje Binde, VIII. Aust-Agder fylke, IX. Vest-Agder fylke, X. Rogaland fylke, M. Olsen (ed.), with additional material from S. Bugge, O. Rygh, I. Undset, utgitt for Kjeldeskriftfondet, Norsk Historisk Kjeldeskrift-Institutt (Oslo).

Sveriges runininskrifter. 1924–36. Trejde bandet. Södermanlands runinskrifter. Granskade och tolkade av E. Brat, och E. I. Wessen, Text. Utgiven av Kungliga Vitterhets Historie och Antivitets Akademin (Stockholm).

Sveriges runinskrifter. 1935. Fjärde bandet. Smålands ruininskrifter. Första häftet. Kronobergs läns runinskrifter. Granskade och tolkade av Kinander, R. Utgiven av Kungliga Vitterhets Historie och Antivitets Akademin (Stockholm).

Sveriges runinskrifter. 1940–43. Sjätte bandet. Upplands runinskrifter. Första delen. Granskade och tolkade av E. Wessen och S. B. F. Jansson, Utgiven av Kungliga Vitterhets Historie och Antivitets Akademin (Stockholm).

Sveriges runinskrifter. 1949–1951. Åttonde bandet. Upplands runinskrifter. Tredje delen. I. Text. Granskade och tolkade av E. Wessen och S. B. F. Jansson, Utgiven av Kungliga Vitterhets Historie och Antivitets Akademin (Stockholm).

Sveriges runinskrifter. 1953–1958. Nionde bandet. Upplands runinskrifter. Tredje delen. I. Text. Granskade och tolkade av E. Wessen och S. B. F. Jansson, Utgiven av Kungliga Vitterhets Historie och Antivitets Akademin (Stockholm).

Sveriges runinskrifter. 1964. Trettonde bandet. Västmanlands runinskrifter. Granskade och tolkade av S. B. F. Jansson, Utgiven av Kungliga Vitterhets Historie och Antivitets Akademin (Stockholm).

Secondary Bibliography

Aðalbjarnson, B., 1941–51. *Heimskringla* (Islenzk Fornrit vols 26–28) (Reykjavik).

Andersson, T. M., 1985. 'Kings' sagas (Konungasögur)', in Clover & Lindow (eds) 1985: 197–238.

Clover, C. J., 1985. 'Icelandic family sagas (Islendingasögur)', in Clover & Lindow (eds) 1985: 239–315.

Clover, C. J., & Lindow, J. (eds), 1985. *Old Norse-Icelandic Literature.* (Islandica XLV) (London).

Cooper, J. (ed.), 1993. *The Battle of Maldon: Fiction and Fact* (London).

Frank, R., 1978. *Old Norse Court Poetry. The Dróttkvætt Stanza.* (Islandica XLII) (London).

—— 1985. 'Skaldic poetry', in Clover & Lindow (eds) 1985: 157–96.

Jakobsson, M., 1992. *Krigarideologi och vikingatida svärdstyplogi* (Stockholm Studies in Archaeology 11) (Stockholm).

Jónsson, F., 1973. *Den norsk-islandske skjaldedigtning* vol. IB *(rettet tekst),* (Copenhagen, reprint: original Copenhagen, 1912).

Kock, E. A., 1923–44. *Notationes Norrœnae: Anteckningar till Edda och skaldediktning* (Lund Universitets Årsskrift new ser., sec. 1) (Lund).

Lund, N., 1986. 'The armies of Swein Forkbeard and Cnut: *leding* or *lið*?', *Anglo-Saxon England* 15: 105–18.

—— 1993. 'Danish military organisation', in Cooper (ed.) 1993: 109–26.

Poole, R. G., 1987. 'Skaldic verse and Anglo-Saxon history: some aspects of the period 1009–1016', *Speculum* 62: 265–98.

—— *Viking Poems on War and Peace. A Study in Skaldic Narrative* (Toronto).

Sawyer, P. H., 1987. 'The processes of Scandinavian Christianisation in the tenth and eleventh centuries', in B. Sawyer, P. H. Sawyer & I. N. Wood (eds), *The Christianization of Scandinavia* (Alingsås), pp. 68–87.

—— 1993. 'The Scandinavian background', in Cooper (ed.) 1993: 33–42.

Whaley, D., 1991. *Heimskringla. An Introduction* (Viking Society for Northern Research Text Series vol. VII) (London).

CHAPTER 8

Violence and the creation of socio-political order in post-conquest Yorkshire

S. J. Speight

The Norman Conquest did not follow a set pattern; it adapted itself to each region's circumstances. In some areas it was relatively peaceful, in others a protracted and bloody affair. In the earldom of Northumbria, of which Yorkshire formed the southern sector, conquest took the latter course. Its completion can be judged by two criteria; the eventual acceptance of William I's rule, and the replacement of the native aristocracy, both secular and ecclesiastic, by Normans, Bretons and Frenchmen (in general, see now Dalton 1994). In its course, we see a clear example of the use of violence to change and regulate early medieval society.

The new invaders did not initiate unrest in Northumbria, they stumbled into a continuing, bitter saga that had its immediate origins in the struggle of the English and Scottish kings to establish their rule in the north, countered by the north's struggle to retain its independence (Palliser 1993: 3). William hoped to succeed where both previous monarchies had failed.

Unrest actually began in 1065, when the leading men of Yorkshire and the north rebelled against Earl Tostig and replaced him with Morcar. One reason for the revolt, a recurring reason for unrest throughout the 1070s, was Tostig's attempt to impose a new tax, probably Danegeld, that went against Northumbrian 'custom' (*ASC s.a.* 1065; Higham 1993: 233–37). 'Custom' is a key to explaining the mentality and bloodshed of the late eleventh-century; many of the assassinations and massacres that litter the region's history in this period can be attributed to the imposition of non-customary dues and practices. Violence did not occur because the new ruling party was French, but because it followed the preceding government in trying to impose a new political settlement on the north (Kapelle 1979; Lomas 1992: ch. 1).

The unrest of the late 1060s, 'historical' rather than 'anti-Norman', forced William to turn his attention northwards. His reluctance to intervene personally was revealed by his early actions. His initial appointees were native aristocrats, yet they were still unable to calm the area and halt the spiralling murder and revenge. Modern historians assume the king had inaccurate knowledge of the region, hence his ill-chosen candidates, and that he was trying to be conciliatory appointing locals (Lomax 1992: ch. 1; Kapelle 1979: ch. 3; Palliser 1992: 2). Yet the suspicion lingers that William willed the northern nobles to cull themselves via internal squabbles, until he had the time and resources to impose Norman rule. By commanding natives to raise new taxes, he split the malcontents into two parties instead of uniting them in opposition to his rule. William perhaps gambled upon the disunity of the northern nobility and upon a Scottish king more interested in raiding than in political solutions; Malcolm III invaded Northumbria five times during his reign but made no permanent gains.

Soon after Hastings, William replaced Morcar with Merlesveinn, sheriff of Lincolnshire and a wealthy Yorkshire landowner. Merlesveinn, however, declared for Edgar Atheling and was succeeded in March 1067 by Copsi, Tostig's former colleague, who was soon murdered (*ASC s.a.* 1067,1068; OV II: 222; Palliser 1992: 2). William's next choice was Cospatric, a scion of the Scottish and Northumbrian royal houses, but his tax-raising duties doomed him and his loyalty was suspect. In 1068 he joined Edwin and Morcar's revolt in favour of Edgar Atheling (*ASC s.a.* 1067, 1068; OV II: 222). This pushed William into his first Northumbrian journey whereupon he built the earliest castle at York, garrisoned it with 500 men under Robert FitzRichard and William Malet, and dispatched his first Norman earl of Northumbria, Robert de Commines, to Durham (*HR* 153; Palliser 1993: 2–3). The Norman grip on the north was extended with a chain of crucial castles from Nottingham, Lincoln and York to Durham.

Revolt flared again in January 1069 with the massacre of Commines and his men, FitzRichard's murder and the seizure of York (*HR* 153; OV II: 222; *Historia Anglorum* VI.32). William marched north, relieved the York garrison, and built a second castle on the other side of the river entrusted to William FitzOsbern, subduer of Herefordshire and Hampshire (OV II: 222). FitzOsbern's involvement shows how seriously the Yorkshire situation was viewed. In September a Danish fleet arrived led by Osbeorn, son of King Sveinn. They attacked York but were forced back by the castle garrison who fired the city (*HR* 153; OV II: 224–28).

Eventually, William paid the Danes off (*HR* 153). He spent Christmas restoring order to the burnt city (OV II: 232).

The Danish invasion may have been the catalyst that forced William's hand and heralded the 'harrying of the north'. While the local aristocrats squabbled amongst themselves (Morris 1992 for the region's long tradition of 'feuding') and staged small, easily put-down revolts, he could defer large-scale action. However, once they began to invite in outsiders, decisive military action was required. Because of the opposition's disparate nature, its preference for subterfuge and assassination, a pitched-battle like Hastings was impossible. Instead William ravaged the land on either side of his route north from the Aire (near Pontefract), destroyed crops and settlements and forced the rebels into hiding. In the New Year of 1070 he split his army into smaller units and sent them out from York to burn, loot and terrify (Palliser 1992: 3).

This was brutally successful. There followed a grand-scale redistribution of estates to chosen Norman aristocrats, some of whom must have led harrying parties. Domesday Book hints at the role of William de Percy, telling us that he expropriated property in the city of York 'after he returned from Scotland' (DB30, Part 2, C10). Scotland became a refuge for leading Anglo-Saxon dissidents like Edgar Aetheling and this would have been one reason for William's 1072 campaign against the Scots (*ASC s.a.* 1072). If William de Percy was involved in this, it is likely that he participated in the Yorkshire campaigns as well. Percy and his like were given large honours and extensive powers, and left to 'run' the north (OV II: 260–66).

MILITARY CONQUEST: EARLY TWELFTH-CENTURY ATTITUDES TO THE HARRYING OF THE NORTH

The terrible harrying, and the motives for it, defied categorization at the time and cannot be neatly pigeon-holed today. Too many of our sources are questionable. In particular, Palliser has assessed the historical evidence whilst Wightman expounded the myth that all Domesday 'waste' was harrying damage (Palliser 1993: 2–5; Wightman 1975; Speight 1993: 11–14). The conclusions drawn from irregular or irregular village plans are also tentative and archaeology is simply absent (Sheppard 1976; Speight 1993: 14–17; Palliser 1993: 5). But it is clear from our chronicle sources, however late they may be (most date from the 1120s), and from the Yorkshire Domesday, however experimental in format this may be, that the harrying was a significant occurrence (Palliser 1992: 8–15; 1993: 16–20).

In Hugh the Chantor's words: 'The man who would relate all the unhappy accidents and bitter misfortunes which befell the city and church of York after the conquest of England by William, Duke of Normandy, would find his story both painful and long' (*Historia*: 2). Hugh then describes the effect of the harrying upon York itself: 'But the city of York and the whole district round it, in spite of having given hostages to the king for keeping the peace, was disloyal, hostile, and wickedly and violently destructive, and was on that account destroyed by the French with the sword, famine, and flames. The metropolitan church of St Peter was also burned, and its ornaments, charters, and privileges consumed and lost' (*Historia*: 2).

The key word in Hugh's account is disloyal, *infidelis*. The men of Yorkshire broke an agreement sealed by the deliverance of hostages. This is just one perception of events. A major benefit of the early twelfth-century sources is that although they are consistent in their portrayal of the harrying as a violent, bloody event, they are not consistent in their interpretation of the motives behind it. Thus, although we may never be able to judge the physical extent of the harrying and must accept that the land may have recovered quickly, we have enough evidence to assess its psychological impact upon the population and upon historians writing during the reign of the Conqueror's son, Henry I. Clearly the harrying was still being discussed half a century later. It initially appears as an example of public, state violence, but the views of four twelfth-century chroniclers are less cut and dried.

Symeon of Durham tells us that the Northumbrians revolted against Commines early in 1069 because he had allowed his men to loot and pillage their way through the city 'even slaying some of the yeomen of the church' (*HR* 153). William of Malmesbury (died c. 1143) does not record the event. Orderic Vitalis (c. 1075-1142) mentions the murder ('they were attacked unawares, deceitfully') but not the supposed looting by the Normans (OV II: 222). He is followed by Henry of Huntingdon (c. 1084-1155) (*Historia Anglorum* VI.32).

Symeon attributes the burning of York in September 1069 to the garrison's fear that the combined force of Danes and Northumbrians would use the houses and ditches near the two castles to launch attacks upon them. He condemns the action as wicked and futile; God ensured that the Danes arrived before the whole city had been destroyed and were able to take the castles (*HR* 153). Orderic says nothing about the city being burnt and attributes the loss of the castles to a foolish and doomed sally out of their defences by the garrison (OV II: 228).

During the winter of 1069-1070 Symeon states that the Danes plundered the east coast of Holderness at William's invitation; this was their reward for accepting a bribe to return home in the spring (*HR* 153). William of Malmesbury, by contrast, has the Conqueror laying waste himself to large areas of eastern Yorkshire so that the Danes should find no sustenance and be compelled to leave or suffer hardship (*Gesta Regum* III.249). Henry of Huntingdon states that William drove the Danes back to their boats (*Historia Anglorum* VI.32). Orderic Vitalis describes the Danes as being reduced to wandering pirates, at the mercy

Table 1: A list of prominent Anglo-Saxons and Normans killed as a result of Northumbrian unrest 1065–1080.

1.	Tostig	former Earl of Northumbria – killed at Stamford Bridge, 25th September 1066.
2.	Copsi	earl of Northumbria – murdered 12th March, 1067 at Newburn-on-Tyne by Osulf, Morcar's deputy.
3.	Osulf	former deputy in Northumbria – murdered later in 1067.
4.	Robert de Commines	earl of Northumbria – murdered January 1069 at Durham.
5.	Robert FitzRichard	'governor' of Yorkshire – murdered 1069 at York.
6.	Morcar	former earl of Northumbria – probably died in prison during 1070s (OV II: 216).
7.	Edwin	former earl of Mercia and brother of Morcar – murdered by his own followers while fleeing to Scotland in late 1070.
8.	Waltheof	earl of Northumbria – executed 1076.
9.	Ligulf	adviser to Walcher, bishop of Durham and earl of Northumbria – murdered c. 1078.
10.	Walcher	bishop of Durham and earl of Northumbria – murdered May 1080 at Gateshead.
11.	Leodwin	chaplain to bishop Walcher, the murderer of Ligulf – murdered May 1080 at Gateshead.

of 'winds and waves' (OV II: 232–34). Their fate was an inevitable outcome of the harrying; there is no suggestion that the east coast was harried deliberately to deny them supplies, nor that William bribed them to leave.

These four chroniclers present a set of varying views of the harrying. Symeon's Conqueror is a vengeful monster with a defined enemy, the people of Yorkshire and Northumberland. The Danes are irrelevant to him. This is public violence, but personalized by the author, who presents William's actions in terms of personal retribution, even of vendetta. The north had seen several uprisings since 1065, successive royal appointees had been murdered and William wanted blood for blood (Palliser 1993: 3). Of the eleven men listed in Table 1, nine were Anglo-Saxon and seven of these were killed by fellow Anglo-Saxons;

eight owed their positions to William. William's attempts to conciliate were met with assassination. When we talk about the Norman obliteration of the Anglo-Saxon nobility, we should not forget that the Anglo-Saxons helped!

Malmesbury's Conqueror, by contrast, is equally hostile towards English, Scot and Dane:

> 'He [William] almost annihilated the city of York, that sole shelter for rebellion, destroying its citizens with sword and famine for there Malcolm, King of the Scots with his party, there Edgar, and Morcar and Waltheof, with the English and Danes, often brooded over the nest of tyranny; there they frequently killed his generals' (*Gesta Regum* III.249).

Orderic Vitalis, further from the scene and often betrayed by his lack of accurate information (Palliser 1993: 4-5), does not understand the region's politics or its long history of separatism. He believes the malcontents to be a minority and paints a glowing portrait of Copsi, the earl of Northumbria murdered by his own people in 1067 (OV II: 206-08). His Copsi was killed for refusing to betray the king whereas in reality Copsi was a henchman of the hated Tostig. He had maintained himself after Tostig's exile in 1065 by plundering the Northumbrian coast before deciding to throw in his lot with the Normans (Kapelle 1979: 106).

Whereas Malmesbury sees Malcolm of Scotland as a treacherous oath-breaker (*Gesta Regum* III.250), Orderic praises the king for making peace with William in 1068: 'For the Scottish people, though fierce in war, prefer ease and peace, seek no quarrel with their neighbours, and give more thought to the religion of Christ than to the pursuit of arms' (OV II: 218).

Thus Orderic insinuated that the northerners were wrong to rise against William, that they were led astray by malcontents and should have succumbed to a king established by God (OV II: 206). William was 'filled with sorrow and anger' (*Rex ergo tam dolore quam ira conturbatur*) at the rebellion – his reaction is that of a father bitterly hurt by his children's foolish actions (OV II: 228). This is not to say that the harrying was any less severe; Orderic abhorrs the violence, but he does so because he sees the men of Yorkshire and Northumberland as misguided rather than criminal. He gives the impression that the northerners were afraid of William because they felt guilty.

His portrayal of the harrying is therefore very different from Symeon's; to Orderic it is straightforward 'public' violence, a necessary evil that has to be carried out for the good of the realm after all else has failed. In his obituary of the king, Orderic even has him repent on his deathbed of 'having caused the death of thousands by starvation and war, especially in Yorkshire' (OV IV: 93; Palliser 1992: 3). To Symeon the harrying is a work of royal retribution, perhaps even enjoyed by its perpetrators. Henry of Huntingdon devotes a matter-of-fact few lines to the harrying; his strongest statement is that the king 'destroyed the English of that province' (*Historia Anglorum* VI.32).

Perhaps the most important point to be made is that the harrying was an exception; it does not represent the standard method of 'Normanization'. For this we have to look at more subtle processes.

LAND REDISTRIBUTION

The redistribution of land followed two separate patterns: an inevitable unregulated pillage and seizure and, at the same time, clear indications of royal control with attempts to legitimise the routine expulsion of thegns. Here the violence was both public ('legitimized' government action) and private (the latter sometimes defined as crime).

The Yorkshire Domesday's Claims section provides evidence for individual and state depredations, recording conflicting claims to individual portions of land, often with a local jury's verdict (Roffe 1990). The disputes preserved were between Norman and Norman as well as Norman and Saxon. A Yorkshire manor might pass through three pairs of hands between 1070 and 1086 before its ownership was fixed by Domesday. This, in the admittedly partisan view of the *Anglo-Saxon Chronicle*, was partly the king's fault.

> 'The king granted his land on the hardest terms and at the highest possible price. If another buyer came and offered more than the first had given, the king would let it go to the man who offered him more. If a third came and offered still more, the king would make it over to the man who offered him most of all. He did not care at all how very wrongfully the reeves got possession of it from wretched men, nor how many illegal acts they did' (*ASC s.a.* 1068).

This probably refers to the way in which the king 'farmed' out his demesne estates but it is equally relevant to the process of subinfeudation as a whole. Lesser men no doubt negotiated with the king for their chosen portion, but those destined to become the greater tenants-in-chief seem largely to have taken what they wanted. Domesday Book tells us that William de Warenne seized land and two horses in Bedfordshire and 'has not yet given them back' (DB20, 17.1). The Yorkshire Claims were an attempt by the king to regulate a situation fast becoming uncontrollable.

They reveal Nigel Fossard (died c. 1120) to have been a particularly rapacious land-grabber. Fossard is inveigled in fourteen of the thirty-eight claims concerning the North and East Ridings and seven of the thirty-nine West Riding claims. He had been compelled to relinquish several properties, including land in the royal manor of Great Driffield, which until then he had 'detained by force' (DB30 Part 2, CE4).

Hamelin, perhaps a man of Nigel Fossard, had 'detained by force two carucates and five bovates of land in the same vill ' (DB30 Part 2, CE5). If men were able to treat royal land like this, how much worse must have fared the rest? In Middleton on the Wolds Nigel had held a carucate of land belonging to Mulagrimr; by the time Domesday was drawn up he had 'given it up' (DB30 Part 2, CE3, CE8). In some places the process of restoration or legalization was only just underway.

Giving up land did not mean its restoration to the late Saxon holder. In Croom Nigel relinquished another portion of land formerly held by Mulagrimr to the king (DB30 Part 2, CE10). He was, however, able to retain some ninety-five manors scattered about the North and East Ridings. The Fossard fief was the most dispersed of the early Yorkshire tenancies-in-chief which may indicate not only its origin as a mesne tenancy (it was upgraded in 1088) but also a royal wish not to concentrate any one area in the hands of such a potentially unruly baron.

Phrases such as 'detained by force' hint at the violence inherent in the seizure of land. A lord might be 'legally' enfeoffed in one manor and illegally in possession of neighbouring lands which suited the expansion of his territory. William Percy probably held Hagendebi in Yorkshire simply because it lay close by his caput at Tadcaster (Fleming 1991: 201). Such violence was inflicted by Norman upon Saxons and Normans alike, so fierce was the competition for land.

The case of William Malet is a good example. Constable of the first castle of York from 1068, he seems to have been sheriff of Yorkshire by mid-1069. Soon afterwards, he and his family were captured by the Danes and William fades from our view, although he left a widow and a son (OV II: 228). He was dead by 1086 at the latest and probably by 1071 (Douglas 1943: 138; Palliser 1992: 3). Domesday records William Malet being in possession of Yorkshire land before the destruction of his castle, hence by the first quarter of 1069 or by 20 September the same year when both castles were attacked and the city fell (OV II: 222). The men of Ryedale Wapentake testified that he had been in possession of Havarthr's land 'before the castle was taken' (DB30 Part 2, CN3). In the East Riding he held the land of the lady Asa:

> 'Concerning all Asa's land they testify that it ought to be Robert Malet's because she herself had her land separate and free from the control and power of Bjornulfr her husband, even when they were together, so that he could make neither gift nor sale of it, nor forfeit it. Indeed after their separation she herself withdrew with all her own land and possessed it as a lady. Moreover the men of the county saw William Malet in possession both of that (land) and the whole of her land, until the castle was attacked. This they attest concerning all the land of Asa which she had in Yorkshire' (DB30 Part 2, CE15).

Perhaps Asa was dead by 1086; perhaps William had pensioned her off? The testimony forced from her compatriots suggests a lawful descent, making clear that Asa's husband had no claim to her land. But a little further on the position becomes clearer: 'Concerning seven carucates of land in North Duffield which Nigel [Fossard] has, they say William Malet was in possession [of them] and had the land and service until the castle was destroyed.'

> 'The two carucates of land which Nigel has in South Duffield they say belong to the king's lordship in Pocklington. But the remaining six carucates in the same place William Malet had as long as he held the castle of York and men rendered service to him' (DB 30 Part 2, CE 19–20).

William Malet had been a major power in the region. He possessed considerable property prior to the harrying; indeed he had organized his estates remarkably well in a short space of time. The customary dues and renders were being delivered. Then there was a revolt, his castle was damaged, and he and his family captured. His authority was removed from the scene, allowing men like Nigel Fossard to step in; not only did Nigel usurp Saxon landowners, but he also usurped the rights of Malet's son Robert. There was a period of increased lawlessness, the king installed his chief troubleshooter, William FitzOsbern in a second castle and, once the harrying was over, the king reviewed the distribution of land, deciding to take some of Nigel Fossard's gains into his own hands. Robert Malet's inheritance was central to several of the claims, providing clear evidence of a struggle for land between rival Norman families (DB30 Part 2, CE21, 23, 30, CW2, 3, 24–32). But the Malet's legitimate possession of these lands was a problem that even Domesday could not quite explain away: 'Likewise they testify that they saw William Malet in possession and holding (them) and men performed service to him in respect of the land and were his men, but they do not know in what manner he had it' (DB30 Part 2, CW32).

The situation within York itself was a microcosm of the county-wide picture. Nigel Fossard was active again: 'Nigel Fossard appropriated [*intercepit*] two dwellings but he said that he had given them back to the bishop of Coutances' (DB30 Part 1, C9).

William Percy, also in possession of portions of Malet land, was in dispute with the burgesses.

> 'The same William has from Earl Hugh two dwellings of two reeves of Earl Harold, but the burgesses say that one of these had not been the earl's, but [they say] the other had been forfeited to him. . . . Furthermore concerning one dwelling of a certain Uhtred, the burgesses say that William of Percy had carried it off for himself into the castle after he returned from Scotland. But William himself denies that he had had the land of this Uhtred,

but he says that through [the orders of] Hugh the Sheriff he had borne off the man's [Uhtred's] house into the castle in the first year after the destruction of the castles' (DB30 Part 1, C10).

At last we have a blatant mention of land being forfeited [*forisfacta*] and of the theft of property. Presumably Uhtred's dwelling was dismantled to provide rebuilding materials for the castles. This is a rare example of local people standing up to the new powers and protesting at their arbitrary actions. In the 1080s Percy's shabby treatment of the monks of Whitby Abbey, of which he was the principal patron, may have been the cause of their abandonment of the site for a temporary home at Lastingham (EYC 2, Earl of Chester's Fee: 199).

A major function of Domesday Book was to confirm in writing (hence in custom and law) who owned what in 1086, thereby reducing the opportunities for future conflict. It confirms that few natives survived long as tenants-in-chief (but see Sawyer 1985: 71–85; Faull & Moorhouse 1981: 252).

Reduction to tenant status and the adoption of non-native names were two common effects of land-redistribution. The former process is scantily recorded; land changed hands at 'kangaroo courts' set up from 1067 onwards. The Claims section of the Yorkshire Domesday hints time and again, with phrases like 'the men who have sworn', 'they testify', 'they say', that local juries were present at these courts and forced to help disinherit their own friends and relatives by providing tenurial information (DB30 Part 2, CN2, CE13, CE14, CE15, CE18). Throughout all the disputes listed, between the Malets and Nigel Fossard, William Percy and Osbern de Arches, it is the local people, the ordinary tenants, who are having to provide the crucial facts, to relive the nightmares of the late 1060s and tell the Domesday Commissioners who held the land 'until the castle was attacked' (DB30 Part 2, CE15).

These tenurial changes, although rubber-stamped and legalized by the sheriffs, represented a sinister form of oppression, almost mental violence, using the knowledge of the dispossessed in order to legalise their disinheritance. At such courts thegnly families were re-labelled as tenants on their own land. The alternatives to acceptance were poverty, exile or death. Although the native retained his status as a 'freeman', the increased rents demanded frequently forced his sons into bondage on the lord's demesne. The maintenance of free status in 1070 did not mean a family had fallen as far as it would – servitude was often only a short step away. By such means a whole generation of people were subjected. This was a country-wide occurrence but the evidence for it is particularly strong in Yorkshire. Domesday Book lists a high proportion of natives among the under-tenants of Yorkshire's territorial fees.

Domesday did not end unlicensed land-grabbing. The honorial

charters of many men reveal repentant restitutions well into the 1120s (for the case of Nigel d'Aubigny and Roger de Mowbray see Mowbray Charters nos 2–5, 6–7, 102–03, 318; Speight 1993: 216–17).

SOCIAL CHANGE

In examining military conquest and land re-distribution, the definition of violence broadens to include psychological intimidation and humiliation, weapons easily as potent as physical violence. The psychological element is even stronger in the area of social change. Here, 'violence' is intimate and domestic, permeating every working day. Such violence occurred throughout the length and breadth of the county, at the lowest level, affecting every peasant. One of its chief tools was religion; another was segregation.

In rural and urban settlements alike the incomers had to make choices between continuity and change. Many changes were physical. Fortification necessitated the destruction of large swathes of housing, industrial and farm-land. At York, the newly dammed River Foss destroyed two town mills, whole streets made way for the Old Baile (the first castle) in 1068–1069, and a large commercial district was divided (DB30 Part 1, C22; Hall 1988: 234). Further homes were removed for the second castle in 1070. All these factors contributed to the state of York in 1086 when it possessed 1000 waste plots (Palliser 1990: 12,18). Similar destruction occurred in rural settlements where the cottages clustered around the church. These were physical changes with deep psychological effects.

Few castles built in the county by 1086 can have avoided destruction of someone's property for the simple reason that, in the main, they were built in the heart of the community. Pontefract was erected over an extensive Saxon cemetery, a sacrilege that recalls the horror expressed by the author of the *Gesta Stephani* when, in 1140, the graveyard of Hereford was disturbed to create siege-works (*Gesta Stephani* 53).

The first castle of Sheriff Hutton, built either by Nigel Fossard or his mesne tenant Bertram de Bulmer, overlies ridge-and-furrow, showing that it intruded into cultivated land (Beresford & St Joseph 1979: 154–55). Domesday details for the manor of Cleeton in Holderness suggest that its berewick, the hamlet of Dringhoe, had already been depopulated to make way for Skipsea castle (DB30 Part 1, 14E8).

The late Saxon urban church suffered badly in the initial post-conquest period. Domesday Book records land in Sandburn being held by Ralph Paynel alongside the plaint 'the Canons (of York) say that they had it before 1066' (DB30 Part 2, C25). Early in his reign, even before the harrying, the king felt it necessary to issue a charter re-stating the rights of Archbishop Ealdred (Regesta: 10, no. 33). The charter contained the phrase 'no man is to wrong him or his tenants'. This is perhaps an empty phrase. It is also issued in English, but there are enough charters from the first twenty years of the twelfth century to suggest that the Saxon church found itself at a disadvantage (EYC I: 118, no. 128; Chibnall 1976).

A telling writ of Henry I is addressed to Nigel d'Aubigny, Anshetil de Bulmer and the barons of Yorkshire concerning the lands of the canons of St-Peter of York, St-John of Beverley, St-Mary of Southwell and St-Wilfrid of Ripon and Hexham. The writ states that they shall be quit of demands for carrying service and castle works *tempore patris et fratris mei* (EYC 1: 119, no. 130). It is immediately noticeable that all the houses in question are Saxon foundations. The phrase 'as in the time of my father and brother' further suggests that an earlier writ had been issued to free the minsters from the specified services. It had clearly failed so that by the period c. 1115–1123 it was for Henry I to raise the matter again. A similar charter was issued in favour of St-Cuthbert of Durham by William Rufus c. 1096–1100 (Regesta: 116, no. 480).

Within the towns of Yorkshire Norman aggression expressed itself in the violent seizure of property, in compelling local people to perform castle-works, and perhaps most of all in the intimidation of the native church. If the church was forced to kowtow, then the other orders in Yorkshire society had little choice but to follow. Urban society was the victim of a fundamental, tried and tested, Norman policy. Towns inevitably bore the brunt of any violence, as in Normandy so in England and Wales they were the principal tools used to control territory. French became the language of commerce and borough affairs (Loyn 1967: 173). There were French boroughs at Pontefract, Doncaster and Richmond; the French settlers were granted French borough customs, (i.e. those of Breteuil), while the English community maintained their ancient traditions (Beresford 1967: 523–24; Buckland *et al.* 1989; Fieldhouse & Jennings 1978; Bateson 1900). Gradually the two would merge.

The Normans used native traditions to control local people; the Anglo-Saxon *trimoda necessitas* could be retained with the simple substitution of castle-works for burh-building (Stenton 1971: 289–92). It did not matter that a public duty thereby became a private one. Such methodology was still in use a century later in Ireland. Two-tier systems were being set up. Superficially, they may appear as compromises, but the long-term effect was to segregate and distinguish between two communities, thereby making it much easier to preserve the superiority of one. The 'French boroughs' postponed urban integration for a generation.

Outside the towns, the incoming nobility made particular use of 'magnate-core' villages – settlements based around a church and thegn's residence. These offered an opportunity to emphasise continuity of lordship/seigneurial power, ready-made defences that could quickly be improved, and an existing residence in the core of the local community.

The possession of a church and a defended manor were among the pre-requisites of thegnly rank. The Normans requisitioned these symbols and made them even more elitist by the imposition of the castle.

Such a scenario may be envisaged at Kippax in the West Riding, held in 1066 by Earl Edwin. This became an early estate centre within the Lacy honour of Pontefract. The church of St Mary stands adjacent to a small ringwork which may have been the site of the late Saxon seigneurial residence. The church has a tall aisleless nave, chiefly composed of herringbone masonry. The Taylors were not sufficiently convinced to call the church Anglo-Saxon, but its position next to the ringwork suggests a potential pre-conquest 'magnate core' to the village, providing a convenient set-up for the use of the village's first Norman lords (Taylor & Taylor 1980: 719).

Thegns seem to have lived expansively, spreading their buildings over a large area (Hinton 1990: 110). By contrast, Norman lords occupied smaller spaces within the midst of the community; night and day their tenants lived within their shadow. This was often not the end of the process.

The ringwork at Kippax, whatever its origins, late Saxon or early Norman, was not a particularly awesome edifice. At Laughton-en-le-Morthen by contrast a much clearer symbol of Norman 'domination' was erected. Here, Roger de Busli 'succeeded' to the manor and '*aula*' of Earl Edwin of Mercia. The *aula* probably stood next to the church of All Saints which seems to have originated as a private estate-church, planned around a central space (a crossing transept). The north porticus and door of the crossing transept survive in the modern church (Ryder 1982: 72–79). Roger de Busli entrenched his position by building a motte-and-bailey castle just a few feet away from the church, perhaps on the site of Edwin's *aula*.

Post-conquest Laughton therefore saw its former lord's *aula* either abandoned or refortified. Any access the locals may have had to the church was diminished by the intimidation of a motte-and-bailey castle built in front of it. Within fifty years the Saxon church itself was being swept away and replaced by a more acceptable 'Norman' version.

In a large majority of instances early castles were built within half a mile of a parish church. In many cases, as at Kippax and Laughton, the two are adjacent. Whatever the practicalities of the site choice, it can only have increased the tension inevitable in the early months of the Norman take-over. There is also the problem of who had to build the castle. Charters bestowing exemption from castle-works on religious houses and towns are quite frequent (see above: 168) and indicate that the purveyance of labour for castle construction was equally common. The labour may well have been impressed but it seems more likely that castle-construction and maintenance simply slipped into the normal rental agreement so that every tenant of every castle-building lord was liable for it. A handful of professionals, men like the count of Mortain's *fossarius* recorded by Domesday Book, would oversee the labour (DB12, 15.1; Golding 1990: 134); very few specialist craftsmen would have been required.

Castle-labour would become an occasional but onerous service added to the weekly and seasonal work of a villein tenant. A structure like the motte at Laughton-en-le-Morthen, ten metres high with a ten metre summit diameter and a ten metre deep ditch, plus a bailey of half an acre, would entail considerable labour (McNeill 1992: 40). Such service would have been arduous and seriously detrimental to the tenant's strips and plots awaiting his attention.

Yorkshire was not a region dense in castles in the late eleventh and twelfth centuries; current knowledge gives only one to every 48.9 square miles (King 1983: 511). Landholdings were larger and major tenants fewer than elsewhere. Yet where castles were built they were central to settlements, villages and towns. Every donjon, small and large, timber and stone, was a powerful symbol of new lordship, a sign of elitism, a potential source of oppression. In the perception of the *Anglo-Saxon Chronicle*, William the Conqueror caused castles to be built 'which were a sore burden to the poor' (*ASC s.a.* 1086). The burden encompassed both loss in earnings as valuable farm time was requisitioned, and loss of self-esteem.

The Norman take-over of village churches was not an expression of piety – that came later in the twelfth century when churches were rebuilt in the Romanesque style. Some late Saxon tower-naves probably began their lives as deliberately defensible structures, displaying the social status of the owner. Earls Barton in Northamptonshire is a good example, set within a ringwork of uncertain date (Davison 1967: 208, 209–10). By building castles next to these, and later by destroying much of these churches and replacing them with 'Norman' architecture, the Normans intimidated their tenants, forcibly reminding them at every mass who was now in charge. They removed status symbols and even community refuges that had been an essential feature of late Saxon social culture (they were also able to make personal use of a stone structure with its own defensive capabilities).

CONCLUSION

A combination of the evidence for post-harrying waste and village planning suggests that while Yorkshire suffered military devastation in the post-conquest decade, its effect was patchy and economic recovery quick (Wightman 1975: 55–71). The most significant factor was the wholesale replacement of the local gentry and the introduction of a class of landowners themselves prone to dispute. The revolts of Odo of Bayeux in 1088 and Robert de Mowbray, earl of Northumbria, in 1095, each involved the newly settled aristocracy of Yorkshire. The Mowbray revolt indicates how alike the Norman and Saxon aristocracies were. A protest against strong government from the south, it was the last in a long line of separatist rebellions and pushed William Rufus into abolishing the earldom. 'Conquest' was achieved by military action but 'Normanization' was far more subtle. It was vital that the usurpers present themselves as the true heirs to their Saxon ancestors in order to claim the rights enjoyed by the latter. Sometimes they married the heiresses of the Saxon lords they displaced. Even for Henry I it was politic to marry a princess of the house of Cerdic. The pope had given his approval to the conquest and Duke William enjoyed a blood descent from the Confessor. To the outside world this was not conquest but a legitimate expansion of the 'Norman empire'. Every attempt was made to cloak the routine expulsion of Anglo-Saxon thegns and the virtual destruction of the native aristocracy. But the new aristocracy were well aware of their guilt. The post-Hastings penances imposed by Ermenfrid, bishop of Sitten, purportedly during a visit to England in 1070, included a clause specifically dealing with violence committed after the consecration of the king at Christmas 1066: 'Those who have killed men after the consecration of the king must do penance as for homicides wilfully committed, always with this exception, that if the men thus killed or wounded were in arms against the king, then the penalties will be as before stated.' Hence the penances enjoined upon the Norman army in Yorkshire would be less, because those it killed were in rebellion against their lawful king. The pattern of significant religious foundation and refoundation after this date may perhaps represent acts of penance for the bloodshed in the north (Dobson 1969; Spence & Spence 1981: 101–02; *HD* III.21–22; Platt 1990: 24–25). The harrying itself took two main forms: the brutal short-term effect of a major military campaign, and the subsequent more subtle and varied processes whereby the people of the north were 'Normanized'. The campaign can be seen as an inevitable side-effect of Hastings. The bloodshed of Senlac Hill was unavoidable from the moment Harold was crowned. William, with a claim to the throne in many ways the strongest, now had to fight for a crown he perceived as rightfully his. He therefore needed to reward the reluctant Norman nobles who crossed the channel with him. Yorkshire became one such reward, a vast expanse of land, conveniently far from Winchester and Westminster, an area known to be troublesome, that could be handed over to the less stable members of the king's entourage. The military violence that followed resulted in part from this decision, from a fatal combination of northern separatism and foreign greed. The harrying re-asserted royal control but a heavy price was paid. Yet in the long term it was the burgeoning Norman settlement that sealed the fate of the populace. The castle, in the twelfth century a welcome employer, was in the late eleventh century a new and frightening interloper. It towered over the community, destroyed agricultural land, and dismantled urban and rural housing. In many cases it usurped the residence of the familiar lord and threw a sinister arm around the parish church. Local people, intimidated by the ferocity of the harrying, watched helplessly as brash incomers disputed amongst themselves for prize parcels of land and, a generation later, were called upon themselves to settle the longer-running disputes. This was the most significant part of the harrying. As a result of political decisions made far away the people of Yorkshire were punished with fire and sword, physically and psychologically. Their land was taken from them, their status was lowered, their lords were removed and their spiritual freedom was curtailed. The punishment for rebellion did not end with military defeat but continued with a thorough re-organization of the status quo, with small-scale, domestic and spiritual intimidation that was far more enduring and violent.

BIBLIOGRAPHY

Primary Sources

Anglo-Saxon Chronicle: D. Whitelock, D. Douglas & S. Tucker (trans.), *The Anglo-Saxon Chronicle: A Revised Translation* (London, 1961).

Burton. J. E., 1988. *English Episcopal Acta V: York 1070–1154.*

Domesday Book: M. Newman & S. Wood (eds), vol. 12, *Hertfordshire* (Chichester, 1976); V. Sankaran & D. Sherlock (eds), vol. 20, *Bedfordshire* (Chichester, 1977); M. Faull & M. Stinson (eds), vol. 30, part 1, *Yorkshire* (Chichester, 1986); M. Faull & M. Stinson (eds), vol. 30, part 2, *Yorkshire* (Chichester, 1986).

Early Yorkshire Charters: W. Farrer (ed.), *Early Yorkshire Charters* I (Edinburgh, 1914); C. T. Clay (ed.), *Early Yorkshire Charters IV: Honour of Richmond* part 1 (Yorkshire Archaeological Society Extra Series vol. 1) (1935).

Ermenfrid of Sitten, Penitential: D. C. Douglas, & G. W. Greenaway, (eds), *E.H.D.* vol. 2 *(1042–1189)* (London, 1961), pp. 649–50.

Gesta Stephani: K. R. Potter (ed.), *Gesta Stephani* (Oxford, 1976).

Hugh the Chanter's *Historia:* C. Johnson (ed. & trans.), *Hugh the Chanter, The History of the Church of York 1066–1127* (revised edition) (Oxford, 1990).

Henry of Huntingdon, *Historia Anglorum:* T. Arnold (ed.), *Henry of Huntingdon, Historia Anglorum* (Rolls Series) (London, 1879); T. Forester, (trans.), *The Chronicle of Henry of Huntingdon* reprinted (Lampeter, 1991).

Mowbray Charters: D. E. Greenway (ed.), *Charters of the Honour of Mowbray, 1107–1191* (London, 1972).

Orderic Vitalis: M. Chibnall (ed. & trans.), *The Ecclesiastical History of Orderic Vitalis* (6 vols) (Oxford, 1968–80).

Regesta: H. W. C. Davis (ed.), *Regesta Willelmi Conquestoris et Willelmi Rufi, 1066–1100* (Oxford, 1913).

Simeon of Durham, *Historia Regum:* T. Arnold (ed.), *Symeonis Monachi. Opera Omnia* vol. 2 (Rolls Series) (London, 1885); J. Stephenson (trans.) *Simeon of Durham. A History of the Kings of England* reprinted (Lampeter, 1987).

Simeon of Durham, *Historia Dunelmensis*: T. Arnold (ed.), *Symeonis Monachi. Opera Omnia* vol. 1 (Rolls Series), (London, 1882); J. Stephenson (trans.), *Simeon of Durham. A History of the Church of Durham* reprinted (Lampeter, 1987).

William of Malmesbury, *Gesta Regum*: W. Stubbs (ed.), *William of Malmesbury. De Gestis Regum Anglorum* 2 vols (Rolls Series) (London 1887–89); J. Stephenson (trans.), *William of Malmesbury. A History of the Norman Kings 1066–1125* reprinted (Lampeter, 1987).

Secondary Bibliography

Bateson, M., 1900. 'The Laws of Breteuil', *English Historical Review* 15: 73–78, 302–18, 496–523, 754–57.

Beresford, M., 1967. *New Towns of the Middle Ages* (London).

Beresford, M., & St Joseph, J. K., 1979. *Medieval England: An Aerial Survey* (Cambridge).

Buckland, P. C., Magilton, J. R., & Hayfield, C., 1989. *The Archaeology of Doncaster 2: The Medieval and Later Town* part 1 (British Archaeological Reports, British Series 202.1) (Oxford).

Chibnall, M., 1976. 'Robert of Bellême and the Castle of Tickhill', in R. Aubreton, R. Carabie, O. Guillot & L. Musset (eds), *Droit Privé et Institutions Régionales: Études Historiques offertes à Jean Yver* (Rouen), pp. 151–56.

Dalton, P., 1994. *Conquest, Anarchy and Lordship. Yorkshire, 1066–1154* (Cambridge).

Davison, B. K., 1967. 'The origins of the castle in England', *Archaeological Journal* 124: 202–11.

Dobson, R. B., 1969. 'The first Norman abbey in England', *The Ampleforth Journal* 74: 161–76.

Douglas, D. C., 1943. 'Companions of the Conqueror', *History* 28: 129–47.

—— 1964. *William the Conqueror* (London).

Faull, M. L., & Moorhouse, S. A. (eds), 1981. *West Yorkshire: An Archaeological Survey to AD 1500.* vol. 3, *The Rural Medieval Landscape* (Wakefield).

Fieldhouse, R., & Jennings, B., 1978. *A History of Richmond and Swaledale* (Chichester).

Fleming, R., 1991. *Kings and Lords in Conquest England* (Cambridge).

Golding, B., 1991. 'Robert of Mortain', *Anglo-Norman Studies* 13: 119–44.

Hall, R. A., 1988. 'The making of Domesday York', in D. Hooke (ed.), *Anglo-Saxon Settlements* (Oxford), pp. 233–47.

Higham, N. J., 1993. *The Kingdom of Northumbria AD350–1100* (Stroud).

Hinton, D. A., 1990. *Archaeology, Economy and Society: England from the Fifth to the Fifteenth Century* (London).

Kapelle, W. D., 1979. *The Norman Conquest of the North: the region and its transformation 1000–1135* (London).

King, D. J. C., 1983. *Castellarium Anglicanum* (New York).

Lomas, R., 1992. *North-East England in the Middle Ages* (Edinburgh).

Loyn, H., 1967. *The Norman Conquest* (London).

McNeill, T., 1992. *Castles* (London).

Morris, C. J., 1992. *Marriage and Murder in Eleventh-Century Northumbria: A Study of 'De Obsessione Dunelmi'* (University of York Borthwick Paper 82) (York).

Palliser, D. M., 1990. *Domesday York* (University of York Borthwick Paper 78) (York).

────── 1992. *An Introduction to the Yorkshire Domesday* (London)

────── 1993. 'Domesday Book and the 'Harrying of the North', *Northern History* 29: 1–23.

Platt, C., 1990. *The Architecture of Medieval Britain: A Social History* (Yale).

Roffe, D., 1990. 'Domesday Book and northern society: a reassessment', *English Historical Review* 55: 310–36.

Ryder, P. F., 1982. 'Saxon churches in South Yorkshire', *South Yorkshire County Council Archaeology Monographs* 2: 72–79.

Sawyer, P., 1985. '1066–1086: A tenurial revolution?', in P. H. Sawyer (ed.), *Domesday Book: A Reassessment* (London), pp. 71–85.

Sheppard, J., 1976. 'Medieval village planning in northern England: some evidence from Yorkshire', *Journal of Historical Geography* 2.1: 3–30.

Speight, S. J., 1993. 'Family, Faith and Fortification: Yorkshire 1066–1250', University of Nottingham PhD Thesis.

Spence, J., & Spence, B., 1981. *The Medieval Monasteries of Yorkshire* (Helmsley).

Stenton, F. M., 1971. *Anglo-Saxon England* 3rd edition (Oxford).

Taylor, H. M., & Taylor, J., 1980. *Anglo-Saxon Architecture* vol. 2 (Cambridge).

Wightman, W. E., 1975. 'The significance of "waste" in the Yorkshire Domesday', *Northern History* 10: 55–71.

CHAPTER 9

'These are things that men do, not women': the social regulation of female violence in Langobard Italy

Ross Balzaretti

'Throughout the Middle Ages all social relations were character-
ised by violence and aggression, a fact that is familiar to us . . .
The social and psychological implications of the prevalence of
violence between individuals have been little explored' (Fumagalli
1994: 39).

Early medievalists rarely discuss violent relations between the sexes.[1] We
seem content to agree with our texts: violence was something 'that men
do, not women' [*istas causas viri faciunt, nam non mulieres*] (*Liut. Leg.* AD
734, 141). Historians have concentrated on violence between men: war,
'feuding' and plundering (Fumagalli 1994: 39–52; Gasparri 1990a: 271–
73; Leyser 1979: 9–47; Reuter 1985; 1990; Nelson 1992: 160–89). Male

---

1. This chapter is inspired by the work of Joan Scott (esp. Scott 1986: 1057). Sewell
1990 and Gordon 1990 also discuss Scott's ideas. The Editorial Statement of
Gender and History 6, no. 1 (1994): 1–6 considers recent developments in
historical gender studies. I have drawn also on Bennett 1989, Kelly 1981 and
Scott 1991, which provide differing, sometimes opposing, feminist approaches
to historical study.

violence towards women, for which there is a shocking quantity of evidence throughout the substantial corpus of 'barbarian' edicts, has been
noticed, but still awaits extended treatment (Colman 1983; Payer 1984:
38, 60–61; Brundage 1987: 127–49; McNamara & Wemple 1987: 135).
Female violence, the subject of this chapter, has been almost completely
ignored.[2]

This neglect stems only partly from poor evidence.[3] Certainly, the investigation of early medieval social behaviour is made difficult by written
sources which are frequently formulaic or dependent on distant models,
with laws and charters at once amongst the most problematic and re-
warding texts. Explanations of how and why these texts were made vary
widely from one temporal and spatial context to another (Wormald
1977; Davies & Fouracre (eds) 1986: 1–5; Van Caenegem: 1992: 16–29).
In the Langobard kingdom, one of the better evidenced early medieval
societies, the earliest surviving legal text is *Rothari's Edict* (643), with
charters reasonably common from the early eighth century.[4] As is well
known the laws, preserved in sixteen earlier medieval manuscripts, are
by no means straightforward.[5] *Rothari's Edict*, issued as a single corpus of
codified custom (whether Langobard, Roman or whatever), looks like a

---

2. De Beauvoir 1953: 353–55 is the classic treatment of the role of 'possible
   violence' in social and sexual relationships between women and men. Connell
   1987 provides a helpful guide to the sociological study of gendered violence
   (especially pp. 11–14, 57–58, 85–86). Segal 1990: 233–71 is an important
   examination of 'male violence'.

3. For reasons of space I have concentrated on legal and charter texts to the exclusion of other useful material (especially narrative histories and penitentials) and
   have not discussed the many technical problems presented by Langobard
   written material in the detail they deserve (see Capo 1990; Delogu 1972; Diurni
   1988; Harrison 1993; Petrucci 1973). The archaeological investigation of gender
   is tricky (Wylie 1991) and, in Langobard context, needs more explicit study. For
   a simple illustration of how gender can be represented archaeologically, compare the seventh-century site of Trezzo sull'Adda (between Milan and Bergamo),
   where there is clear linkage between men and weaponry (Roffia 1986) with the
   lavish contemporaneous female burial at Borgo della Porta (near Parma) (Bierbrauer 1984: 484; Catausi Dall'Aglio 1993: 37).

4. Baudi di Vesme 1855, Bluhme (ed.) 1868 and Moschetti 1954 are essential for
   detailed discussion of manuscript tradition and early glossing. Translations are
   from Drew 1973 with my own modifications. For the charters I have used *CDL*,
   old but more comprehensive and easily available than most recent editions.
   About 320 charters survive from the Langobard kingdom as a whole; 75 of these
   are from eighth-century Lombardy.

5. The question of Roman influence on the content and form of Langobard law,
   and the application of that law to Romans and Langobards, has dominated
   discussion. There can be little doubt that some Roman traditions survived in the
   Langobard edicts (above all, see Del Prisco 1991: 171–73; Sinatti D'Amico 1968:
   137–44).

rather idealized statement of intent.[6] The later laws (of Grimwald, Liut-prand, Ratchis, Aistulf and the Beneventan and Carolingian additions), containing many more examples of case law, often frame their decisions with reference to Rothari (although some have argued for the latter's practicality too).[7] Whether or not the laws reflect actual practice, although somewhat easier to assess in the later period, with the survival of court cases and charters for comparison, is, in the end, not resolvable with certainty.[8] Similarly, the early charters' palaeography and diplo-matic are much studied (Diurni 1988; Harrison 1993: 99–104; Sinatti D'Amico 1968: 135–200, based largely on Tuscan charters; Violante 1982) and their contents much used in local histories but, because of their formulaic structure, some historians doubt whether they reflect 'real life' any more than do the laws.

Whilst these texts will never provide a comprehensive picture of everyday 'real life' they can, for all their frustrations, afford some insight into the ideas and beliefs of those who caused them to be made and, in particular, the ways in which these beliefs are presented in the surviving texts. Historians of Langobard Italy have therefore, unsurprisingly, made much use of legal material. Most argue that the Langobard state, as it had evolved by Liutprand's time, was a sophisticated one: a bureau-cracy centralized at Pavia, and successfully integrated with neighbouring dukedoms; justice regulated by numerous courts manned by royal officials: judges, gastalds and the like; a flourishing urban culture, part-icularly at Pavia, Milan, Verona and Cividale; royal and aristocratic power based on extensive fiscal properties, helped by tribute and toll-taking; and a well-developed military organization. Put simply, historians

---

6. The early importance of this Edict is clear from the way it was remembered in many historical texts, especially narratives of Langobard history (and from the considerable number of surviving medieval manuscripts). The *Historia Lango-bardorum Codicis Gothani* (an epitome of Lombard and early Carolingian history written c. 807 most probably at Pippin's Italian court) is characteristic: 'Rothari ruled sixteen years; by whom laws and justice were begun for the Langobardi; and for the first time judges followed a written [code]; for before cases were decided by custom [*cadarfada*], by arbitration [*arbitrium*] or by ordeal [*ritus*] (ch. 7).'

7. Franca Sinatti D'Amico (1980: 640) has argued persuasively that all Langobard law had a practical purpose. Important discussions (in addition to those already cited) are: Drew 1988; Gasparri 1983: 93–133; Gasparri 1990b; Guerra Medici 1986; Sinatti D'Amico 1968; Wickham 1986.

8. Since the majority of surviving manuscripts of these laws are post-Langobard in date, it is far from clear which laws were actually current in which places in seventh- and eighth-century northern Italy. The Langobard edicts were certainly known in the vicinity of Pavia and Milan as some charters directly quote clauses from them (Gualazzini 1969; Sinatti D'Amico 1980: 645). It is quite likely that the vulgarized Roman law of Chur (*Lex Romana Curiensis*) was in use in Alpine areas north of Milan (Vinogradoff 1929: 21–22; Lear 1965: 165–66).

concentrate on what might be termed the public activity of adult men
(for all this see Sinatti D'Amico 1980; Wickham 1981; Gasparri 1990a;
Harrison 1993).

Langobard women's political activities have been much less studied,
as though these were of secondary importance. After the mid-seventh
century, lack of information about these activities is not an insurmount-
able problem, although in absolute terms we know less about women
than men (Drew 1988; Guerra-Medici 1986; Veronese 1987). Whether
our information about men is more representative of widespread social
customs than that about women is an issue not easily resolved without
drawing on other historical contexts or indeed other disciplines. As
completely new written evidence is unlikely to emerge, I have tried to
show instead that these well-known texts have much that is new to tell us
about gender relations, once questions about gender are asked of them.
When gender is regarded as a relational process the Langobard material
can be seen to contain enough information about women and men to
enable us to comment on gendered relationships (Scott 1986: 1054).
The problem is what significance to attribute to these relationships and
how to relate them to ideas of 'vertical' social status, the categories
normally evoked when early medieval violence is discussed.

MALE PROTECTION AND VIOLENCE TOWARDS WOMEN

Langobard women were legally subordinate to men, if the evidence of
Rothari's Edict is to be believed. Every woman was protected or 'tutored'
by her male guardian, or *mundoald*. [9] *Ed. Roth.* 204 states this clearest:

> 'No free woman who lives according to the law of the Langobards
> within the jurisdiction of our realm is permitted to live under her
> own legal control, that is, to be legally competent [*selpmundia*],
> but she ought always to remain under the control of some man or
> of the king. Nor may a woman have the right to give away or
> alienate any of her moveable or immovable property without the
> consent of him who possesses her *mundium*'.[10]

Most women's guardians were drawn from their immediate family:
fathers, husbands, adult brothers or sons (*Liut. Leg.* 5 for a typical

---

9. Note that this word appears for the first time in *Liut. Leg.* 12. Rothari uses
mundius or *mundium*. The impact of this particular codified custom is supported
by the evidence of charters. Langobard women's legal status is thoroughly
examined in Guerra-Medici 1986, a wide-ranging synthesis which only came to
my attention during the final preparation of this paper.

10. Similar rules applied to Roman women (Gardner 1986: 5-29). It has recently
been argued (Clark 1993: 15) that such guardianship had been severely eroded
in the Mediterranean Roman world by the fourth century. Nevertheless, women
as a group continued to be regarded as weak and irresponsible (Clark 1993: 59).

example). Although couched in terms of protection from external threat, mistreatment of women by their ostensible 'protectors' was apparently not rare. Rothari's law-makers realized that, even within this context, powers of guardianship might be open to abuse, especially in cases of non-consensual marriage and violent attack (*Ed. Roth.* 182 and 187). Domestic violence is quite well evidenced throughout the legal material and we should be wary of assuming, as has much recent work, that the family at this period was a place of refuge for most women (Wemple 1981).[11] For example:

'We now state that it is mistreatment if he [a male guardian] lets her [i.e. his ward] go hungry or does not give her clothes or shoes according to the quality of his wealth, or if he presumes to give her as a wife to someone else's slave or *aldius*, or if he strikes her dishonourably [*battederit turpiter*] (unless she is still a child and in honest discipline he is trying to show her a woman's work [*pro honesta disciplina ostendendum muliebre opera*] or is correcting her evil ways just as he would do with his own daughter), or if he sets her forcefully to indecent work, or if he has intercourse with her. If anyone presumes to do any of these things, we say it is ill treatment . . . Therefore we decree that in the case of such treatment or injury or intercourse, the *mundoald* shall pay composition to that woman and he shall lose her *mundium* . . .' (*Liut. Leg.* 120 (AD 731)).

This permissable domestic violence towards unmarried girls by their fathers, uncles or other guardians contrasts completely with unacceptable violence outside the home involving mature women under the protection of their husbands (or adult sons). When one such woman had to walk home naked in full view of everyone because a man had stolen her clothes whilst she was bathing (*Liut. Leg.* 135, AD 733) the man had to pay a high fine directly to the woman instead of, as was normally the case for crimes against the female person, to her family (Drew 1988, IV: 84–85). The exposure of a naked female body for everyone to see transgressed the norms of public decency to such an extent that usual compensation procedures were deemed inappropriate. For the law-makers male protection of women seemingly assumed its greatest significance when women left the home, when they appeared in the public, male, world.

The transferance of property rights was one such occasion. Indeed, women generally appear only in charters recording the disposition of property (both land and people) by sale, gift or bequest, which might

---

11. For example, 'By the mid-eighth century . . . the private rights of women to the control of property had been established, giving them as daughters, sisters, mothers, and wives, a position of economic equality within the family' (McNamara and Wemple 1988: 90).

appear to be an essentially non-violent activity.[12] However, violent ex-propriation of property was common in this period and the use of written charters by non-royal individuals (increasingly encouraged by Langobard rulers) may have been intended to set the authority of the witnessed written word against any attempts at extortion.[13] Although this could have worked in a woman's favour as a protective device, it apparently frequently did not.

A classic Carolingian case of such extortion is described by Paschasius Radbertus in his *Life of Wala* (I.26), written c. 836. He tells a long story (probably relating to the early 820s when Wala was in Italy with Lothar) about a widow in Italy whose property was taken from her by a group of noblemen:

> 'A certain noble woman entrusted her possessions and herself to a justiciar as her defender [*defensori suo*]. By instrument of sur-render she also assigned him almost half her possessions so that the rest would remain safe for her. Soon he craftily laid hold on absolutely all the deed for himself and produced witnesses. When the woman wanted to return to her properties and make use of her possessions, there were guards to prevent her from entering her own lands, claiming that she had assigned everything to her defender.'

Seeking help from Louis the Pious, the woman was murdered before it arrived. This story, like most of our material about propertied Lango-bard women, applies to a woman of high social class. The need to pro-tect such women's property rights is repeatedly stressed in early Carol-ingian legislation, including that specifically directed at Italy (*MGH, Capit. I*, 89, 90, 91, 95). Very often, as in this case, it did not work.

This is a well-documented case of an old problem. The role of violence in property dealings is the subject of an early law of King Liut-prand (AD 721, 22), stating that acts of sale in which women have been compelled to sell are not legally valid:

> 'If a woman wishes to sell her property with the consent of her husband [*consentiente viro suo*] or in community with him, the man who wishes to buy or those who wish to sell to her shall notify two or three relatives of the woman who are the nearest in relation ship to her. If in the presence of these relatives the woman says that she has acted under compulsion, then that which she sold

---

12. This role is clear from the c. 75 eighth-century charters for Lombardy of which 15 (c. 20%) involve women in property transactions.

13. The *Codex Theodosianus* (2,29,2; Pharr 1952: 60) had made provision for instances where land held by written instrument was violently seized. Both Rothari and Liutprand attach importance to written records (*Ed. Roth.* 243; *Leg. Liut.* 91 [AD 727]).

shall not be valid [*Et si in presentia de ipsis parentibus suis mulier illa violentias aliquas se dixerit pati, non sit stabilem quod vindederit*]. But if in the presence of her relatives or of the judge who presides in that place she claims that she did not act under compulsion but voluntarily (*volontate*) sold her property, then that which she sold ought to remain valid' (*Liut. Leg.* 22 (AD 722)).

This law was apparently quickly taken up, for its crucial formula is reproduced in several charters from Lombardy in which the woman states that she sells her property freely and that no violence was employed to force her to sell it (Skinner 1993: 145 has tenth-century southern Italian parallels).[14] Furthermore, this formula is clearly gender-specific for the linkage of 'no violence and free consent' is not made in similar charters from this area in which men dispose of property (e.g. *CDL* 10 and 53); nor do the laws make provision for this eventuality (in contrast to Visigothic Spain; García Moreno, above: 47).[15] One example comes from a Milan charter written only three years after this law's promulgation, in which Ermendruda sells a slave: 'The sign of the hand of Theoperto . . . in whose presence she proclaimed that she was under no constraint, giving consent' (*CDL* 4 (AD 725)). Another example, from Pavia in 769 (*CDL* 37), records a sale between two high status women, Natalia and Amelberga. In this document Natalia completes the act of sale *nulla me violencia pati, sed bona et spontanea mea voluntate nullius cogentis imperio accepissim.*[16] In view of the coincidence of law and charters we may presume that, although the law-makers' concerns were respected in some cases, Langobard women could be pressured violently to sell their property. Men, in contrast, were apparently thought to be less vulnerable to violent intimidation and more able to look after themselves,[17] a small but important difference which helped define and maintain male

---

14. Whether such formulae afford any glimpse into real life or not is not really knowable in the absence of much comparative material from other types of text or artefact. It at least seems likely that the repetition of basic ideas in standardized phraseology helped to validate fundamental beliefs for document-using groups.

15. Nick Everett has kindly pointed out to me that two Farfa charters (Schiaparelli 196 and 198, both of 766) do in fact apply a rather shortened version of this formula to a man. However, the phrases used [*bona et spontanea mea, libera potestate, vendidi* and *virum honestum venditionem libera potestate vendidisse*] are less elaborate than those used in the cases of women cited above, perhaps suggesting that threats of violence were less effective against men.

16. The formula continued in use after the Carolingian conquest. See *CDL* 117, of 833, from Milan. The phrase becomes, in variant versions, quite standard in Lombardy by the tenth century (*CDL* 503, 612, 724, 744, 758, 764, 781, 843, 917) and continues well into the twelfth (Baroni 1984: 25, 38 and 45).

17. It is interesting that even those laws (*Liut. Leg.* 19, 58 and 149) and charters (*CDL* 267, AD 876) concerning the disposition of property by minor male children do not raise the possibility of force being brought to bear against them.

and female roles.

It is important to note the presence of violent undertones in charters precisely because it is *not* from charters that the long-standing image of the especially savage, 'barbarian' Langobards has been derived. Historians have turned much more readily to the laws and chronicles, notably Paul the Deacon's *Historia Langobardorum*, for evidence of widespread threatened and actual physical violence (Wallace-Hadrill 1952: 56; Wickham 1981: 64-65; Gasparri 1990a: 271-73). Langobard violence has long been implicitly characterized as male and mostly non-domestic: war, plundering, raiding and inter-family 'feuding' in which even royal women normally took no active part. Whatever we may think now about the frequency with which actual physical violence occurred in these societies it remains true that the use of arms was carefully regulated in later Langobard society, with women explicitly barred from carrying weapons. Deprived of the means for self-defence women were clearly more vulnerable than most men.

Thus it is not very surprising that women of all social ranks were subjected to male sexual violence (*Ed. Roth.* 205-07). In legal and charter texts most clauses dealing with face-to-face violence between persons of different sex describe violence of male subjects towards female objects. Rape, or abduction (*raptus*), is assumed to be a crime committed by men against women and their kin (Clark 1993: 34-38; Colman 1983; Payer 1984: 38; Brundage 1987: 148-49). Women of high socio-political status were perhaps particularly at risk of violent abduction since here the sexual violation of a female, normally dealt with as a family matter, could take on wider political significance (Paul the Deacon *H.L.* V, 8; *Liut. Leg.* 31; Colman 1983). This is clearly shown by *Ed. Roth.* 186, where the sum demanded as compensation (900 *solidi*) would only have been available to the very rich. [18]

This law, like Paschasius Radbertus' tale, illustrates explicitly the link between the possession of substantial property and the potential for violence against the female person. Violent abduction could be a way for a man to appropriate precisely those property rights recorded in charters as held by rich women. It was left to the woman's kin to obtain compensation, presumably not easy if the attacker had been willing to use violence in the first place. Apparently, the abduction of a free man by another free man was not thought worthy of notice by the lawmakers, perhaps because no one had protective rights over free adult males and so no one was dishonoured as a result. [19]

---

18. Azzara & Gasparri 1992: 114, n. 90. If the woman consented to abduction the penalty was less (100 *solidi* and separation, *Ed. Roth.* 185). 900 *solidi* is the penalty prescribed for serious crimes of treason, murder, the violation of graves and the violation of peace in the countryside (*Ed. Roth.* 5, 8, 13, 14, 15, 19, 237).

19. I owe this point to Jinty Nelson.

Nor was rape or violent abduction always thought to be wrong (Payer 1984: 38): the idea that women deserved rape is sometimes expressed in non-legal texts. The portrayal of women and men in Paul the Deacon's *Historia Langobardorum* predictably reproduces many clerical stereotypes of women, ultimately der̄ ⁓d from Patristic authors (Salisbury 1992). Paul's women can be both good and bad because they are naturally unpredictable and quixotic whilst men can legitimately be both kind and violent to women depending on the circumstances. Certainly many women are violently treated by men in his stories, perhaps the most lurid of which concerns Romilda, wife of Gisulf, Duke of Friuli, and relates to the Langobard-Avar wars of the early 600s (Fumagalli 1994: 43–44):

> 'Romilda gazed upon him [the Avar khagan] from the walls, and when she beheld him in the bloom of his youth, the abominable harlot was seized with desire for him and straightaway sent word to him by a messenger that if he would take her in marriage she would deliver to him the city with all who were in it.'

This she duly did with (presumably) fatal results.

> 'Romilda indeed, who had been the head of all this evil-doing, the king of the Avars, on account of his oath, kept for one night as if in marriage as he promised her, but upon the next he turned her over to the Avars, who abused her through the whole night with their lust, succeeding each other by turns. Afterwards too, ordering a stake to be fixed in the midst of a field, he commanded her to be impaled upon the point of it, uttering these words, moreover, in reproach: "It is fit you should have such a husband." Therefore the detestable betrayer of her country who looked out for her own lust more than for the preservation of her fellow citizens and kindred, perished such a death' (Paul the Deacon, *HL* IV.37).

This story is primarily about treasonable betrayal. Men as well as women could betray their families and their king and the laws made harsh provision for such behaviour (normally death and property confiscation, *Ed. Roth.* 1–4; Lear 1965),[20] but the story would surely have been different if Romilda had been a man; sex would probably not have played so crucial a part. Whilst the sexual violence is extreme because the Avars are pagans and Paul wants to convey their especial nastiness, the first sexual move was Romilda's and Paul condemns her for it.[21]

Not all dukes' wives were seen as evil. Earlier in the text Paul tells the

---

20. Paul seems to have known *Rothari's Edict*, *HL* IV.42.
21. He praises her daughters for defending their chastity by 'wearing' rotten chicken flesh and so making themselves sexually unattractive. The onus was firmly on the girls to prevent rape: the potential rapists are not condemned here.

story of Ratperga, model wife of Pemmo, the Duke of Friuli, whose 'behaviour and humility and reverent modesty pleased him more than beauty
of body [*plus euis mores et humilitatem verecundamque pudicitiam quam cor-
poris pulchritudinem sibi conplacere*]' (*HL* VI.26; Fumagalli 1994: 27).

From these episodes it seems clear that Paul had definite ideas about
the correct behaviour of women and men towards each other, ideas
which differed little from those implicit in the laws. Taking this evidence
into account it could be argued that the laws sought to protect women
like Ratperga, and to scapegoat women like Romilda.[22]

Unacceptable behaviour could result in a woman's death, sanctioned
by the state. Severe penalties were extracted for improper killing of both
women and men (*Ed. Roth.* 200–03, 376), but complicit adultery by a
wife, even where the man had enticed his wife to bed with another man,
resulted in her death at the hands of her husband and, probably, her kin
(*Ed. Roth.* 212), with the husband paying a penalty to her relations:

> 'The husband . . . shall pay composition to the wife's relatives
> such an amount as would be paid if she were killed in a brawl
> [*scandalum*], since, because of her evil nature, she participated in
> *scandalum* when she consented to commit this deed – indeed she
> could not participate in greater *scandalum* if she were killed in a
> brawl (*Liut. Leg.* 130 AD 733).'[23]

Thus we come full circle: the law-makers thought the man had engin-
eered his wife's adultery and her resulting death in order to take possession of her property [*ut ipsam mulierem perdat, et res eius habebat*]. The
transfer of property could be dangerous for a woman, especially if she
was from a rich family and was surrounded by men with claims on her

---

22. The operation of gender in Paul's works, or indeed other Langobard narratives
    such as the *Origo Gentis Langobardorum* or the *Historia Langobardorum Codicis
    Gothani*, has been little studied. In addition to violence suffered passively by
    women it is notable that some women are portrayed as murderers and poisoners
    (*HL* I.20; II.28) and as wise rulers (notably Theudelinda, *HL* IV.5, 6, 22, 23).
    However, men are also cast in these roles, whereas it is only women who use
    their sexuality to gain power (*HL* III.30), who are attacked sexually or who are
    facially mutilated to destroy their allure (*HL* VI.22). That this was traced back to
    the sin of Eve is clear from *Historia Langobardorum Codicis Gothani* 5, where the
    anonymous clerical author departs from his source (the *Origo*) in telling of King
    Alboin's murder by his wife Rosemund and her accomplice Helmechis, and Hel-
    mechis' subsequent murder by Rosemund and the prefect Longinus, in attribut-
    ing the initiative to her rather than Longinus: 'just as the first introduction of sin
    was brought about by the evil persuasion of woman and so up to the present day
    it is customary for women to sin [*ut per femineum primum exordium accidit mala
    suasio peccati, inde usque ad presentem diem feminalis tenet consuetudo peccandi*].'

23. *Scandalum* was an all-purpose word in *Rothari's Edict* for violent breach of the
    peace (Drew (trans.) 1973: 239, n. 3; Azzara & Gasparri 1992: 107, n. 14). It could
    mean participating in a fight or in treason or in making war (*Historia Lango-
    bardorum Codicis Gothani*, 4: '*Gibites scandalum commiserunt cum Langobardis*').

land. Charters reveal (as noted) a concern with the potential for coercion which could be exerted by male relatives on a propertied woman. Yet charters must have provided little real protection for women with violent relatives. Unsurprisingly, therefore, laws and narrative histories record cases of extremely serious physical violence in which property interests, kin and marital relationships were closely linked, and which, in the process of the telling, reveal deep-rooted, and perhaps widespread, beliefs about what was, and what was not, correct social behaviour for both men and women. We have established too that physical violence could be used by adult males, largely those of high social status, against women of all ranks. Much, including killing, was legitimized by the state through its legislation. Kings, the issuers of laws made in collaboration with the leading nobles, had an ambivalent role as far as violence against women was concerned. They were ultimately responsible for the maintenance of proper relations between women and their male guardians and they had a duty to step in when these relations broke down. Yet, although compensation for crimes committed against non-royal women was overwhelmingly paid to the woman's family or to her guardian (who could be the king), not to her or her female relatives, at the same time kings could profit from women's misfortune: fines were paid to the king's fisc for unjustified violence against women, without, or so it would seem, much consent from the woman or indeed much benefit to her. The situation was perhaps worst of all for women in a king's immediate social circle (queens, princesses and nuns) who were subject to the attacks, rapes and other forms of violence which royal men carried out as frequently as any others in the pages of Paul the Deacon – unless they were especially demure, stayed at home, were 'good' – without having explicit protection written into the laws. Laws (and even charters) were made about women, about the dealings of men with women, but arguably not, for all the language of protection, for women and certainly not by women. The consequences of this are only too obvious in the surviving narratives.

Here, it is as well to recall that some scholars (notably Ennen and Wemple) have viewed male 'protection' of women in a very positive way: 'The high value placed on feminine honour by the law was matched in reality' (Ennen 1989: 36). In this characterization women were genuinely protected by men, both their kinsmen and the king. That 'protection' may have oppressed women does not seem to be an issue. Why women needed 'protection' at all is clearly a crucial question and part of the answer must be that they needed protecting from the violence of men which was one of the basic facts of their world.

These are merely a few of the norms, customs and agreed beliefs surrounding gender roles that can be extracted from these texts. Yet, however prevalent such ideas and actions were, they do not account for all the material in the laws. The view that these texts simply reflect the classic binary oppositions that many modern scholars have seen in biblical and patristic authors (men/women; active/passive; masculine/feminine; public/private; ruler/ruled and so on) needs modification. Straightforward echoes of simple binary ideas about society are not usually reproduced in Langobard legal or charter texts, because 'real life' was more complex.

VIOLENT WOMEN

In the material just outlined we should not expect to find much evidence of women who resisted these intense socio-cultural pressures. Therefore, it is worth noting carefully evidence for apparent resistance when it exists. Two cases deserve deeper consideration.

In 734 King Liutprand and his *iudices* issued four laws 'covering a few cases which have recently arisen and were found not to be covered in the edict before this time' (a standard formula). Three of these concern marriages of dependent women and are of a type quite commonly found in early medieval edicts. The other case is different:

> 'It has been related to us that certain perfidious and evil-minded men, not presuming themselves to enter armed into a village or into the house of another man in a violent manner since they fear the composition which has been set up in an earlier law [*Ed. Roth.* 19, 279, 280], gather together as many women as they have, both free and bond, and set them upon weaker men [*homines, qui minorem habebant virtute*]. Seizing these men the women rain blows upon them and commit other evil deeds in a violent manner more cruelly than men might do.
>
> Since this has been brought to our attention and these less strong men have entered an accusation on account of this violence [*et ipsi homines pro sua violentia, qui minus potebant*], we add to the edict that if, in the future, women presume to do this, if they receive any injury or dishonour [*obprobrium*], wounds or injuries, or even death there, those who, in defending themselves, inflicted this injury or caused destruction to them shall pay no composition to the women themselves or to their husbands or to their *mundoalds*. And in addition the public agent [*publicus*] who is established in that place shall seize those women and shave [*decalvare*] them and drive them with beatings [*frustare*] though the neighbouring villages of that region in order that other women shall not presume to commit such evil deeds.[24] If the women in this situation inflict wounds or cause other injuries to any man, their husbands shall pay composition for the wounds or injuries they inflicted according to the provisions of the code [*Ed. Roth.* 19, 279].

---

24. Gasparri (1983: 140–51) argues, unconvincingly, that the so-called *decalvatio* was scalping rather than shaving. Leyser 1992 points up the link between cropped hair and humiliation in Merovingian Francia.

We have decreed this rather on account of the discipline than the composition because we cannot equate the collecting together of the women with a breach of the peace with an armed band (*arschild*) [*Ed. Roth.* 19; *Liut. Leg.* 35, 134] nor with the sedition of rustics [*Ed. Roth.* 280], because these are things that men do, not women; therefore it shall be done concerning such women as provided above. If a woman rushes into a brawl (*scandalum*) and receives there death or a blow or injury, justice shall be done for her as our predecessor King Rothair provided and adjudged [*Ed. Roth.* 378]' (*Liut. Leg.* 141). [25]

It is hardly surprising that none of the 138 decisions issued by Liut-prand since 717 helped in deciding what to do about this disturbance: no exact precedent was known to any of the law-makers. *Ed. Roth.* 378, referred to in the last sentence, is the only other chapter, of the many hundreds penned for Langobard kings since 643, to provide penalties for physical violence actively perpetrated by women:

'If a free woman [*mulier libera*] participates in a brawl [*scandalum*] where men are arguing, and if she inflicts some blow or injury and perhaps in turn is struck or killed, she shall be valued according to her rank [*adpretietur secundum nobilitatem suam*] and composition shall be paid for her as if the deed had been done to a brother of that woman. But the penalty for such injury, for which 900 *solidi* have been adjudged, shall not be required since she had participated in a struggle in a manner dishonourable for women [*quod inhonestum est mulieribus facere*].'

Female violence clearly puzzled the law-makers as much as it has perplexed historians. Their shock was caused by the disjunction of ideal and real, of the collision of marginal situations with central beliefs. The boundaries beyond which women were not meant to tread come into the open in these two texts: public violence was 'dishonourable for women' because it was something 'that men do, not women'. These sentiments occur elsewhere in the edicts. *Ed. Roth.* 278 makes it quite clear that women, like servants and slaves, were not allowed to carry arms: 'On *hoberos*, that is violation of an estate. A woman is not able to take violent possession of an estate, which is *hoberos*, for it is clearly absurd that a woman, free or servile, could commit a forceful act with arms as though she were a man' [*quasi vir cum armis vim facere possit*] (my translation). *Liut. Leg.* 13 (AD 717), in stating that 'daughters, since they are of the feminine sex, are unable to raise the feud', brings home the degree of censure faced by women who acted forcefully in public. There

---

25. I have modified Drew's translation slightly. Ennen's (1989: 35–36) translation is mostly very misleading. The Italian translation (Azzara and Gasparri 1992: 203–05) is close in sense to Drew's.

is surely an implicit link made here between the inappropriateness of female violence and the appropriateness of female domesticity. Free adult men were the only members of society who could, with state approval, legitimately behave violently in public situations. This was an essential aspect of their manhood and all others (women, male children, slaves and other dependants) were defined against this fact. It was a matter of honour that these less powerful groups be silent and accept this state of affairs passively. For this reason transgression ('gender trouble' in Butler 1990), signalled in the laws by words such as *obprobrium, inhonestum, absurdum* and *inpossibile*, was severely punished, here with the state's backing. [26]

In *Ed. Roth.* 378 and *Liut. Leg.* 141 women are blamed for fighting. This may not surprise us after two decades of feminist historical research into, 'how and why . . . the oppression of women (has) endured for so long and in so many different historical settings' (Bennett 1989: 259). Judith Bennett's question may begin to be answered if we consider why there is no rational reason for the blaming of women in these two texts. In *Liut. Leg.* 141 we are told at the start that men trying to dodge compensation payments were the initiators of the disturbance reported to Liutprand. Yet by the third sentence the women (who are 'more cruel than men') are already blamed. This is interesting because it belies the rational explanations usually deemed characteristic of Langobard legal mechanisms (Wickham 1986: 111–12). This text does not 'make sense' as a record for it is not clear why the women are blamed more than the men. After all, in these laws the initiator of an action is often deemed as guilty as the perpetrator (when these are different). The law-makers, apparently unsettled by the whole case, had to fall back on gendered type-casting: women were blamed because they were that most dangerous of things, women trying to be men. Here we have one of Victor Turner's liminal situations where beliefs common to society as a whole (in this case gender roles based on biology) are highlighted in the course of threatening, puzzling and troubling episodes. The law's response was to maintain clearly gendered subjects (women and men), with distinct feminine and masculine qualities, defined most of all through their relationships with each other (Scott 1986: 1064). Violence's role in maintaining these artificial creations was important; consequently woman and man were, in this respect, categories created and maintained violently.

The processes which created and continually reproduced these gen-

---

26. Another instance of 'gender trouble' is seen in Liutprand 129 where mature women [*mulieres*] are accused of trying to seduce [*copolabant*] small boys [*puerolus parvolus*] into marriage. In addition to what it reveals of family and property relationships this law is important for our understanding of Lombard attitudes to sexuality. It is clear that women's sexuality, when not properly channelled towards reproduction, is feared. There is no such censure of relationships between an older man and a sexually immature female [*puella/infantula, Liut. Leg.* 12].

dered subjects were complex in all early medieval societies. This chapter has concentrated on relations between women and men, on the one hand because man-man relations are what the history of the Langobards has hitherto been about, and on the other because material for studying woman-woman relationships is largely lacking in Langobard sources.[27]

Whilst women would be punished for any violence towards men, the idea that women who are violent to other women should be punished does not, apparently, find its way into any Langobard text. Woman-woman violence was simply of no concern to the Langobard state, the public manifestation of men's opinions and actions. Patriarchy may represent disunity amongst women as much as solidarity between men (Damsholt 1989) and although some women did disrupt the established social order, as constructed in the legal texts, by escaping temporarily from the domestic into the public sphere, in attempting to escape from their class (Wittig 1992: 15) they succeeded simply in reinforcing male opinion against it, and were violently repressed.

We observe much more in these texts than mere 'sexual double standards' (Wemple 1992: 176). The occurrence of much of the violence highlighted here in explicitly sexual situations reminds us that gender often was (and is) a violently constructed category (Butler 1990: 166, n. 26). Gender and violence were mechanisms, institutionalized in law and family custom, through which women were kept subordinate, and the literal, as much as the figurative, reproduction of Langobard society ensured (Wittig 1992: 20). The view of these Langobard texts is that violence was a sexually constructed activity which produced and defined the categories of women and men.

The law's social subjects had to be clearly demarcated as men and women for male law-makers to be able to maintain power over women and 'unmen' (the term coined by Walters 1993: 29 for people 'male in sex' but 'not men in gender'); women had, therefore, to be non-violent because men were violent. In this way, women and men remained classes politically apart and the Langobard state was, at least partly, constructed upon this gender difference. Thus, in this example, gender affected 'those areas of life that do not seem to be connected with it' (Scott 1986: 1057).[28]

---

27. The only explicit example of woman-woman interaction in the laws is *Leg. Grim.* 8 where a woman who seduces another woman's husband loses all her property, half of which goes to the king and half to the other woman's relatives.

28. Versions of this paper were read at the Women's History Network Conference (Nottingham, September 1992) and the University of Birmingham Postgraduate Medieval Seminar (November 1993). I am immensely grateful for all the suggestions made on those occasions. I want to thank Nicola Donn, Nick Everett, Guy Halsall, Jinty Nelson, Patricia Skinner and Geoff West for their acute criticisms on various written drafts, and above all Giorgio and Antonia Ausenda for their hospitality in Milan and Lanzo d'Intelvi, where much of this was written.

BIBLIOGRAPHY

Primary Sources

Capitularia Regum Francorum, A. Boretius (ed.), *MGH Capitularia Regum Francorum, I.* (Hanover, 1883).

Codex Diplomaticus Langobardiae: G. Porro-Lambertenghi (ed.), (Turin, 1873).

Codex Theodosianus: C. Pharr (trans.), *The Theodosian Code* (Philadelphia, 1952).

Codice Diplomatico Longobardo: L. Schiaparelli (ed.), 2 vols (Rome, 1929-1933).

Edictum Rothari and *Liutprandi Leges*: F. Beyerle (ed.), *Leges Langobardorum 643-866* 2nd edition (Witzenhausen, 1962); F. Bluhme (ed.), *Leges Langobardorum, MGH Leges* 4 (Hanover, 1868); K. F. Drew (trans.), *The Lombard Laws* (Philadelphia, 1973).

Historia Langobardorum Codicis Gothani: L. Bethman and G. Waitz (eds), *MGH. Scriptores Rerum Langobardorum* (Hanover, 1878), pp. 7-11.

Lex Romana Raetica Curiensis: K. Zeumer (ed.), *MGH Leges in Folio* V (Hanover, 1874-89).

Paul the Deacon, *Historia Langobardorum*: L. Bethman & G. Waitz (eds), *MGH. Scriptores Rerum Langobardorum* (Hanover, 1878), pp. 12-187; L. Capo (ed. and trans. into Italian), *Storia dei Longobardi* (Vicenza, 1992); W. D. Foulke (trans.), *History of the Langobards* (Philadelphia, 1906).

Paschasius Radbertus, *Ex vitis Adalhardi et Walae*: G. Pertz (ed.), *MGH Scriptores*, II (Berlin, 1829); A Cabaniss (trans.), *Charlemagne's Cousins. Contemporary Lives of Adalard and Wala* (New York, 1967).

Secondary Bibliography

Azzara, C. and Gasparri, S., 1992. *Le leggi dei Longobardi. Storia, memoria e diritto di un popolo germanico* (Milan).

Baroni, M., 1984. *Le carte di Santa Maria D'Aurona* (Milan).

Baudi di Vesme, C., 1855. *Edicta Regum Langobardorum edita ad fidem optimum codicum opera et studio, Monumenta Historiae Patriae* 5 (Turin).

Bennett, J. M., 1989. 'Feminism and history', *Gender and History* 1: 251-72.

Bierbrauer, V., 1984. 'Aspetti archeologici di Goti, Alamanni e Longobardi', in *Magistra Barbaritas. I Barbari in Italia*, (Milan).

Brundage, J. A., 1987. *Law, Sex, and Christian society in Medieval Europe* (Chicago).

Butler, J., 1990. *Gender Trouble. Feminism and the Subversion of Identity* (London).

Cammarosano, P., & Gasparri, S. (eds), 1990. *Langobardia* (Udine).

Capo, L., 1990. 'Paolo Diacono e il problema della cultura dell'Italia longobarda', in Cammarosano and Gasparri (eds) 1990: 169-236.

Clark, G., 1993. *Women in Late Antiquity* (Oxford).

Colman, R. V., 1983. 'The abduction of women in barbarian law', *Florelegium* 5: 62-75.

Connell, R. W., 1987. *Gender and Power* (Cambridge).

Cortese, E., 1955-56. 'Per la storia del mundio in Italia', *Rivista Italiana per le scienze giuridiche* 8: 323-474.

Damsholt, N., 1989. 'Theories of patriarchy and women's history', in K. Glente & E. Jensen (eds), *Female Power in the Middle Ages* (Copenhagen), pp. 55-76.

Davies, W., & Fouracre, P., 1986. *The Settlement of Disputes in Early Medieval Europe* (Cambridge).

De Beauvoir, S., 1953. *The Second Sex* (London; original French edition 1949).

Del Prisco, A., 1991. *Il latino tardoantico e altomedievale* (Rome).

Delogu, P., 1972. 'I langobardi e la scrittura', in *Studi storici in Onore di O. Bertolini*, I (Pisa), pp. 313–24.

Diurni, G., 1988. *Le situazioni possessorie nel medioevo. Età longobardo-franca* (Milan).

Drew, K. F., 1988. *Law and Society in Early Medieval Europe. Studies in Legal History* (London) (chapters, referred to by Roman numeral, each have separate pagination).

Ennen, E., 1989. *The Medieval Woman* (Oxford).

Fumagalli, V., 1994. *Landscapes of Fear. Perceptions of Nature and the City in the Middle Ages* (S. Mitchell, trans.) (Cambridge).

Gardner, J., 1986. *Women in Roman Law and Society* (London).

Gasparri, S., 1983. *La cultura tradizionale dei Longobardi. Struttura tribale e resistenza pagane* (Spoleto).

—— 1990a. 'Il regno longobardo in Italia. Struttura e funzionamento di uno stato altomedievale', in Cammarosano and Gasparri (eds) 1990: 237–305.

—— 1990b. 'Il regno e la legge. Longobardi, Romani e Franchi nello sviluppo dell'ordinamento pubblico (secoli vi-x)', *La cultura* 28/2: 243–66.

Gordon, L., 1990. Review of J. Scott, *Gender and the Politics of History*, *Signs* 15: 853–58.

Gualazzini, U., 1969. 'La scuola Pavese, con particolare riguardo all'insegnamento del diritto', in *Pavia capitale del regno, IV Congresso internazionale di studi sull'altomedioevo* (Spoleto), pp. 19–31.

Guerra Medici, M. T., 1986. *I Diritti delle donne nella società altomedievale* (Naples).

Harrison, D., 1993. *The Early State and the Towns. Forms of Integration in Lombard Italy AD 568–774* (Lund).

Jarnut, J., 1990. 'I Longobardi nell'epoca precedente dell'occupazione dell'Italia', in Cammarosano and Gasparri 1990: 3–33.

Kelly, J., 1981. *Women, History, Theory* (Chicago).

Lear, F. S., 1965. *Treason in Roman and Germanic Law. Collected Papers* (Austin).

Leyser, C., 1992. 'Long-haired kings and short-haired nuns: power and gender in Merovingian Gaul', *Medieval World* 5: 37–42.

Leyser, K., 1979. *Rule and Conflict in an Early Medieval Society* (London).

McNamara, J., & Wemple, S., 1988. 'The power of women through the family in Medieval Europe, 500–1100', in M. Erler & M. Kowaleski (eds), *Women and Power in the Middle Ages* (Athens & London), pp. 83–101.

—— 1987. 'Sanctity and power: the dual pursuit of medieval women', in R. Bridenthal, C. Koonz and S. M. Stuard (eds), *Becoming Visible* (Boston), pp. 90–118.

Moschetti, G., 1954. *Primordi esegetici sulla legislazione longobarda nel secolo ix a Verona secondo il codice Vat. Lat. 5369* (Spoleto).

Nelson, J., 1992. *Charles the Bald* (London).

Payer, P. J., 1984. *Sex and the Penitentials* (Toronto).

Petrucci, A., 1973. 'Scrittura e libro nell'Italia altomedievale', *Studi Medievali* series III, 14: 961–1002.

Reuter, T., 1985. 'Plunder and tribute in the Carolingian empire', *Transactions of the Royal Historical society* 35: 75–94.

—— 1990. 'The end of Carolingian military expansion', in R. Collins & P. Godman (eds), *Charlemagne's Heir* (Oxford), pp. 391–405.

Roffia, E. (ed.), 1986. *La necropoli longobarda di Trezzo sull'Adda* (Florence).

Salisbury, J., 1992. *Church Fathers, Independent Virgins* (London).

Scott, J., 1986. 'Gender: a useful category of historical analysis', *American Historical Review* 91: 1053–75 (reprinted in *Gender and the Politics of History*, Chicago, 1988).

—— 1991. 'Women's history', in P. Burke (ed.), *New Perspectives on Historical Writing* (Cambridge), pp. 42–66.

Segal, L., 1990. *Slow Motion. Changing Masculinities, Changing Men* (London).

Sewell, V. H., 1990. Review of J. Scott, *Gender and the Politics of History*, *History and Theory*, 29: 71–82.

Shaw, B. D., 1993. 'The passion of Perpetua', *Past and Present* 139: 3–45.

Sinatti D'Amico, F., 1968. *Le prove giudiziarie nel diritto longobardo* (Milan).

—— 1980. 'I longobardi nella "Langobardia": una società laica?', in *Longobardia e Lombardia: aspetti di civiltà longobarda, VI Congresso internazionale di studi sull'alto medioevo*, II (Spoleto), pp. 639–58.

Skinner, P., 1993. 'Women, wills, and wealth in medieval southern Italy', *Early Medieval Europe* 2.2: 133–52.

Van Caenegem, R. C., 1992. *An Historical Introduction to Public Law* (Cambridge).

Veronese, A., 1987. 'Monasteri feminili in Italia settentrionale nell'alto medioevo. Confronto con i monasteri maschili attraverso un tentativo di analisi "statistico"', *Benedictina* 34: 355–416.

Vinogradoff, P., 1929. *Roman Law in Medieval Europe* (Oxford).

Violante, C., 1982. *Atti Privati e Storia Medioevale. Problemi di Metodo* (Rome).

Wallace-Hadrill, J. M., 1952. *The Barbarian West* (London).

Walters, J., 1993. ' "No more than a boy": the shifting construction of masculinity from ancient Greece to the Middle Ages', *Gender and History* 5 (1): 20–33.

Wemple, S., 1981. *Women in Frankish Society. Marriage and the Cloister, 500–900* (Philadelphia).

—— 1992. 'Women from the fifth to the tenth centuries', in C. Klapisch-Zuber (ed.), *A History of Women. II, Silences of the Middle Ages* (Cambridge, Mass.), pp. 169–201.

Wickham, C. J., 1981. *Early Medieval Italy* (London).

—— 1986. 'Land disputes and their social framework in Lombard-Carolingian Italy', in W. Davies & P. Fouracre (eds), *The Settlement of Disputes in Early Medieval Europe* (Cambridge), pp. 105–24.

Wittig, M., 1992. *The Straight Mind* (London).

Wormald, P., 1977. '*Lex Scripta* and *Verbum Regis*: legislation and Germanic kingship from Euric to Cnut', in P. H. Sawyer & I. N. Wood (eds), *Early Medieval Kingship* (Leeds), pp. 105–38.

Wylie, A., 1991. 'Gender theory and the archaeological record: why is there no archaeology of gender?', in J. M. Gero & M. W. Conkey (eds), *Engendering Archaeology. Women and Prehistory* (Oxford), pp. 31–56.

CHAPTER 10

Rape in Anglo-Saxon England[1]

Julie Coleman

For the Anglo-Saxons, rape was a crime which touched at least three other parties as well as the raped woman herself: the king, the woman's family or guardians, and the rapist. This study is based on material drawn from historical texts, laws, penitentials, sermons, personal correspondence and literature, each of which refers to rape with different intentions and treats it from a different point of view. The evidence from these disparate sources is drawn together to give us a clearer understanding of the various meanings of the crime during the period.

One of the main problems involved in studying rape in Anglo-Saxon England is the question of definition. For us it seems relatively straight-forward: rape is an act of intercourse which takes place against the woman's will. Closer examination of legal practice, however, indicates that this represents a simplification of the application as well as the letter of the law in Britain and America. State laws across America differ as to whether ejaculation, full or partial penetration or mere genital contact constitute rape. During the thirteenth century, on the other hand, a woman who became pregnant as the result of rape was considered to have consented, since it was believed that pregnancy could not result without each party contributing its seed (Carter 1985: 121) but penitentials used during the Anglo-Saxon period show that pregnancy was not considered to disprove a rape charge (Frantzen 1983: 56; McNeill & Gamer 1938: 196). The earliest attempt to provide a legal definition of rape in Anglo-Saxon England is found in the late ninth-century laws of King Alfred.

---

1. I would like to thank Elaine Treharne of Leicester University for discussing this paper with me and for her numerous helpful suggestions.

Putting aside consideration of what physical act constitutes rape, modern British law still departs from the straightforward definition given above in its treatment of marital rape, which is only recognized in Scotland. The rape of a prostitute, moreover, is an offence which is rarely prosecuted, and raped women who are not prostitutes often face intrusive questioning about their sexual histories, since a promiscuous past is seen to undermine the credibility of a woman's claim that she did not consent. There is little evidence of prostitution during the Anglo-Saxon period (Coleman 1989: 181–96), but by the late ninth century the rape of a non-virgin was considered a lesser offence than the rape of a virgin. Although Anglo-Saxon laws do stress that couples should marry by choice, their constant reiteration of this suggests that it was not successfully enforced. Since marital sex was a duty which one owed to one's spouse, it can probably be assumed that even where the marriage was consensual, some acts of intercourse took place against the woman's will. Similarly, slaves and women unprotected by male kinsfolk would probably have been unable to enforce their refusal, while nuns were not at liberty to consent. Acts which we would consider as abduction, elopement or adultery are often grouped with rape by the Anglo-Saxons, and so it is frequently impossible to determine from the context whether or not the woman was a consenting party.

Most OE rape words are of forms cognate with the two elements *niman* 'to take' and *nid* 'force', and are used indifferently of both rape and abduction. The OE lexis of this field suggests that the consent of a woman's family or guardian was at least as important as her own. After the Norman Conquest, however, 'rape in the sense of *violentis concubitus* is soon treated as a crime for which the woman and only the woman can bring an appeal' (Pollock & Maitland 1968 II: 490). The penalty by then was often, but not consistently, castration or death.

Rape, like all criminal acts during the Anglo-Saxon period, was an offence against the king's peace. In his description of the reign of the saintly King Edwin, Bede writes:

> '*Tanta autem eo tempore pax in Brittania, quaquauersum imperium regis Eduini peruenerat, fuisse perhibetur ut, sicut usque hodie in prouerbio dicitur, etiam si mulier una cum recens nato paruulo uellet totam perambulare insulam a mari ad mare, nullo se ledente ualeret.*'

> 'It is related that there was so great a peace in Britain, wherever the dominion of King Edwin reached, that, as the proverb still runs, a woman with a new-born child could walk throughout the island from sea to sea and take no harm' (Bede *EH* II.16).

The underlying assumption is that in Bede's own degenerate days such a trip was no longer possible without fear of molestation. It is likely that it never was, of course, and that Bede is looking back at the good old days through a haze of admiration for the early English royal saints. This wistful longing for a peaceful past becomes more marked after the Viking raids begin, and appears as early as Alcuin's letter to Æthelred on the subject of the raid on Lindisfarne:

> '*Non dico quod fornicationis peccata non essent in populo, sed a diebus Ælfwaldi Regis fornicationes, adulteria, et incestus inundaverunt supra terram ita ut absque omni verecundia etiam et in ancillis Domino dicatis hæc peccata perpetrabantur.*'

> 'I do not say that formerly there were no sins of fornication among the people. But from the days of King Ælfwold fornications, adulteries and incest have poured over the land, so that these sins have been committed without any shame and even against the handmaids dedicated to God' (Alcuin, *Letter to Æthelred*).

Rape is frequently found as a rhetorical device in Anglo-Saxon texts, where it serves as one indication, among many, of the decline from earlier and holier times. While we do not tend to find references to specific and actual rapes, the crime is frequently used as a symbol of contemporary godlessness and a symptom of the general break-down of order. It is still used in this way at the very end of the Anglo-Saxon period:

> '*And oft tyne oððe twelfe, ælc æfter oþrum, scendað to bysmore þæs þegenes cwenan & hwilum his dohtor oððe nydmagan þær he on locað þe læt hine sylfne rancne & ricne & genoh godne ær þæt gewurde*'.

> 'And often ten or twelve, one after another, will disgracefully insult the thegn's wife, and sometimes his daughter or near kinswoman, while he who considered himself proud and powerful and brave enough before that happened, looks on' (Wulfstan *Sermo Lupi*, ll. 113–17).

Here another victim of the rape is considered: the woman's male relations who are lessened by their inability to protect her. The unprotected woman with her child, as described by Bede, could rely upon respect for the king's peace for her protection, but by the early eleventh century, Wulfstan asserts, even the presence of her own previously powerful male relations could not protect her.

Rape is a frequent by-product of warfare, and the inability to protect its women acts as a powerful symbol of a nation's weakness. Power struggles between the Anglo-Saxons and the Britons, the Danes and the Normans, as well as among the various Anglo-Saxon kingdoms, must have provided many opportunities for the opportunist soldier-rapist (Barlow 1983: 157), but contemporary historical texts do not give us much information about this (but see Schulenberg 1986). In his *Life of King Alfred* (c. 49), for instance, Asser writes that Vikings settled in convents in Britain and on the continent, but does not dwell on the likely consequences of this. Reference is made to the capture of women by both the Anglo-Saxons and the Vikings in the *Anglo-Saxon Chronicle*, but no attention is paid to their fate (*ASC s.a.* 893, 895, 1009, 1010).

Viking rapists, whether involved in the early raids from Scandinavia or sheltering in the Danelaw in the later period, were usually beyond the reach of Anglo-Saxon law-makers, who concerned themselves instead with sexual offenders within their own jurisdiction. The earliest written Anglo-Saxon laws are those of Æthelberht, dating from the late sixth or early seventh century:

> '*Gif man wið cyninges mægdenman geligeþ, L scillinga gebete*'.

> 'If a man lies with a maiden belonging to the king, he shall pay fifty shillings compensation' (Æthelberht, Laws 10).

The amount of compensation to be paid varies according to the value of the slave, with further variations introduced by the status of the slave's master. The penalty for 'lying with' a nobleman's serving maid is twelve shillings, six shillings for a commoner's serving maid, down to thirty sceattas for lying with the lowest slave of a commoner. To put these penalties into context, thirty sceattas are to be paid in compensation for the loss of a big toenail, six shillings for the laceration of an ear, twelve for injury to the power of speech and fifty for knocking out an eye.

Abduction is also treated in Æthelberht's law-code:

> '*Gif man mægþmon nede genimeþ: ðam agende L scillinga & eft æt þam agende sinne willan ætgebicge. Gif hio oþrum mæn in sceat bewyddod sy, XX scillinga gebete. Gif gængang geweorðeþ, XXXV scill' & cyninge XV scillingas. Gif man mid esnes cwynan geligeþ be cwicum ceorle, II gebete*'.

> 'If a man forcibly carries off a maiden, [he shall pay] fifty shillings to her owner, and afterwards buy from the owner his consent. If she is betrothed, at a price, to another man, twenty shillings shall be paid as compensation. If she is brought back, thirty-five shillings shall be paid, and fifteen shillings to the king. If a man lies with the woman of a servant, during the lifetime of the husband, he shall pay a twofold compensation' (Æthelberht, Laws 82-85).[2]

The abductor of a woman must pay fifty shillings in compensation, but

---

2. The term *agende* would probably be better translated by 'guardian' than 'owner' (Fell 1984: 62-63), which means that this passage does not apply only to slaves.

he may also buy the right to keep her. If he decides to return her instead, her guardian has suffered only a temporary loss, so his compensation is reduced by fifteen shillings, which is paid instead to the king. Where the woman is betrothed in *sceat*, the offence is against both her guardian and her prospective husband, so the compensation is increased by twenty shillings. Unless the use of force is understood to be carried over, the last offence is one of simple adultery rather than rape. Here both the husband and the employer/owner of the woman are compensated.

Alfred's laws, dating from the late ninth century, deal with another type of abduction:

> '*Gif hwa nunnan of mynstere ut alæde butan kyninges lefnesse oððe biscepes, geselle hundtwelftig scill', healf cyning, healf biscepe & þære cirican hlaforde, ðe ðone munuc age*'.

> 'If anyone takes a nun from a nunnery without the permission of the king or bishop, he shall pay 120 shillings, half to the king, and half to the bishop and the lord of the church, under whose charge the nun is' (Alfred, Laws 8).

The severity of the offence is suggested by the fact that the same penalty is demanded for public disregard of the laws of the church during Lent, for breaking into the fortified premises of the king, for drawing a weapon and disturbing a meeting called by an ealdorman, or for employing the escaped slave of an ealdorman, all serious offences against secular or ecclesiastical authority.

Alfred's laws also deal with sexual offences against free women:

> '*Gif mon on cirliscre fæmnan breost gefo, mid V scill. hire gebete. Gif he hie oferweorpe & mid ne gehæme, mid X scill. gebete. Gif he mid gehæme, mid LX scill. gebete. Gif oðer mon mid hire læge ær, sie be healfum ðæm ðonne sio bot. Gif hie mon teo, geladiege hie be sixtegum hida, oððe ðolige be healfre þære bote. Gif borenran wifmen ðis gelimpe, weaxe sio bot be ðam were*'.

> 'If anyone seizes by the breast a young woman belonging to the commons, he shall pay her 5 shillings compensation. If he throws her down but does not lie with her, he shall pay [her] 10 shillings compensation. If he lies with her, he shall pay [her] 60 shillings compensation. If another man has previously lain with her, then the compensation shall be half this [amount]. If she is accused [of having previously lain with a man], she shall clear herself by [an oath of] 60 hides, or lose half the compensation due to her. If this [outrage] is done to a woman of higher birth, the compensation to be paid shall increase according to the wergeld' (Alfred, Laws 11).

While Æthelberht's laws punish sexual offences according to the status of the woman's guardian, Alfred's laws punish them according to a free woman's own rank: moral as well as social. All penalties are halved if the woman is not a virgin or cannot produce sufficiently wealthy character-witnesses to swear that she is. If she is a nun, it states elsewhere, they are doubled. A distinction is now made between rape and attempted rape, and another advance is that compensation is paid to the woman herself. Where the offence is one of adultery, however, the penalty is still paid to the husband. The amount of compensation depends on the husband's wergeld: the amount which would be paid to his kin in compensation for his murder. The penalty for lying with the wife of a man whose wergeld was 1200 shillings was 120 shillings, 100 for the wife of a 600 shilling man, and forty shillings for the wife of a commoner. It is not clear how these laws were applied to rape committed against a married woman. If it were treated as adultery the fine would be forty shillings; if as rape the fine would be only thirty shillings because she was no longer a virgin. While the rape of a married woman may well have been considered a lesser crime than the rape of a virgin, this implies that because adultery was an offence in itself, the woman's consent or refusal was irrelevant.

However, Alfred's laws do deal with consent, even where it is only a slave who is raped, although the slave is still not treated as the injured party:

'Gif mon ceorles mennen to nedhæmde geðreatað, mid V scill. gebete þam ceorle; & LX scill. to wite. Gif ðeowmon þeowne to nedhæmde genede, bete mid his eowende'.

'If anyone rapes the slave of a commoner, he shall pay 5 shillings to the commoner, and a fine of 60 shillings. If a slave rapes a slave, castration shall be required as compensation' (Alfred, Laws 25).

The use of nedhæman (literally 'to have sex by force') indicates that it is now considered significant whether a slave consents to sex or not, but the compensation is still paid to her owner and the fine to the king. Free men who were unable to pay fines were able to sell themselves into slavery in order to raise the money, but this option was not available to the already enslaved, so physical punishments are usually provided for them in place of monetary penalties.

Lower penalties for offences committed against children than against adults seem to be normal in Anglo-Saxon law, but where a rape is committed the penalty is not reduced:

'Gif mon ungewintrædne wifmon to niedhæmde geðreatige, sie ðæt swa ðæs gewintredan monnes bot'.

'If anyone rapes a girl who is not of age, the same compensation shall be paid to her as is paid to an adult' (Alfred, Laws 29).

It seems strange, in the light of modern attitudes, to treat the rape of a child as if it were no worse a crime than the rape of a woman, but where the size of a fine for any offence was related to the social worth of the victim, the fact that the penalty is the same does indicate that raping a child was considered to be a serious offence.

The third of the four groups suffering the consequences of a rape is the rapist himself. The significance of the rapist's offence against his own soul is indicated by the length of penance suggested in penitentials. Theodore's penitential, dating from 668–690, was the basis of many others used in Anglo-Saxon England.[3] It prescribes a penance of one year for fornication with a virgin, which increases to three years for a vowed virgin, four for a married woman and fifteen for fornication with one's sister or mother. For the purposes of comparison, the penance for killing by accident was one year, three for killing in anger, seven for murder without malice aforethought and ten if the murder was the result of a quarrel. Frantzen (1983: 80) writes that Theodore's penitential raises women to a higher position than the roughly contemporary law-codes of Æthelberht, because it considers the woman's own status rather than that of her guardian, but since the woman's status is largely determined by reference to her relationships to men, this is not a major advance. The penitential also joins Æthelberht's laws in failing to distinguish clearly between consensual and non-consensual sex. Where a man has sex with a slave, however, a penance of only six months is supplemented by an admonition to set the woman free, which would hardly be appropriate if she had consented.

In his *Sermo Lupi*, quoted above, Wulfstan goes on to describe the purchase, gang-rape and subsequent resale of a slavewoman:

'And scandlic is to specenne þæt geworden is to wide & egeslic is to witanne þæt oft doð to manege þe dreogað þa yrmþe, þæt sceotað togædere & ane cwenan gemænum ceape bicgað gemæne, & wið þa ane fylþe adreogað, an æfter anum & ælc æfter oðrum, hundum gelicost þe for fylþe ne scrifað, & syððan wið weorðe syllað of lande feondum to gewealde Godes gesceafte & his agenne ceap þe he deore gebohte'.

'And it is shameful to speak of what has too commonly happened, and it is dreadful to know what many too often do, who practise that wretchedness that they club together and buy one woman in common as a joint purchase, and with the one commit filth one

---

3. Neither Bede's nor Egbert's penitential has much to contribute to an understanding of the spiritual significance of rape during the Anglo-Saxon period.

after another and each after the other just like dogs who do not
care about filth; and then sell for a price out of the land into the
power of enemies the creature of God and his own purchase that
he dearly bought' (Wulfstan, *Sermo Lupi*, ll. 85–91).

Wulfstan's emphasis in this passage is on the men's bestial filthiness
and lust, rather than on the rape as an offence against the woman. Of
the two offences committed against her, her sale into slavery among
heathens, which had been forbidden since the earliest written Anglo-
Saxon laws (Pollock & Maitland 1968: 35) seems to be the greater. This
suggests that the woman's soul was not endangered by physical assault,
but only by her exclusion from Christendom. According to this interpretation, the main victim of rape, the woman herself, suffered only a
physical assault, with no spiritual repercussions.

In *Apollonius of Tyre*, however, the daughter of King Antiochus does
appear to be defiled when he rapes her:

'Ða gewearð hit þæt þæs mædenes fostormodor into ðam bure eode and
geseah hi ðar sittan on micelre gedrefednesse and hire cwæð to: "Hwæt
eart þu, hlæfdige, swa gedrefedes modes?" þæt mæden hyre andswerode:
"Leofe fostormodor, nu todæg forwurdon twegen æðele naman on þisum
bure." Seo fostormodor cwæð: "Hlæfdige, be hwam cwist þu þæt?" Heo
hyre andwirde and cwæð: "Ær ðam dæge minre bridgifta ic eom mid
manfulre scilde besmiten".'

'Then it happened that the girl's nurse went into her chamber
and saw her sitting there in great perturbation, and said to her:
"Why are you so troubled in spirit, lady?" The girl answered her:
"Dear nurse, today two noble names have now perished in this
chamber." The nurse said: "Of whom do you say that, lady?" She
answered her and said: "I am polluted with wicked sin before the
day of my marriage"' (Apollonius 2, ll. 20–25).

In this case, however, the pollution the girl complains of may be as
much the defilement of incest as of rape. It would be difficult to determine from these two passages whether the victim of rape was spiritually
defiled if the offence was uncompounded by incest or sale into heathen-
dom.

Avoidance of rape is, however, a characteristic feature of the lives of
many popular female saints (Schulenberg 1988: 121), and the Anglo-
Saxons were not immune to its appeal. The audience of a female saint's
life would have known that her faith would protect her from rape and
could, therefore, have sat back to enjoy a vicarious pleasure in the
attempt, its failure, and the punishment of the malefactor. Lingering descriptions of sexual torture and heroic acts of defiance are elements of
the most common approach, but farce is also employed. In the life of

Rape in Anglo-Saxon England 201

saints Agape, Chionia and Irene, for instance, the would-be-rapist, Dulcitus, makes love to kitchen implements after mistaking them for the holy virgins *þurh godes miht* (Martyrology: 52–55). Although they were intended to educate and exhort, saints' lives also provided entertainment.

While it is evident that saints' lives cannot be considered reliable historical accounts, they can throw light on contemporary secular and ecclesiastical attitudes (Schulenberg 1988: 103). Of the saints considered in this paper, only Ætheldryda is an Anglo-Saxon, but their stories were all translated into English between the late ninth and the early twelfth centuries, and must have had some appeal or perceived relevance. The general outline of many of these stories is that a beautiful young Christian girl is desired, sexually or maritally, by a powerful heathen who is prevented from fulfilling his desires by the power of her faith. He does succeed, however, in inflicting various imaginative tortures upon her, resulting in her glorious martyrdom (Treharne 1990: 222–23).

St Agnes, for instance, in Ælfric's account of her life, rebuffs the judge Sempronius who commands his men to strip her and lead her to a harlot's house. Although they follow his orders, Agnes's body is covered by her hair and she is met at the brothel by an angel so bright that no man could look upon her or touch her. Sempronius is not impressed by his followers' fear:

'Þa ðreade he hi þearle. forðan þe hi þæs scinendan leohtes./ swa swiðe wundrodon. and hi gewemman ne dorston./ Arn þa him sylf inn. mid sceand-lican willan./ ac he feol astreht ætforan þam mædene adyd./þurh ðone deofol þe he dwollice gehyrsumede.'

'Then he reproached them furiously because they had wondered so much at the shining light, and had not dared to defile her. Then he himself ran in with shameful intent, but he fell prostrated before the maiden, struck down by the devil whom he foolishly obeyed' (Ælfric 7, ll. 168–72).

After Sempronius' fatal attempt upon her chastity, Agnes is also protected from fire, but finally dies by the sword (see also Martyrology: 28–29). St Cecilia too, although God allows her to be boiled in a bath and finally to die after an unsuccessful beheading, is protected against rape. On their wedding night she announces to her husband, Valerian, that:

'Ic hæbbe godes encgel þe gehylt me on [lufe]./ and gif þu wilt me gewemman. he went sona to ðe./ and mid gramum þe slihð þæt þu sona ne leofast.'

'"I have God's angel who holdeth me in love, and if thou pollute me he will quickly turn to thee and will slay thee in anger, that thou wilt soon cease to live"' (Ælfric 34, ll. 32–34).

An angel does appear and Valerian, understandably, is converted. Saints Irene and Theodota (Martyrology: 54–55, 136–37) are also protected from rape by angels. Like St Ætheldryda (*EH* IV.19), however, Cecilia is protected even from marital intercourse. As Treharne (1990: 232) writes of St Margaret, Cecilia's protection from rape 'is less a testament to reality than a narratological device protecting the virgin (for virgin she must remain for the purpose of her sanctification), and exposing a favourable reception by God of the saint's prayers that she remain undefiled.'

Although the rape of a saint appears to be an impossibility, Ælfric has St Lucy discuss the spiritual implications of her defilement with her would-be-rapist, Paschasius:

'*Se apostol behet þam ðe healdað clænnysse. þæt hi synd godes templ. and þæs halgan gastes wunung./Þa cwæð se arleasa. Ic hate þe ardlice lædan to þæra myltestrena huse þæt ðu þinne mægð-had forleose./þæt se. halga gast þe fram fleo./ðonne þu fullice byst gescynd./Lucia andwyrde þus. ne bið ænig gewemmed. lichama to plihte. gif hit ne licað þam mode. . . . gif þu me unwilles gewemmen nu dest./me bið twifeald clænnysse. geteald to wuldre./Ne miht þu gebigan minne willan to þe./swa hwæt swa þu minum lichaman dest. ne mæg þæt belimpan to me.*'

'"The apostle promised those who preserve chastity, that they are God's temple, and the Holy Ghost's habitation." Then the impious one said, "I shall straightaway bid men lead thee to the house of harlots, that thou mayst lose thy maidenhood, that the Holy Ghost may flee from thee, when thou art foully dishonoured." Lucy thus answered, "No one's body is dangerously polluted, if it pleases not the (possessor's) mind . . . if now, against my will, thou causest me to be polluted, a twofold purity shall be gloriously imputed to me. Thou canst not bend my will to thy purpose; whatever thou mayest do to my body, that cannot happen to me"' (Ælfric IX, ll. 79–93).

Lucy is not raped, of course (but see Chance 1990: 254): when Paschasius' men attempt to move the saint the Holy Ghost will not allow them to, no matter how many men or oxen pull on the ropes tied to her hands and feet. Black magic and fire also fail to harm her, and although she finally falls prey to a fatal sword-blow, she does not die until after Paschasius has been beheaded and she has received the last rites. The treatment of rape in saints' lives therefore suggests, firstly, that a saint may not be raped because, whatever other torments she suffers in the process of her martyrdom, God will preserve her virginity; and secondly, that even if she were raped it would make no difference to her sanctity. It is unlikely, given the first of these assumptions, that a woman who had been raped would have been considered a candidate for either papal or popular canonization.

To attempt to sum up attitudes to rape in a period ranging from the earliest English law-codes to the Norman Conquest is probably unwise: the historical period is too long, and the geographical disparities too great. It is possible, however, to see some general trends. The first is that rape was considered as a symptom of general lawlessness and the break-down of order. In this it is associated with offences such as robbery and murder, but also with spiritual transgressions like lust and gluttony. The second is that the woman's consent was not as essential a defining feature of rape as it is today. Nuns did not have the right to give consent, a woman without the protection of her kin did not have the means to enforce her refusal and wives, unless particularly saintly, may not have had the right to refuse. Through the early part of the Anglo-Saxon period, it seems that the consent of a woman's owner or guardian was more important than her own. By the late ninth century, law-codes are concerned with the woman's consent, although the severity of the punishment depended upon her own moral standing. Rape of a non-virgin was merely rape; rape of a virgin was both rape and defilement; rape of a nun was rape, defilement, and an offence against God and the Church; rape of a saint was, apparently, impossible.

BIBLIOGRAPHY

Primary Sources

Ælfric, *Lives of the Saints*: W. W. Skeat (ed. & trans.), *Ælfric's Lives of the Saints* vol. I, Early English Text Society 76 (London, 1881); vol. II (Early English Text Society 94/114) (London, 1890).

Æthelberht, *Laws*: F. L. Attenborough (ed. & trans.), *The Laws of the Earliest English Kings* (Cambridge, 1922).

Alcuin, Letter to Æthelred, king of Northumbria: A. W. Haddan & W. Stubbs, (eds), *Councils and Ecclesiastical Documents Relating to Great Britain and Ireland* vol. 3 (Oxford, 1871); D. Whitelock (trans.), *EHD* vol. 1 ?nd edition (London, 1979).

Alfred, *Laws*: F. L. Attenborough (ed. & trans.), *The Laws of the Earliest English Kings* (Cambridge, 1922).

Anglo-Saxon Chronicle: D. Whitelock, D. Douglas, & S. Tucker (trans.), *The Anglo-Saxon Chronicle: A Revised Translation* (London, 1961).

Apollonius of Tyre: P. Goolden (ed.), *The Old English Apollonius of Tyre* (Oxford 1958); M. Swanton (trans.), *Anglo-Saxon Prose* (London, 1979), pp. 158–73.

Asser, *Life of King Alfred*: S. Keynes & M. Lapidge (trans.), *Alfred the Great* (London, 1983).

Bede, *Ecclesiastical History*: B. Colgrave & R. A. B. Mynors (eds & trans.), *Bede's Ecclesiastical History of the English People* (Oxford, 1969).

Martyrology: G. Herzfeld (ed.), *An Old English Martyrology* (Early English Text Society 116) (London, 1900).

Wulfstan, *Sermo Lupi ad Anglos*: D. Bethurum (ed.), *The Homilies of Wulfstan* (Oxford, 1958); M. Swanton (trans.), *Anglo-Saxon Prose* (London, 1979), pp. 116–25.

204   Coleman

Secondary Bibliography

Barlow, F., 1983. *The Norman Conquest and Beyond* (London).

Carter, J. M., 1985. *Rape in Medieval England. An Historical and Sociological Study* (New York & London).

Chance, J., 1990. 'Structural unity in Beowulf', in Helen Damico & A. Hennessey Olsen (eds), *New Readings on Women in Anglo-Saxon Literature* (Indiana, 1990), pp. 248-61.

Coleman, J., 1989. 'A Study of the Semantic Fields of LOVE, SEX and MARRIAGE in OE' (King's College, University of London MA Thesis).

Fell, C. (with Clark, C., & Williams, E.), 1984. *Women in Anglo-Saxon England and the Impact of 1066* (London).

Frantzen, A. J., 1983. *The Literature of Penance in Anglo-Saxon England* (New Jersey).

McNeill, J. T., & Gamer, H. M. (trans.), 1938. *Medieval Handbooks of Penance* (New York).

Pollock, F., & Maitland, F. W., 1968. *The History of English Law* 2 vols 2nd edition (Cambridge).

Schulenberg, J. T., 1986. 'The heroics of virginity: brides of Christ and sacrificial mutilation', in M. B. Rose (ed.), *Women in the Middle Ages and the Renaissance* (Syracuse), pp. 29-72.

—— 1988. 'Female sanctity: public and private roles, ca. 500-1100', in M. Erler & M. Kowaleski (eds), *Women and Power in the Middle Ages* (Athens & London), pp. 102-25.

Treharne, E. M., 1990. '"They should not worship devils which can neither see, nor hear, nor walk": the sensibility of the virtuous and the Life of St Margaret', *Proceedings of the PMR Conference, Augustinian Historical Institute, Villanova University* 15: 221-36.

CHAPTER 11

Selective female infanticide as partial explanation for the dearth of women in Viking Age Scandinavia[1]

Nancy L. Wicker

'So you are with child. If you should bear a girl, it shall be exposed, but if a boy, then it shall be raised.'

Þorsteinn to Jófríðr in *Gunnlaugs saga*

This thirteenth-century Icelandic saga gives an example of 'exposure', or the abandonment of an unwanted child. Though the saga was written well within the Christian period, Þorsteinn's directive to his wife Jófríðr contradicts Christian medieval teachings that dictate raising all children and perhaps recalls ninth-century norms. From his declaration we may infer that men in this society had the right to make such decisions and that women were compelled to accept their judgement. His apparently cavalier attitude also suggests that female offspring may have routinely been disposed of in this manner. The action advised by Þorsteinn, exposure, represents a category of violence rarely documented in Viking culture. Public violence in warfare and plunder was exalted and

---

1. I have presented some of this material at the 1992 annual meeting of the Society for American Archaeology and at the 1993 Scottish Archaeological Forum meeting on 'Death and the Supernatural.' Proceedings of the Scottish Archaeological Forum paper will be published.

mentioned frequently in the sagas and in history, tending to form our views of violence in this society, while other forms of more private violence at home are little known.

The Viking world has been considered one of powerful men, and we may question whether there even is such a concept as 'Viking women'. Though the etymology is unclear, the word 'Viking' apparently refers specifically to the seafaring men who pillaged and established colonies throughout much of Europe and beyond from 800 to 1150 (Jesch 1991: 1). We know much less about women and children of the Viking period than about men because they were not similarly commemorated in life or in death in the extant histories and sagas that we read or in the burial remains that we find.

Here, female infanticide will be considered as contributing to any explanation of the scarcity of archaeological remains of women in some Scandinavian regions from the late Iron Age, c. AD 600, through the end of the saga period, c. AD 1300. Infanticide is recorded in Scandinavian literary and proto-historical sources during and shortly after the period of conversion to Christianity, around AD 1000, but the practice is difficult to trace in the archaeological record. Literary and historical scholars have noted infanticide in the form of exposure of infants, and archaeologists have detected a dearth of adult female burials in the late Iron Age, but these disparate studies have yet to be correlated with indirect archaeological evidence such as finds of scattered infant bones that may indicate exposure of infants.

THE WRITTEN EVIDENCE

Though possibly repugnant to us, infanticide has been widespread throughout history and prehistory (Langer 1974; Ehrenberg 1989). Explanations for its occurrence revolve around tradeoffs pertaining to demography, ecology, and culture (Dickeman 1975; Hrdy 1992; Scrimshaw 1984). Elimination of infants of either sex, especially deformed or sickly individuals, may occur, but widespread parental favour for male children has also led to selective female infanticide (Williamson 1976).

Methods of infanticide vary. It often does not take the form of the cold-blooded murder of babies, occurring instead as the intentional abandonment or 'exposure' of undesired children or as the uncalculated preferential treatment of the favoured sex and neglect of the other sex. Exposure was perhaps the most prevalent form in ancient Rome and Greece as well as Europe, but in other parts of the world drowning, suffocation, and strangulation were also customary (Lee 1981: 163). 'Deferred' infanticide by withholding adequate food and other resources from unwanted children, which is less actively violent, also has been widespread (Johansson 1984; Miller 1981). While not explicitly insinuating infanticide, Elisabeth Iregren suggests that withholding breast-feeding may account for the unusually high mortality of infants from three to six months of age at Västerhus in Jämtland, Sweden (1988: 22–25). Infanticide in all its manifestations has had a powerful effect as a conscious or unconscious mechanism of population control and the maintenance of social power.

A cross-cultural examination of infanticide reveals a polarity between societies where infanticide is condoned, and those wherein it is condemned. Historical examples of the first type are known from ancient Greece and Rome where infanticide may have been an acceptable method to control inheritance and dowry responsibilities (Bennett 1923; Golden 1990: 179; Harris 1982). A letter from Alexandria in the first century BC closely resembles the words of *Gunnlaugs saga* in the introduction to this chapter: 'If – good luck to you – you bear offspring, and it is a male, let it live; if it is a female, expose it' (Lefkowitz & Fant 1982: 111). As this selection informs us, newborns rarely were murdered with direct violence; instead, they were abandoned 'on garbage heaps or in public places' (Anderson & Zinsser 1988: 30; Bennett 1923). Following the so-called 'law of Romulus', many Roman families were unwilling to keep more than one daughter though they were obliged to raise all sons (Pomeroy 1975: 164). In Roman society, the *pater familias* performed a ritual to recognize the newborn as a member of the family. He had the prerogative of deciding which children would be allowed to live, just as in Scandinavia, and if he chose not to recognize the infant, he ordered its exposure (Gardner 1986: 153–58; Pomeroy 1975). Since it was not yet a member of the family, the action was not considered murder. While exposure was not censured, it was carried out discreetly. Pomeroy asserts that ancient Greek and Roman court records and citizenship lists reveal only that daughters were much scarcer than sons, but never refer directly to exposure. As would be expected with a dearth of daughters, it seems that adult women are under-represented in the archaeological record in both Greece and Rome (Anderson & Zinsser 1988: 30–31).

In Christianized early medieval Europe, attitudes shifted toward vigorous social rejection of infanticide. Infanticide has been suggested in tax and census records (Coleman 1976, though problematic) and in clerical exhortations against infanticide (Sawyer 1987: 84). The vehemence with which clergy and law-makers attempted to eradicate the practice reveals their repugnance at this remnant from the pagan past. Rather than the father's prerogative, infanticide becomes more and more the desperate recourse of an unmarried mother forced to kill her child single-handedly to avoid social pressure upon herself and the child. Roslund (1990: 290) suggests this scenario to explain an infant skeleton discovered under the floor of an eleventh- or twelfth-century house in Lund, Sweden. The tide turns from an action supported by communal values to one vilified by Christian societies (see Wrightson 1982 for discussion of this shift in attitudes). Christian authorities developed ways of attempting to deal with exposed children.

These historical European instances of infanticide emanate from societies thoroughly conditioned by Christian condemnation of the practice. The Scandinavian written sources reflect a hybrid world where a veneer of moralizing teachings of the church met long-standing local tradition head-on. The topic of female infanticide in Scandinavia during and shortly after the period of conversion, around AD 1000, has been discussed by Carol Clover (1988), Juha Pentikäinen (1968; 1990), and, most recently, by Jenny Jochens (1995: 85–93). Clover calls attention to infanticide in eleven Old Norse sources, including references to laws and customs as well as narratives describing specific incidents. The most straightforward Scandinavian accounts of infanticide, usually in the form of exposure, occur in Icelandic sagas. One such example (*Gunnlaugs saga*, 3) is cited at the beginning of this chapter. Another example relates that 'Now it will be told that Earl Bjartmarr's daughter bore a baby girl, and it seemed advisable to most that it be exposed' (*Hervarar saga*, 3; Clover 1988: 158). Apparently exposure was considered appropriate simply because the child was a girl, not because it was deformed or sickly.

We have assumed that exposure is a method of infanticide, thus resulting in death for the exposed newborns. Boswell (1984; 1988) maintained that exposure in the sagas does not amount to infanticide and that exposed infants were meant to be found. Parents who exposed their offspring may have hoped for a propitious outcome for them. However, one must keep in mind that exposure in the cold harsh climate of the north could be deadly to a newborn much sooner than in Christian southern Europe, where the climate is kinder and the church's attitude was more pervasive. Each of the children intended to be exposed in the sagas was either prevented from being exposed, or discovered and saved before being harmed. In four instances, boys were put out to die but were discovered; these exposures clearly were considered unusual even within the saga context explicitly because the children were healthy males. Clover (1988: 150–58) contends that these saga examples were exceptional and that the discovery and adoption of foundling infants in Scandinavia must not have been common. These incidents were included only because the outcome was extraordinary and the child crucial to the story. Such stories may have been influenced by hero legends or the Oedipus folklore motif (Pentikäinen 1968: 69–73; Aarne 1964: no. 931). Children of special portent, such as Romulus and Remus, Oedipus, Moses, and Jesus, have often been the focus of infanticidal intent.

Clover (1988: 151) also counters Boswell's thesis by pointing out that medieval law-codes, such as the Swedish *Gutalagen*, written down in the 1350s, included prohibitions against infanticide. *Gutalagen* (ch. 2) states: 'Every child born in our country shall be raised and not gotten rid of'

(Thomson 1960: 6). The practice of exposure was apparently common enough that laws against it became necessary in the Christian period. Pentikäinen sees criminalization of exposure of infants as an indication of growing Christianization. The Icelandic governing body, or *thing*, specifically allowed the heathen practice of the exposure of children during the conversion period, according to Ari Thorgilsson's *Íslendinga-bók* (ch. 7; Hovstad 1956: 348). Its tacit acceptance underscores its existence. According to Icelandic sagas, a child could be abandoned until a name-giving rite was carried out: after this ceremony death by exposure was considered murder even in the pre-Christian period (Pentikäinen 1990: 79). With Christianization, exposure even before a child was named was criminalized. In the saga examples, perhaps the overlay of Christianity has affected the acceptability of such violence, since various people try to prevent exposure and save the child.

The level of direct violence in these cases of intended infanticide is usually low. Normally the father orders the mother to abandon the child. Though expected to obey his command, she was not required to carry out the deed herself. Either parent usually orders someone inconsequential to the story to carry out the dastardly deed (e.g. *Finnboga saga* 2) or, more commonly, the child is ordered borne out without specifying by whom (e.g. *Gunnlaugs saga*).

Passages in some sagas suggest that violence or the threat of violence may be used to dominate and regulate women in this society. Although usually coerced into submission, occasionally women seek actively to redress the situation and resist their husbands' orders. In *Finnboga Saga*, a mother's objection is overruled by her fear of her husband, but Jófríðr in *Gunnlaugs saga* defies Þorsteinn and arranges to save the child. In at least one case, a woman could use the threat of exposure to control another woman's behaviour, as in *Vatnsdœla saga*, in which the wife of a man who fathered an illegitimate child from an extramarital relationship orders the child exposed.

Besides indirect infanticide by abandonment, other more violent methods are attested in the literature. In *Harðar saga ok Holmverja* (ch. 8), orders were given for a child to be thrown into a river. An Arab traveller, Al Tartushi, reported that infanticide was performed at Danish Hedeby, where unwanted infants were thrown into the sea to save the costs of bringing them up (Birkeland 1954: 104). A Christian apologist in *Reykdœla saga* (ch. 7) indirectly substantiates the custom of ritual infanticide by his report of the assembly's decision not to resort to sacrificing infants and elderly persons to propitiate the weather (Clover 1988: 152).

Old Norse literary sources also mention fewer females than should be the case according to natural sex ratios. A suspicious preponderance of male children and a lack of female children, perhaps indirectly reflecting selective female infanticide, has been noted by Clover (1988: 167–

68) in lists of household membership in the medieval Icelandic *Land-námabók*, a book detailing the tenth-century settlement of Iceland. The lists of household membership show that there were not as many girls and women as would be expected. Clover estimates that sons usually out-number daughters at a ratio of four or five to one, occasionally even nine to one, perhaps indirectly reflecting the effects of female infanticide. Swedish Upplandic runestones, as counted by Anne-Sofie Gräslund, display similar ratios of sons to daughters. Gräslund (1989: 233–40) suggests that female infanticide may account for this scarcity of daughters.

Some scholars have attempted to discount evidence of infanticide by explaining that women and girls only seem to be lacking because they were not important enough to be mentioned as often. In either case, 'hidden' practice contributes to the relative invisibility of women. But even slaves were enumerated in *Landnámabók* (Karras 1988: 80), pre-sumably because of their economic significance. It would seem logical, therefore, that each girl should also be noted due to the future negative economic impact that her dowry, the woman's inheritance which was handed over by her father at marriage, would represent (Frank 1973: 475–76). While the scarcity of women and girls in written sources is not conclusive proof of infanticide, this testimony supports the proposition of female infanticide when considered alongside other evidence.

THE ARCHAEOLOGICAL EVIDENCE

Archaeological evidence that might demonstrate the existence of infant-icide is almost all indirect; the most pervasive testimony is the dearth of women's remains, as we find for Iron Age Scandinavia as well as for Merovingian Gaul (Halsall 1996: 15–16). John Boswell has called the analysis of sex ratios from cemetery remains 'a particularly treacherous methodology' (1988: 44, n. 107). While archaeological data have limita-tions, the source materials of historical demography, such as taxation lists, court lists, and ecclesiastical records, have their own weaknesses too (Welinder 1979: 33). Although estimating population from archae-ological remains is fraught with difficulties, it should not be overlooked. Before discussing the scarcity of women's graves in Scandinavia, let us first examine how the sex or gender of a burial is determined.

Identification of sex or gender in graves

There are two major methods to determine the sex or gender of a buried person: by analysis of skeletal remains, and by investigation of grave-goods. For Viking finds, both means are used because often the preservation of human remains is not satisfactory to permit conclusions on the basis of osteological analysis alone, due to cremation or soil conditions affecting preservation. However, archaeologists are fortunate that many Scandinavians of the Viking period buried their dead with grave-goods. Vikings practised both inhumation and cremation, but even cremation graves with only fragments of burnt bone may contain grave-goods that may allow gender identification.

The gender of the dead is often ascertained by grave-goods when skeletal remains are inadequate. Binford (1971: 22) proposed that the most important way of displaying gender to the so-called 'invisible society' of burial was by the objects in the grave: clothes, jewellery, other personal equipment and characteristic tools. However, it is debatable exactly which grave-goods can be used reliably as indicators of gender and, indeed, the whole basis for our assumptions of the gender specificity of artefact correlates needs to be re-examined (Brush 1988).

In Scandinavia, weapons and certain tools buried with skeletons normally indicate males, and jewellery and domestic implements signify females, but it is difficult to make these assignments with certainty. The usual practice has been to assume that a grave is male if, for instance, as few as one weapon was found, or female if five or more beads were found (Solberg 1985: 63). The numbers of objects decided upon may be arbitrary, but regardless of the number chosen as diagnostic, the artefacts used for gender determination normally are jewellery and weapons (Henderson 1989).

Often there is substantial agreement between results from sexing graves by grave-goods and by analysis of skeletal material, but there is not complete accord (Henderson 1989; Pader 1981). A study of all unburnt Danish Iron Age burials (Sellevold *et al.* 1984; Sellevold 1985) compared results arrived at by skeletal analysis to results indicated from grave-goods and determined that for the Viking Period there was a strong correlation between the sex of the deceased and artefacts buried with them. The objects that could be used to distinguish men's graves consisted of weapons such as swords and spears; axes; riding equipment including stirrups, bits, and spurs; blacksmith's tools such as shears, hammers, tongs, and files; and penannular brooches. Women's graves can be distinguished by the inclusion of jewellery including paired oval brooches, trefoil buckles, disc brooches, arm rings, and necklaces; jewel boxes or caskets; and spindle whorls. Objects common to both sexes included buckles, combs, clay pots, wooden vessels, knives, whetstones, coins, and, contrary to common assumptions, beads, sewing needles, and various jewellery types (Sellevold 1985: 67). Even the common assumption that weapons necessarily indicate males needs to be reassessed in light of a few problematic graves such as at Gerdrup in Denmark (Hemmendorff 1985) and Aurland in Norway (Dommasnes 1982: 77) in which women, as determined by skeletal analysis, have been found with a sword and arrowheads, respectively. Ultimately, however, sexing graves by either grave-goods or skeletal analysis indicates that women were scarce.

Indirect evidence of infanticide: the dearth of female graves

A relative shortage of adult female mortuary remains compared to the expected sex ratio of nearly 1 : 1 has been noted in many regions of Scandinavia for the late Iron Age. Norway's population seems to diverge most markedly from average sex ratios. Dommasnes (1979; 1982; 1991) found a much smaller representation of women in studies of burials in four regions of the country. The women's share of graves identifiable by gender in the four areas of Sogn, Gloppen, Nordland, and Upper Telemark varied from only 6% to 32%. Dommasnes (1979: 99–100) found ratios of eight males to one female in Sogn in the seventh century and six to one in the eighth century. The ratios are typical of graves throughout most of Norway in that period. For instance, Ellen Høigård Hofseth (1988: fig. 11) found that women represented only from 8% to 18% of the late Iron Age graves in Hordaland. In another study, Trond Løken (1987) found three times as many male as female graves in Iron Age material from Ostfold and Vestfold in Norway.

In Denmark, sex ratios from cemetery analysis also are skewed toward males. The study of all unburnt Danish Iron Age skeletal remains found during the previous one hundred and fifty years identified 158 individuals of the Viking period for which sex could be determined by skeletal analysis (Sellevold *et al.* 1984). Of these, 85 were found to be males and 73 females. The numbers represented are small and reflect quite a sampling problem in Denmark where preservation is poor, but notably fewer women than men were identified and the sex imbalance is even more pronounced in earlier Iron Age material. In addition, just across the Danish-German border at Viking Hedeby, 62% of adult dead (47 individuals) that could be sexed skeletally were men and only 38% (29 individuals) women (Schaefer 1963).

For Sweden there has been no country-wide re-evaluation of Iron Age skeletal material as completed for Denmark and in progress for Norway (Sellevold & Næss 1987), though there is a project underway for the medieval period (Iregren 1988: 25). The situation appears to differ with a marked qualitative rather than quantitative difference between women's and men's graves. Studies of Swedish material have concentrated on extraordinary sites such as boat graves at Valsgärde, as well as the large number of burials at Birka dating to Viking times. At Valsgärde, men were inhumed in chamber graves and boat graves, but women were cremated (Arwidsson 1942; 1954). At Birka where more than 2,000 grave mounds are visible, sex has been determined for only 415 burials. Gräslund (1980) reports that women's graves there actually outnumber men's, representing 58% of the inhumations (308 burials) and 61% of the cremations (107 burials). However, women were buried in the generally richer chamber graves less frequently (44%) than men, so there was at least a qualitative differentiation between women's and men's graves.

Women also made up most (68%) of those interred without coffins. Rather than indicating a preponderance of women at Birka, Gräslund has suggested that the greater number of women's graves there may merely indicate that their graves are easier to identify because of their contents, especially jewellery. However, Birka is anomalous; the trading community there should not be considered representative for the Viking period as a whole because of its unusual wealth and early missionary activity; the relatively large number of women's remains found at Birka might be explained by the missionaries' success.

In her analyses of Norwegian material, Dommasnes (1982: 73) assumed that there was a 1:1 ratio of men to women, but perhaps that was not so. The sex ratio from cemetery analysis could be skewed if a portion of the population died elsewhere, away from home (Ehrenberg 1989: 127). One might expect that many men of Viking-Age Scandinavia died in foreign lands (Gräslund 1989: 236–37), and at least some such deaths are memorialized on runestones commemorating men, listing where they travelled and who they fought (Morris, above: 149, 152). Warfare and migration could have taken such a toll on men that their remains would be scarce in cemeteries at home (perhaps such as at Birka). However, in many Scandinavian regions, men are not lacking: women are. Divale and Harris have hypothesized that preferential female infanticide compensates for the loss of adult males due to extra deaths in warfare (Divale 1970; Divale & Harris 1976). Such a functionalist explanation could explain the mirroring effects of public and private violence to regulate Viking society, a population in which heavy male outward migration and warfare might have led to an overabundance of women if not for the levelling effect of female infanticide at home.

Perhaps because infanticide is so distasteful to us, some scholars have attempted to discount the dearth of women's remains in Scandinavia by explaining that women only seem to be lacking because they were not memorialized as often with large grave mounds or visible stone settings, so their graves go unnoticed. Dommasnes (1982), for instance, assumes she has not dealt with a representative sample of the Iron Age population. Women may have been given a different, less ostentatious, burial rite, as at Birka and Valsgärde. Yet it is also possible that men actually outnumbered women due to selective female infanticide or other factors. We may be witnessing the results of preferential female infanticide compounded by the relative invisibility of low status female graves.

Mortuary remains of infants and children

Very little direct archaeological evidence of infanticide exists, as the practice is rarely traceable in the physical record. Infant mortality was high in prehistory and the Middle Ages, often around 50% for Scandinavia (such as Welinder 1979: 83), so infant bones do not necessarily indicate infanticide as the cause of death. The frustrations in locating adult female graves wane compared to the difficulties of tracing children and infants in the archaeological record. Throughout much of prehistory, children's mortuary remains apparently were disposed of in an archaeologically invisible manner, as at Udby on Sjælland in Denmark, where no children under age five were discovered in a Roman Iron Age cemetery (Ethelberg 1989: 7; cp. Morris 1987: 62).

Iron Age children's graves are rare in Scandinavia. Gender- and age-specific grave-goods are often all that remain since children's and specifically infants' bones may disintegrate easily depending upon soil conditions. The unossified, cartilaginous skeletal material of infants may be totally destroyed during cremation; all that remains may be the unerupted tooth crowns and the densest temporal area of the skull (Henderson 1989; McKinley 1989: 242). Such scanty remains from earlier excavations may often have been missed altogether or discarded as apparent animal bones. Even when bones are preserved, they are fragmentary and have not developed the characteristic sexual dimorphism of adult specimens, so they rarely can be sexed osteologically (Lillehammer 1986: 12; Welinder 1989: 59). The only remaining method for assigning gender to them is according to grave-goods, with all the attendant problems of this approach for adult graves.

Some Iron Age children's graves are very wealthy, as at Luistari in Finland (Lehtosalo-Hilander 1982: 44–46), Birka in Lake Mälaren in Sweden (Gräslund 1973; 1980), and Store Ihre on Gotland, where a young boy was buried with an adult-sized long-sword and a horse (Stenberger 1961). A newborn cremated at Mulde in Fröjel parish on Gotland was buried in adult fashion but accompanied by jewellery sized to fit an infant (Lindquist 1989). Many children were not given an adult-type burial; some may have been deposited without any funerary ritual (Lillehammer 1986: 13). In many cultures, children are not considered fully human until some culturally recognized threshold has been passed, such as when the child walks, talks, or is named (Williamson 1978: 64). Saga evidence reveals that children could be exposed until the name-giving rite was carried out, and those who died before this formality might not be considered fully-fledged humans deserving burial (Pentikäinen 1968: 75).

Occasional anomalous treatments of infant remains from diverse settings have been identified as the results of infanticide. Phoenician Carthage, well-known from Biblical and other references, is a notable instance where extensive infanticide is attested by archaeological as well as literary evidence (Brown 1986; Stager & Wolff 1984). Other examples of possible infanticide are recognized only through archaeological remains. Skeletal remains of numerous newborns found in a Late Roman/Early Byzantine sewer in Israel have been identified as the victims of infanticide (Smith & Kahila 1992). Robbins (1977) has suggested that ritual infanticide occurred at the Incinerator site of the Fort Ancient culture in North America, where some infant bones were found in isolated burials unlike other infants buried in household cemeteries with diverse age groups. According to Robbins, these individuals exhibit cranial depression fractures consistent with being violently thrown into pits as sacrifices. Mays (1993) deduces the practice of infanticide in Roman Britain by demonstrating that the age at death of newborn infant remains is not consistent with the distribution of modern stillbirths and natural deaths.

Direct archaeological evidence of infanticide in Scandinavia is limited. Malin Lindquist (1981) has proposed that infant bones in stone packings of cairns may be remains of infanticide victims. Inger Saelebakke (1986: 24) suggests that apparently haphazard bone scatters in middens may be interpreted as remains of exposed infants. At a Norse site at Buckquoy, Orkney, infant bones dispersed through middens may testify to infanticide (Ritchie 1976–1977: 188, 220–21). The scattered remains initially were mistaken for animal bones upon discovery; only during osteological analysis were they identified as human. Other examples from such contexts include five infant skeletons strewn through a garbage pit excavated at Sörby Skola, Gärdslösa, Sweden (Sjöberg & Marnung 1976). Many middens as well as other bone caches from earlier excavations were not investigated as thoroughly as these examples, and one wonders how many infant bones have thus escaped discovery. Archaeologists should carefully investigate bone scatters, particularly from middens, to search for infant remains, as suggested by Larje (1989: 70–74), who cites an example of infant bones from Frösön in Jämtland, Sweden, mistakenly identified as animal bones in 1910.

Infant bones also have been found in wells and bogs, such as at Röekillorna, Skåne, where the skull of a small child was found in a well (Stjernquist 1987) and Bø in Hå *kommune*, Rogaland, where four newborn skeletons were found in a bog (Haavaldsen 1989). Discoveries of bones in these watery contexts often have been interpreted as evidence of sacrificial infanticide, but also concur with Al Tartushi's description of infanticide by drowning at Hedeby (Birkeland 1954).

Children's burials become more numerous in Scandinavian medieval cemeteries than in the pagan grave-fields, perhaps in part because the church's opposition to infanticide limited the practice somewhat (Sawyer 1987: 4). As an explanation for the increased number of older children's graves, Ole Benedictow (1985: 23) has pointed out that 'the prohibition of exposure of neonatals . . . possibly might have led to an increase in the death rates of somewhat older children through malign neglect.' An example of this cited earlier may be demonstrated by the cemetery remains at Västerhus (see above) where Elisabeth Iregren (1988: 22–25) attributes numerous remains of infants from age three through six months to early cessation of breast-feeding. However, the most important reason why more child burials of the Christian period are found is that according to medieval laws, the baptized were required to be buried in consecrated ground. The law also excluded the unbaptized from burial in Christian cemeteries, so dying infants usually were baptized quickly so that they could receive Christian rites (Karlsson 1988; O'Connor 1991; Sigurðardóttir 1983). At the medieval site of Helgeands-holmen in Stockholm, some skeletons of newborns were found just out-side the wall surrounding the cemetery (Jacobzon & Sjöberg 1982: 122–23). That they were not interred in the cemetery suggests they had not been baptized. If they were not baptized, we may hypothesize that they did not die by natural causes; perhaps they were victims of infanticide, as Roslund (1990: 286–90) proposed for the newborn (above: 207) that was buried under the clay floor of a house in Lund, Sweden, dating to the early Christian period there.

CONCLUSION

The interpretation of these scattered archaeological traces of infants who were not buried with an adult-type burial rite is problematic. Even if we can demonstrate that infanticide was practised, we have only in-direct grounds for discussing the existence of preferential female infant-icide. However, we should not underestimate their worth in detecting this practice. Carol Clover (1988: 165) has called archaeological evidence one of the 'lesser forms of evidence'. I would suggest that the testimony of hundreds of graves seen within the context of the literary and histor-ical evidence is a potent source of information. Female infanticide could account for the dearth of women in literature and in cemetery remains, and all the data serve as supporting evidence in an interdisciplinary in-vestigation.

Infanticide is so pervasive throughout history that it should not be surprising that it occurred in Scandinavia. Examining this hidden practice of violence in the Iron Age and Middle Ages may complement our view of the outward violence in these societies. Viking men were re-viled for their pillage of Christian Europe, but women most directly suffered the effects of the ruthless regulatory mechanism of infanticide, since many Viking girls apparently were not allowed to live to become 'Viking women'.

BIBLIOGRAPHY

Primary Sources

Ari Thorgilsson, *Íslendingabók*: J. Benediktsson (ed.), *Íslendingabók. Landnámabók. Íslenzk fornrit* 1.1 (Reykjavik, 1968).
Finnboga saga: In J. Halldórsson (ed.), *Kjalnesinga saga, Íslenzk Fornrit* 14 (1959), pp. 251–340.

Gunnlaugs saga Ormstungu: S. Nordal and G. Jónsson (eds), *Borgfirðinga sogur*. *Íslenzk fornrit* 3 (Reykjavik, 1938), pp. 51–107; G. Jones (trans.), *Erik and Red and Other Icelandic Sagas* (London, 1961, reprint 1980), pp. 171–217.

Gutalagen: C. J. Schlyter (ed.), *Corpus iuris sueo-gothorum antiqui. Samling Af Sweriges Gamla Lagar* 7 (Lund, 1852).

Harðar saga ok Hólmverja: S. Hast (ed.), *Editiones Arnamagnaeanae A* 6. (Copenhagen, 1960); A. Boucher (trans.), *The Saga of Hord and the Holm-Dwellers* (Reykjavik, 1983).

Hervarar saga. Heiðreks saga (Hervarar saga ok Heiðreks konungs): J. Helgason (ed.), *Samfund til Udgivelse af Gammel Nordisk Litteratur* 48 (Copenhagen, 1924, rpt. 1976).

Landnámabók: J. Benediktsson (ed.), *Íslendingabók. Landnámabók. Íslenzk fornrit* 1 (Reykjavik, 1968); H. Pálsson and P. Edwards (trans.), *The Book of Settlements: Landnámabók* (Winnipeg, 1972).

Reykdœla saga ok Víga-Skútu: B. Sigfússon (ed.), *Ljósvetninga saga. Íslenzk fornrit* 10 (Reykjavik, 1940), pp. 149–24; W. H. Vogt (trans.), 'Die Geschichte von den Leuten aus dem Rauchtal', in F. Niedner and G. Neckel (eds), *Thule: Altnordische Dichtung und Prosa* vol. 11 (Düsseldorf-Köln, 1921, reprint 1964), pp. 297–372.

Vatnsdœla saga: E. O. Svinsson (ed.), *Vatnsdœla saga. Íslenzk fornrit* 8 (Reykjavik, 1939); G. Jones (trans.), *The Vatnsdalers' Saga* (Princeton, 1944).

Secondary bibliography

Aarne, A., 1964. *The Types of the Folktale. A Classification and Bibliography,* trans. and enlarged by S. Thompson 2nd revised edition (FF Communications 184) (Helsinki).

Anderson, B. S., & Zinsser, J. P., 1988. *A History of Their Own: Women in Europe from Prehistory to the Present* vol. 1 (New York).

Arwidsson, G., 1942. *Valsgärde 6. Die Gräberfunde von Valsgärde,* 1 (Uppsala).

—— 1954. *Valsgärde 8. Die Gräberfunde von Valsgärde* 2 (Uppsala).

Benedictow, O. J., 1985. 'The Milky Way in history: breast feeding antagonism between the sexes and infant mortality in medieval Norway', *Scandinavian Journal of History* 10: 19–53.

Bennett, H., 1923. 'The exposure of infants in ancient Rome', *Classical Journal* 18: 341–51.

Binford, L. R., 1971. 'Mortuary practices: their study and their potential', in J. A. Brown (ed.), *Approaches to the Social Dimensions of Mortuary Practices* (Memoirs of the Society for American Archaelogy 25) (Washington, DC), pp. 6–29.

Birkeland, H., 1954. *Nordens Historie i Middelalderen efter Arabiske Kilder* (Norske Videnskapsakademis Skrifter) (Oslo).

Boswell, J., 1984. '*Expositio* and *oblatio*: the abandonment of children and the ancient and medieval family', *American Historical Review* 89: 10–33.

—— 1988. *The Kindness of Strangers: The Abandonment of Children in Western Europe from Late Antiquity to the Renaissance* (New York).

Brown, S. S., 1986. 'Late Carthaginian Child Sacrifice and Sacrificial Monuments in Their Mediterranean Context' (Ph.D. Dissertation, Indiana University).

Brush, K., 1988. 'Gender and mortuary analysis in pagan Anglo-Saxon archaeology', *Archaeological Review from Cambridge* 1: 76–89.

Clover, C. J., 1988. 'The politics of scarcity: notes on the sex ratio in early Scandinavia', *Scandinavian Studies* 60: 147–88.

Coleman, E. K., 1976. 'Infanticide in the early Middle Ages', in S. M. Stuard (ed.), *Women in Medieval Society* (Philadelphia), pp. 47–70.

Dickeman, M., 1975. 'Demographic consequences of infanticide in man', *Annual Review of Ecology and Systematics* 6: 107–37.

Divale, W. T., 1970. 'An explanation for primitive warfare: population control and the significance of primitive sex ratios', *The New Scholar* 2: 173–79.

Divale, W. T., & Harris, M., 1976. 'Population, warfare, and the male suprematist complex', *American Anthropologist* 78: 521–38.

Dommasnes, L. H., 1979. 'Et gravmateriale fra yngre jernalder brukt til å belyse kvinners stilling', *Viking* 1978, pp. 95–114.

——— 1982. 'Late Iron Age in western Norway: female roles and ranks as deduced from an analysis of burial customs', *Norwegian Archaeological Review* 15: 70–84.

——— 1991. 'Women, kinship, and the basis of power in the Norwegian Viking Age', in R. Samson (ed.), *Social Approaches to Viking Studies* (Glasgow), pp. 65–74.

Ehrenberg, M., 1989. *Women in Prehistory* (London).

Ethelberg, P., 1989. 'Skrålbanken', *Skalk* 2: 3–9.

Frank, R., 1973. 'Marriage in twelfth- and thirteenth-century Iceland', *Viator* 4: 473–84.

Gardner, J., 1986. *Women in Roman Law and Society* (Bloomington IN).

Golden, M., 1990. *Children and Childhood in Classical Athens* (Baltimore).

Gräslund, A.-S., 1973. 'Barn i Birka', *Tor* 15: 161–79.

——— 1980. *Birka IV. The Burial Customs. A Study of the Graves on Björkö*. (Birka, Untersuchungen und Studien) (Stockholm).

——— 1989. '"Gud hjälpe nu väl hennes själ:" om runstenskvinnorna, deras roll vid kristnandet och deras plats i familj och samhälle', *Tor* 22: 223–44.

Haavaldsen, P., 1989. 'Pojken må förast ut i kärret . . .', *Frá Haug ok Heiðni* 12: 174–76.

Halsall, G., 1996. 'Female status and power in early Merovingian central Austrasia: the burial evidence', *Early Medieval Europe* 5: 1–24.

Harris, W. V., 1982. 'The theoretical possibility of extensive infanticide in the Graeco-Roman world', *Classical Quarterly* 32: 114–16.

Hausfater, G., & Hrdy, S. B. (eds), 1984. *Infanticide: Comparative and Evolutionary Perspectives*, (New York).

Hemmendorff, O., 1985. 'Gravens bipersoner', in *Skalks Gæstebog* (Højbjerg), pp. 13–20.

Henderson, J., 1989. 'Pagan Saxon cemeteries: a study of the problems of sexing by grave goods and bones', in Roberts, Lee, & Bintliff (eds) 1989: 77–83.

Høigård Hofseth, E., 1988. 'Liten tue velter . . . problemer knyttet til manns- og kvinnegravenes i fordeling i Nord-Rogaland', *Artikkel-samling* II (AmS Skrifter, 12) (Stavanger), pp. 5–38.

Hovstad, J., 1956. 'Barneutbering', in J. Granlund (ed.), *Kulturhistoriskt Lexikon för Nordisk Medeltid från Vikingatid till Reformationstid* vol. 1 (Malmö).

Hrdy, S. B., 1992. 'Fitness tradeoffs in the history and evolution of delegated mothering with special reference to wet-nursing, abandonment, and infanticide', *Ethology and Sociobiology* 13: 409–42.

Iregren, E., 1988. 'Avbruten amning blev barnens död? - Ett försök till tolkning av Västerhusmaterialet', *Populär Arkeologi* 4: 22–25.

Jacobzon, L., & Sjögren, J., 1982. 'Människör i stadens utkanterm-Helgandshusets kyrkogård berättar om liv och död', in G. Dahlbäck (ed.), *Helgeandsholmen - 1000 år i Stockholms ström* (Stockholm), pp. 112–33.

Jesch, J., 1991. *Women in the Viking Age* (Woodbridge).

Jochens, J., 1995. *Women in Old Norse Society* (Ithaca & London).

Johansson, S. R., 1984. 'Deferred infanticide: excess female mortality during childhood', in Hausfater & Hrdy (eds) 1984: 463–85.

Karlsson, I., 1988. 'Barnets Ställning i Norden under Medeltiden - en analys med utgångspunkt från arkeologiskt och osteologiskt material', Uppsats i medeltidsarkeologi Ak 200 vid Lunds Universitet (Lund).

Karras, R. M., 1988. *Slavery and Society in Medieval Scandinavia* (New Haven & London).

Langer, W. L., 1974. 'Infanticide: a historical survey', *History of Childhood Quarterly* 1: 353–65.

Larje, R., 1989. 'Benfynd ur jämländska gravar', in O. Hemmendorff (ed.), *Arkeologi i fjäll, skog och bygd. 2. Järnålder-medeltid* (Fornvårderen 24) (Östersund), pp. 61–77.

Lee, B., 1981. 'Female infanticide in China', *Historical reflections. Reflexions historiques* 8: 163–77.

Lefkowitz, M. R., & Fant, M. B., 1982. *Women's Life in Greece and Rome: A Source Book in Translation* (Baltimore).

Lehtosalo-Hilander, P.-L., 1982. *Luistari III. A Burial-Ground Reflecting the Finnish Viking Age Society* (Suomen Muinaismuistoyhdistyksen Aikakauskirja, Finska Fornminnesföreningens Tidskrift 82: 3) (Helsinki).

Lillehammer, G., 1986. 'Barna i Nordens forhistorie: drøft metodegrunnlaget og kildenes bærekraft', *Kvinner i Arkeologi i Norge* 2: 3–21.

Lindquist, M., 1981. 'Mylingar-offer, utsatta barn eller förhistoriska barnbegravningar?', *Gotländskt arkiv* 53: 7–12.

———— 1989. 'Barngravar vid Mulde i Fröjel sn', *Gotländskt arkiv* 61: 241–42.

Løken, T., 1987. 'The correlation between the shape of grave monuments and sex in the Iron Age, based on material from Østfold and Vestfold', in R. Bertelsen, A. Lillehammer, & J.-R. Næss (eds), *Were They All Men?: An Examination of Sex Roles in Prehistoric Society* (Ams Varia, 17) (Stavanger), pp. 53–63.

McKinley, J., 1989. 'Spong Hill, Anglo-Saxon cremation cemetery', in Roberts, Lee, & Bintliff (eds) 1989: 241–48.

Mays, S., 1993. 'Infanticide in Roman Britain', *Antiquity* 67: 883–88.

Miller, B. D., 1981. *The Endangered Sex: Neglect of Female Children in Rural North India* (Ithaca, N.Y.).

Morris, I., 1987. *Burial and Ancient Society: The Rise of the Greek City-State* (Cambridge).

O'Connor, A., 1991. *Child Murderess and Dead Child Traditions* (FF Communications, no. 249) (Helsinki).

Pader, E.-J., 1981. *Symbolism, Social Relations and the Interpretation of Mortuary Remains* (BAR International Series, 130) (Oxford).

Pentikäinen, J., 1968. *The Nordic Dead-Child Tradition* (FF Communications, no. 202) (Helsinki).

—— 1990. 'Child abandonment as an indicator of Christianization in the Nordic countries', in T. Ahlbäck (ed.), *Old Norse and Finnish Religions and Cultic Place-Names* (Åbo), pp. 72–91.

Pomeroy, S. B., 1975. *Goddesses, Whores, Wives, and Slaves: Women in Classical Antiquity* (New York).

Ritchie, A., 1976–1977. 'Excavation of Pictish and Viking-age farmsteads at Buckquoy, Orkney', *Proceedings of the Society of Antiquaries of Scotland* 108: 174–227.

Robbins, L. M., 1977. 'The story of life revealed by the dead', in R. L. Blakely (ed.), *Biocultural Adaptation in Prehistoric America* (Athens GA), pp. 10–25.

Roberts, C. A., Lee, F., & Bintliff, J. (eds), 1989. *Burial Archaeology: Current Methods and Developments* (BAR British Series, 211) (Oxford).

Roslund, M., 1990. 'Nittiotalets medeltidsarkeologi och det döda barnet', *Fornvännen* 85: 283–92.

Saelebakke, I., 1986. 'Noen förelöbige inntrykk fra en middelalder – kirkegård i Tönsberg', *META* 2-3: 21–25.

Sawyer, P., 1987. 'The process of Scandinavian Christianization in the tenth and eleventh centuries', in B. Sawyer, P. Sawyer, & I. Wood (eds), *The Christianization of Scandinavia* (Alingsås), pp. 68–87.

Schaefer, U., 1963. *Anthropologische Untersuchung der Skelette von Haithabu* (Die Ausgrabungen in Haithabu, 4) (Neumünster).

Scrimshaw, S. C. M., 1984. 'Infanticide in human populations: societal and individual concerns', in Hausfater & Hrdy (eds) 1984: 439–62.

Sellevold, B. J., 1985. 'Knokler, oldsaker og kvinner: fysisk antropolgi som metode til kunnskap om kvinner i middelalderen', in *Kvinnearbeid i Norden fra vikingtiden til reformasjonen* (Foredrag fra et nordisk kvinnehistorisk seminar i Bergen 3–7 August 1983) (Bergen), pp. 63–77.

Sellevold, B. J., Lund Hansen, U., & Jørgensen, J. B., 1984. *Iron Age Man in Denmark* (Nordiske Fortidsminder 138) (Copenhagen).

Sellevold, B. J., and Næss, J.-R., 1987. 'Iron age people of Norway', *Norwegian Archaeological Review* 20: 46–50.

Sigurðardóttir, A., 1983. 'Ret er at en kvinde lærer ham at döbe et barn: Om dåb, konfirmation og fadderskab i Island i middelalderen', in S. Aðalsteinsdóttir & H. Þorláksson (eds), *Förändringar i kvinnors villkor under medeltiden* (Reykjavík), pp. 41–54.

Sjöberg, M., & Marnung, B., 1976. *Fornlämning 126. Gravfält, Äldre Järnålder, Sörby Skola, Öster Sörby, Gärdslösa socken, Öland.* (Riksantikvarieämbetet Rapport, B44) (Stockholm).

Smith, P., & Kahila, G., 1992. 'Identification of infanticide in archaeological sites: a case study from the late Roman-early Byzantine periods at Ashkelon, Israel', *Journal of Archaeological Science* 19: 667–75.

Solberg, B., 1985. 'Social status in the Merovingian and Viking periods in Norway from archaeological and historical sources', *Norwegian Archaeological Review* 18: 61–76.

Stager, L. E., & Wolff, S. R., 1984. 'Child sacrifice at Carthage: religious rite or population control?', *Biblical Archaeology*, Jan.-Feb. 1984, pp. 30–51.

Stenberger, M., 1961. 'Das Gräberfeld bei Ihre im Kirchspiel Hellvi auf Gotland. Der wikingerzeitliche Abschnitt', *Acta Archaeologica* 32: 1–134.

Stjernquist, B., 1987. 'Spring-cults in Scandinavian prehistory', in T. Linders & G. Nordquist (eds), *Gifts to the Gods* (Acta Universitatis Upsaliensis Boreas, 15) (Uppsala), pp. 149–57.

Thomson, A., 1960. *Barnkvävningen: En rättshistorisk Studie* (Skrifter utgivna af Kungliga Humanistiska Vetenskapssamfundet i Lund, 58) (Lund).

Welinder, S., 1979. *Prehistoric Demography* (Acta Archaeologica Lundensia, Series in 8° Minore, 8) (Lund).

—— 1989. 'An experiment with the analysis of sex and gender of cremated bones', *Tor* 22: 29–41.

Williamson, L., 1978. 'Infanticide: an anthropological analysis', in M. Kohl (ed.), *Infanticide and the Value of Life* (Buffalo), pp. 61–75.

Williamson, N. E., 1976. *Sons or Daughters: A Cross-Cultural Survey of Parental Preferences* (Beverly Hills).

Wrightson, K., 1982. 'Infanticide in European history', *Criminal Justice History* 3: 1–20.

INDEX

Lightning Source UK Ltd.
Milton Keynes UK
UKOW03f2125041213

222432UK00006B/308/A